# Now all

are called "BIRDS" but there are *a lot* of them, for just as they **differ** from one another in

so do they in *Variety of* **Nature.**

And, although all *Diverse Wretches* are **grouped** as & & ( or + ) still, the *pheno-menon*

*closest* to *T r u e* 's **WORD** *is the*

# The &NOW Awards 2
## The Best Innovative Writing

[Edited by Davis Schneiderman]

&NOW Books
Lake Forest, IL

First published 2012 by &NOW Books, an imprint of Lake Forest College Press.

&NOW BOOKS

Carnegie Hall
Lake Forest College
555 N. Sheridan Road
Lake Forest, IL 60045

andnow@lakeforest.edu

lakeforest.edu/andnow

"Thieves With Tiny Eyes, A Rebus (p. 1)" by Anna Joy Springer, originally appearing in *NAP (2.9)*.

Lake Forest College Press publishes in the broad spaces of Chicago studies. Our imprint, &NOW Books, publishes innovative and conceptual literature and serves as the publishing arm of the &NOW writers' conference and organization.

ISBN: 978-0-9823156-4-4

Cover designs by Jesssica Berger

Book design by Vasiliki Gerentes

Printed in the United States.

# Acknowledgements

Alyssa Basten

Zakea Boeger

Leah Bowers

Jody Buck

Kaisa Cummings

Thomas Dale

Amy Finn

Vasiliki Gerentes

Ryan Goodwin

Tobi Greenwald

Madeeha Kahn

Tammy Kise

Tyler Lebens

Nicholas Miner

Amanda Muledy

Robert Murphy

Samuel Murphy

Vinisha Puroit

Percy Sandel

Taryn Smith

Hannah Speck

Special thanks to Ian Morris for his enormous help in the early stages of the anthology. Ian taught a section of English 324 during the Spring 2012 semester, and gave shape to the shapeless!

# Table of Contents

# Davis Schneiderman
## And Now &NOW and now And Now?

1. These short bursts of text, signaled by these numbers, may be read in any order.
2. Yes, any order at all.
3. If you start with the second number and then read the first, or if those lines are reversed and renumbered on the page, the second then poses a provocative question: what might this mean, this introduction, which begins, like *The Iliad*, in medias res?
4. Same with the last number.
5. There are two "sides" to the book. These "sides" mirror each other, except when they do not.
6. This anthology is biennial, except when it is not.
7. & so on.
8. This is *THE &NOW AWARDS 2: The Best Innovative Writing*, which is an anthology of the best innovative writing.
9. Do you think this is meant as hyperbole?
10. *The &NOW AWARDS 1* covered the years between 2004-2009. This anthology—volume 2—covers the years between 2009-2011.
11. Read on. Or not. Yawn.
12. The &NOW Festival turns 10 in 2014. Wikipedia says:

**&Now** is biennial traveling literary festival and a publishing organization both focused on innovative literature. The festival's main emphasis is on work that blends or crosses genres, and includes a wide variety of work, such as multimedia projects, performance pieces, criti-fictional presentations, and otherwise. According to the website's description, the festival seeks out "literary art as it is practiced today by authors who consciously treat their work as a process that is aware of its own literary and extra-literary history, that is as much about its form and materials, language, communities, and practice as it is about its subject matter."[1] Most of the work presented by authors is considered experimental literature.[2]

13. Trust Wikipedia. Or not.
14. &NOW Books publishes this anthology. There is no connection between the anthology and the festival. Except when there is.
15. Isn't that clever?

16. This introduction is not particularly inspired.
17. Not every author in this book had attended or will attend a Festival, at any of the locations: the University of Notre Dame (2004), Lake Forest College (2006), Chapman University (2008), the University at Buffalo (SUNY) (2009), University of California-San Diego (2011), The Sorbonne and Paris VII (2002), and (join us!) the University of Colorado Boulder (2013).
18. The Festival is biennial, except when it is not.
19. The anthology includes two reflections from Festival organizers, from Buffalo (2009) and UCSD (2011), as these are the years covered by the works in the anthology.
20. There are many words in this book, and you might read some or all, in any order.
21. All of the work in this volume has been previously published. All of the work is this volume was published between September 2009 and September 2011. Except for one piece, published a few months after. A clinamen.
22. This introduction is already over.

# David Shields

### about Appendix to
### *Reality Hunger: A Manifesto*

*Reality Hunger: A Manifesto* is a book by American writer David   Shields, published by Knopf on February 23, 2010. The book is written in a collage style, mixing quotations by the author with those from a variety of other sources. The manifesto is directed toward increasing art's engagement with the reality of contemporary life through the exploration of new, hybrid genres such as prose poetry and literary collage. Overturning the stigma of artistic appropriation and redefining the relationship between fiction and nonfiction are also central themes.

That is what you will read if you search for the Wikipedia entry concerning David Shields' book *Reality Hunger: A Manifesto*. I highlighted the first paragraph of text within my web browser, clicked Command+C on my keyboard, opened a word document and clicked Command+V. The words appeared in front of me instantly, though I cannot take credit for writing them. Or can I? It was, in fact, my idea to paste them here. The words aren't under copyright by Wikipedia or even Moonriddengirl, the last wiki user to edit the page. I've changed the font and repurposed the words, giving them a new context. Shields does the same thing on a larger scale by appropriating the words of everyone from John D'Agata and Roland Barthes to Dj Spooky and John Mellencamp, then he intersperses his own words in the mix. In effect, Shields has written a "remix" text that is composed partly of "sampled" material and partly of "original" material.

Upon &NOW's request to reprint a section of the book, Knopf indicated that it could permit us to only republish portions of the text written by Shields, and not any of the text he had appropriated from other writers. Random House's argument is that it does not own the copyrights or licenses for the appropriations, and therefore cannot grant authorization for re-reuse here. Accordingly, &Now has reprinted only the last pages of *Reality Hunger*: the bibliography. We have adjusted this text to fit into a smaller space, and we urge you, as Shields does, to remove the pages from this book.

—Tyler Lebens

# appendix

This book contains hundreds of quotations that go unacknowledged in the body of the text. I'm trying to regain a freedom that writers from Montaigne to Burroughs took for granted and that we have lost. Your uncertainty about whose words you've just read is not a bug but a feature.

A major focus of *Reality Hunger* is appropriation and plagiarism and what these terms mean. I can hardly treat the topic deeply without engaging in it. That would be like writing a book about lying and not being permitted to lie in it. Or writing a book about destroying capitalism, but being told it can't be published because it might harm the publishing industry.

However, Random House lawyers determined that it was necessary for me to provide a complete list of citations; the list follows (except, of course, for any sources I couldn't find or forgot along the way).

If you would like to restore this book to the form in which I intended it to be read, simply grab a sharp pair of scissors or a razor blade or box cutter and remove pages 210-218 by cutting along the dotted line.

Who owns the words? Who owns the music and the rest of our culture? We do—all of us—though not all of us know it yet. Reality cannot be copyrighted.

Stop; don't read any farther.

# Numbers refer to sections:

2 Sentence about *Unmade Beds*: Soyon Im, "The Good, The Bad, and The Ugly," *Seattle Weekly* / 4 Thoreau / 5 Roland Barthes, *Barthes by Barthes* (who else would be the author?); "minus the novel": Michael Dirda, "Whispers in the Darkness," *Washington Post* / 6 Walter Benjamin / 7 Lorraine Adams, "Almost Famous: The Rise of the 'Nobody' Memoir," *Washington Monthly* / 8 Mark Willis, "Listening to the Literacy Events of a Blind Reader," http://fairuselab. net/?page_id=635 / 11 Adams / 13 John D'Agata, *The Next American Essay* / 16 Second sentence: paraphrase of information conveyed in the foreword to *The New Oxford Annotated Bible* / 18 D'Agata / 19 D'Agata, in conversation / 21-25 Adams / 26 William Gass, "The Art of Self," *Harper's* / 27 Adams; parenthetical statement: first line, Oliver Wendell Holmes, Jr.; second line: Darwin / 28 first half of passage: D'Agata, *The Next American Essay* / 29 Gass / 32 J. M. Coetzee, *Elizabeth Costello* / 33 Adams / 34 Jonathan Raban, in conversation / 35 Raban assures me that this Greene disclaimer exists, but I can't find it. / 36 Vivian Gornick, *The Situation and the Story* / 37 Kevin Kelly, "Scan This Book," *New York Times* / 38 D'Agata / 39 Alain Robbe-Grillet, *For a New Novel*, the book that in many ways got me thinking about all of this stuff. / 41 Alice Marshall, "The Space Between," unpublished manuscript; cf. last line of my book *Black Planet*: "All that space is the space between us." / 42 Kelly / 43 Robbe-Grillet / 44 Charles Simic, *Dime-Store Alchemy* / 45 Adams / 48 Ozick, interviewed by Tom Teicholz, *Paris Review* / 49 Philip Roth, "Writing American Fiction," *Commentary* / 50 Robbe-Grillet / 51 D'Agata / 52-53 Gornick / 55 Jim Paul, "The Found Life," Bread Loaf lecture / 57 Geoff Dyer, *Out of Sheer Rage* / 58 W.G. Sebald, interviewed by Siegrid Löffler, *Profil* / 59 Peter Bailey, "Notes on the Novel-as-Autobiography," in *Novel vs. Fiction*, eds. Jackson I. Cope and Geoffrey Green / 63-64 Robert Winder, "Editorial," *Granta*'s "Ambition" issue / 65 Ben Marcus, "The Genre Artist," *Believer* / 66 Rachel Donadio, "Truth Is Stronger Than Fiction," *New York Times* / 67 Margo Jefferson, "It's All in the Family, But Is That Enough?" *New York Times* / 69 Saul Steinberg, quoted by Kurt Vonnegut, *A Man Without a Country* / 71 Melville, *Billy Budd* / 72 D'Agata / 73 I'm pretty sure these lines, or something close to these lines, were spoken by Terry Gilliam in an interview, but I can't for the life of me find the source. / 74 William Gibson, "God's Little Toys," *Wired* / 75-76 Kelly / 77 Robert Greenwald, "Brave New Medium," *Nation* / 79 D'Agata / 80 Lauren Slater, *Lying* / 81 Clifford Irving, interviewed by Mike Wallace on *60 Minutes* / 82 Picasso / 84 Slater quoted in David D. Kirkpatrick, "Questionable Letter for a Liar's Memoir," *New York Times* / 85 James Frey / 86 Dorothy Gallagher, "Recognizing the Book That Needs to Be Written," *New York Times* / 88 First two lines: Mary Gaitskill, quoted in Joy Press, "The Cult of JT LeRoy," *Village Voice*; the rest is Stephen Beachy, "Who Is the Real JT Leroy?" *New York* / 89 Elmyr de Hory, quoted in Orson Welles, *F for Fake* / 91 Slater, "One Nation Under the Weather," *Salon.com* / 96 Nic Kelman, quoted in Sara Ivry, "Pick Those Fawning Blurbs Carefully," *New York Times* / 101 First three sentences are from Brian Camp's letter to *New York Times*, "Is It Plagiarism, or Teenage Prose?"; the rest of the passage, except for the last line, is from Malcolm Gladwell, "Annals of Culture," *New Yorker*. / 102 Jonathan Lethem, interviewed by Harvey Blume, *Boston Globe* / 103 Patricia Hampl, interviewed by Laura Wexler, *AWP Chronicle* / 104 Susan Cheever, interviewed by Roberta Brown, *AWP Chronicle* / 106 Gornick, "A Memoirist Defends Her Words," Salon.com / 108 D'Agata, *The Lost Origins of the Essay* / 109 Hampl / 110 Gornick, *The Situation and the Story* / 113, 115-116 Marshall / 119 Except for parenthetical statement, Motoko Rich, "James Frey Collaborating on a Novel for Young Adults, First in a Series," *New York Times* / 121 Cicero / 122 D'Agata, *The Next American Essay* / 124 John Mellancamp (!?) / 125 *The Commitments* (the movie version); I haven't read the novel / 126 Hemingway, interviewed by George Plimpton, *Paris Review* / 128 First sentence: Lynn Nottage, quoted in Liesl Schillinger, "The Accidental Design of Rolin Jones's Career," *New York Times* / 129 Jenni, quoted by Steven Shaviro, *Stranded in the Jungle*—29: http://www. shaviro.com/Stranded/29.html / 130 Otto Preminger, (apocryphal?) advice to Lee Remick / 131 Thomas Pynchon, *Slow Learner* / 132 Ross McElwee, interviewed by Cynthia Lucia, *Cineaste* / 133 Dave Eggers, interviewed by Tasha Robinson, *Onion*; Eggers reminds me that he said this ten years ago in a conversation about semi-autobiographical fiction, and that he no longer subscribes to the sentiment expressed here. / 134 "funny": title of Rick Reynolds CD; "pretty": title of Steve Martin album / 136 Frank O'Hara, quoted in Jim Elledge, *Frank O'Hara* / 137 Janette Turner Hospital, *The Last Magician* / 138 Robert Lowell, "Epilogue" / 139 Robert Towers, review of my novel *Dead Languages* in *New York Review of Books* / 141 D'Agata / 142 Frederick Barthelme, *The Brothers* / 143 Dogme 95 manifesto / 144 McElwee / 146 Last line: Nietzsche / 149 Reynolds, *Only the Truth Is Funny* / 151 Martin, quoted in Bruce Weber, "An Arrow Out of the Head and into a Shy Heroine's Heart," *New York Times* / 152 Lionel Trilling, *The Liberal Imagination* / 153 Adam Gopnik, "Optimist," *New Yorker* / 154 First sentence: Jonathan Goldstein, performing on *This American Life*; I could listen to that self-generating/self-demolishing voice of his forever. / 157 Wittgenstein, *Tractatus Logico-Philosophicus* / 158 *Walk the Line* / 161-162 Patrick Duff, "From the Brink of Oblivion," unpublished manuscript / 163 Mark Doty, "Return to Sender," *Writer's Chronicle* / 164 Duff / 167 David Carr, *The Night of the Gun* / 168 Duff / 169 Edward S. Casey, *Remembering* / 170 Legal brief filed by Libby's lawyers / 171 Naipaul? Nabokov? The human condition? / 172 Marshall / 173 Duff / 174 Elizabeth Bowen, "Mental Annuity," *Vogue* / 175-177 Duff / 178 Tony Kushner, quoted in Adam Liptak, "Truth, Fiction, and the Rosenbergs," *New York Times* / 179 Osip Mandelstam / 180-181, 183 Bonnie

Rough, "Writing Lost Stories" *Iron Horse Literary Review* / 185 Emily Dickinson / 186 Irving Babitt, quoted by D'Agata in conversation as *via negativa* / 188 Dyer, "A Conversation with Geoff Dyer," self-interview, Random House website: http://www.randomhouse.com/catalog/display.pperl?isbn=9780375422140&view=auqa / 190 Raban, *Passage to Juneau* / 191 Raban, interviewed by Dave Weich, Powells.com / 192 Raban, *For Love & Money* / 193 Gallagher / 194 Jefferson, "From Romantic-Comedy Sidelines to Glaring Spotlight," *New York Times* / 195 Sebald, quoted in *The Emergence of Memory*, ed. Lynne Sharon Schwartz / 196 T. S. Eliot, *Four Quartets* / 197 Joseph Lowman, quoted in Jane Ruffin, "Be More Shocked When You Don't Lie," *Raleigh News & Observer* / 198 McElwee / 199 Werner Herzog, interviewed on *Fresh Air*; I am equal parts Terry Gross's investment in explanation and Herzog's striving for mystery. / 200 Picasso; Virginia Woolf / 202 McElwee / 203 Geoffrey O'Brien, introduction to Elizabeth Hardwick, *Sleepless Nights*; as is so often the case with me, I like the book, but I like the introduction as much or more: concision. / 204 Roman Jakobson, "Linguistics and Poetics," in *The Discourse Reader*, eds. Adam Jaworski and Nikolas Coupland / 205 McElwee / 213 Rough / 214 Slater, *Lying* / 215 John Fowles, *The French Lieutenant's Woman* / 216 Tad Friend, "Virtual Love," *New Yorker* / 218 Henry Grunwald, *Salinger* / 219 A. O. Scott, "A Cock and Bull Story," *New York Times* / 220 Stephen Holden, "A Reprieve for Reality in New Crop of Films," *New York Times* / 221 Susan Buice, *Four Eyed Monsters* / 222 The song "Compared to What," written by Eugene McDaniels, was made famous via recording by Les McCann and Ed Harris at the Montreux Jazz Festival; that record sold more than a million copies. An anti-war and civil rights polemic, the song has recently been retooled by Chicago rapper Common and R & B singer Mya as a Coke commercial. / 223 McElwee, *Sherman's March* / 225 V. S. Pritchett / 226 A. Norman Jeffares, *W.B. Yeats* / 228 Jenny Gage, interviewed by Heidi Julavits, *Believer* / 230 Robin Hemley, "A Simple Metaphysics," *Conjunctions* / 232 No comment / 236 McElwee, *Cineaste* interview / 237 First sentence: Raban / 242 I was certain this was Frank Rich; I was astonished to find out it was Andrew O'Hehir, "The Long Goodbye," *Salon.* / 244 Brian Christian, in conversation / 246 Patrick Goldstein, "Lovesick Cruise et al. Is Bad Reality TV," *Los Angeles Times* / 248 Philip Gourevitch, quoted in Donadio / 251 Grégoire Bouillier, *The Mystery Guest* / 252 Michael Moore, 2003 Academy Award acceptance speech / 253 Anonymous White House aide in first term of Bush 43's administration, quoted in Ron Suskind, "Without A Doubt," *New York Times Magazine* / 254 Last three sentences: John Hodgman, "Text Message from the Road," *Stranger* / 255-257 Stacy Schiff, "The Interactive Truth," *New York Times* / 258 Lisa Page, letter to the editor, "In Fiction's Defense," *New York Times Book Review* / 259 Emerson / 260 Commonly attributed to Eliot; put together two statements, one by Eliot and one by Picasso, and you pretty much have it. / 261 Picasso / 264 Paul D. Miller aka DJ Spooky, *Rhythm Science* / 265 Lloyd Bradley, *Bass Culture* / 266 Lee Perry, quoted in Bradley, *This Is Reggae Music* / 271 Peter Mountford, "Alistair Wright," unpublished manuscript / 273 Jean-Luc Godard, in *Cahiers du Cinéma, 1960-1968*, vol. 2, ed. Jim Hillier / 274 Wikipedia entry on Sturtevant / 280 Emerson / 287 Brian Goedde, "Fake Fan," Experience Music Project Pop Music Conference / 288 Lethem / 289 Last sentence: Ralph Ellison, *Collected Essays* / 290 Goethe / 291 Emerson / 293 Felicia R. Lee, "An Artist Releases a New Film After Paramount Blocks His First," *New York Times* / 295 Last sentence: Liz Robbins, "Artist Admits Using Other Photo for 'Hope' Poster," *New York Times* / 297 Charles Baxter, *The Soul Thief* / 298 Laurence Sterne, *Tristram Shandy* / 299 Borges, "Pierre Menard, Author of the Quixote" / 300 Gibson / 304 This isn't me; it's James Nugent / 305 Tony DiSanto, quoted in Laura Bly, "The Real Laguna Beach Disdains its MTV Image," *USA Today* / 306 Donadio / 307 Doctorow quoted in Michiko Kakutani, "Do Facts and Fiction Mix?" *New York Times*; the parenthetical comment is mine (shocker). / 308 Marshall / 310 Steve Almond, *Not That You Asked*; last line: Peter Brooks, *Realist Vision* / 312 James Joyce / 313 Sebald / 314 Donald Kuspit, "Collage: The Organizing Principle of Art in the Age of the Relativity of Art," in *Relativism in the Arts*, ed. Betty Jean Craige / 315 Daniel Dennett, *Consciousness Explained* / 316 Kuspit / 317 Ronald Sukenick, *Out* / 319 Lance Olsen, *10:01* / 320 M. H. Abrams and Jack Stillinger, editors, John Stuart Mill: *Autobiography and Literary Essays* / 323 Djuna Barnes, *Nightwood* / 326 Lorrie Moore, *Self-Help* / 329 Thomas Sobchack and Vivian Carol Sobchack, *An Introduction to Film* / 332 Picasso / 333 Sounds to me like Julian Schnabel, but that might just be because of the broken dishes. / 335 Charlie Parker / 336 Walter Pater, *The Renaissance* / 337 Nicholson Baker, *U and I* / 338 Sven Birkerts, *American Energies* / 339 Nina Michelson, "Silence and Music," unpublished manuscript / 340-341 Simic / 342-343 Michelson / 344 Simic / 345 Thomas Lux, "Triptych, Middle Panel Burning" / 346 Deborah Eisenberg, quoted in Frank Conroy, "Angela's Second Boy," *New York Times* / 348-349 Michelson / 352 Benjamin / 353 Emerson / 354 Olsen, "Notes Toward the Musicality of Creative Disjunction," *Symploke* / 355 Emerson / 356 Goethe / 357 Walter Murch, quoted in Michael Ondaatje and Walter Murch, *The Conversations* / 358 Theodor Adorno, *The Adorno Reader* / 359 David Markson, *Reader's Block* / 362 Annie Dillard, *Holy the Firm* / 363 Viktor Shklovsky, *Theory of Prose* / 364 International Museum of Collage, Assemblage, and Construction (http://collagemuseum.com/COLLAGE-signs-surfaces/index.html) / 365 Gopnik, "What Comes Naturally," *New Yorker* / 366 D'Agata, interviewed by Carey Smith, *Collison* / 368 First sentence: Eliot, *The Waste Land* / 369 Robert Dana, interviewed by Lowell Jaeger in *Poets & Writers* / 370 Marcus / 372 Ellen Bryant Voigt, "Narrative and Lyric," *Southern Review* / 373 Elvis Mitchell, "Fast Food, Fast Women," *New York Times* / 376 Shklovsky / 377 David Mamet, "Hearing the Notes That Aren't Played," *New York Times* / 378 Ezra Pound, *The ABCs of Reading* / 380 Conversation between Janet Malcolm and David Salle, from her profile of him, "Forty-one False Starts," *New Yorker* / 382 Emerson / 383 Nietzsche / 384 D'Agata and Deborah Tall, "The Lyric Essay," *Seneca Review* / 385 Paul / 386 D'Agata, in conversation / 388 Lines 1 and 2: Rebecca Solnit, *Eve Said to the Serpent*; lines three to five, Dyer, *Out of Sheer Rage*; line 6: Solnit, *A Field Guide to Getting Lost* / 389 Malcolm, "The Silent Woman," *New Yorker* / 390 Ozick, introduction to *Best American Essays 1998* / 391 Phillip Lopate, *The Art of the Personal Essay* / 392 Orwell / 393 Doty / 396-397, 399 Hampl / 400 Kierkegaard / 402 Montaigne / 403 Keats / 404 Stuart Hampshire, quoted in Lopate / 405 W. H. Auden, paraphrased and altered by Edward Hoagland / 406 Lopate, interviewed by John Bennion, *AWP Chronicle* / 407 Adorno / 408 Robert Hass, interviewed by Susan Maxwell, University of Iowa Writers' Workshop newsletter / 409 D'Agata, *The Next American Essay* / 410 Lopate / 412 John Berger, *Keeping a Rendezvous* / 413 D'Agata; "or the means . . .": Réda Bensmaïa, *The Barthes Effect* / 414 Fourth sentence: David Foster Wallace, "Host," *Atlantic Monthly* / 416 Gore Vidal, quoted in Lopate / 417 David Richards, "The Minefields in Monologues," *New York Times* / 418 Greene / 421 Wallace, interviewed by Laura Miller, *Salon.com* / 422 Michel Leiris, *Manhood* / 423 Nietzsche / 424 Montaigne / 426 E. M. Forster, *Aspects of the Novel* / 427 Didion / 429 Emerson / 430 Alexander Smith, *Dreamthorp* / 431 Lopate / 433 Sonny Rollins, quoted in Ratliff, "A Free Spirit Steeped in Legends," *New York Times* / 438 D'Agata / 439 "no ideas but in things": William Carlos Williams, *Paterson* / 440 John Gardner, *On Moral Fiction* / 443 David Wojahn, "The Inside" / 444 First part: Wallace, interviewed by Larry McCaffrey, *Review of Contemporary Fiction*; second part: Louise Glück, *Proofs and Theories* / 445-446 Lionel Trilling, *The Liberal Imagination* / 448 Borges, prologue to *Ficciones* / 450 Williams, quoted in Robert Cole, *Bruce Springsteen's America* / 451 Gornick / 452 Emerson / 453 Emerson, except list of names / 454 Heidegger / 458 Nabokov, *Lolita*; in honor of the author's Olympian hauteur, I corrected the grammar and punctuation. / 459 Borges / 461 Coetzee, *Doubling the Point* / 462 Oscar Wilde / 467 Smith / 468 New York Film Festival catalogue copy / 469 Emerson / 470 Yeats / 472 Wilde, preface to *Picture of Dorian Gray* / 474 Gornick / 475 James Shapiro, "The Critic's Teeth," *New York Times*; Shapiro and I were colleagues on the National Book Award nonfiction panel a few years ago: all five of us utterly disagreed about what nonfiction was. / 476 Samuel Butler / 477 Anne Carson, *Glass, Irony, and God* / 478 Emerson / 479 Raban, Powells.com interview / 480 Montaigne / 481 McElwee, *Cineaste* interview / 482 Verlyn Klinkenborg, "Carson, Night by Night," *New York Times* / 483 Lorin Stein, "Loves of the Lambs," *New York Review of Books* / 484 Dan Georgakas, "The Art of Autobiography," *Cineaste* / 485 Dickinson / 488 Lopate / 489 Yeats / 491 Marshall / 492 My crush? Sort of; more Paul Bravmann's. / 493 Mikhail Lermontov, *A Hero of Our Time* / 494 George Bernard Shaw / 495 Dana / 496 Dyer, self-interview / 498 Keats / 499 Emerson / 501 Montaigne / 502 Ad copy for *Curb Your Enthusiasm* / 510 My girlfriend and I shared the house with her brother; it was actually he who was wildly prolific all summer. Makes a better story the other way, though. / 524-525 Alexis de Tocqueville, *Democracy in America* / 526 László Kardos, quoted in *More Reflections on the Meaning of Life*, ed. David Friend / 527 Can't quite remember where this is from, though it sounds like fourth-generation Sartre. Endless is the quest for truth. / 528 Nietzsche / 529 Woody Allen, *Side Effects*, preface to *Cat on a Hot Tin Roof* / 531 Zadie Smith, "The Limited Circle Is Pure," *New Republic*; "information bureau . . .": Adorno / 532 Nietzsche / 533 Nirvana, "All Apologies" / 534 Schopenhauer / 535 Nabokov, *Pnin* / 538 Virginia Woolf, *A Room of One's Own* / 539 Jean Cocteau / 540 Robert Rauschenberg, quoted in Michael Kimmelman, "Robert Rauschenberg, American Artist, Dies at 82," *New York Times* / 541 Steinberg, quoted in Vonnegut / 542 Denis Johnson, in conversation / 543 Saul Bellow, "What Kind of Day Did You Have?" / 544 Fitzgerald, *The Great Gatsby* / 545 Barry Hannah, interviewed by James D. Lilley and Brian Oberkirch, *Mississippi Review* / 546 Jennifer Jason Leigh, quoted in Sylviane Gold, "Ready to Play Anyone but Herself," *New York Times* / 547 Paul Elie, *The Life You Save May Be Your Own* / 548 Hass / 549 Emerson / 550 Adam Phillips, *Equals* / 551 Bellow / 552 Beckett / 554 Jim McBride, *David Holzman's Diary* / 555 Robert Capa / 556 Kierkegaard / 557 Gass / 558 Dillard, in praise of Maggie Nelson's *The Red Parts* / 559 Gordon Lish, quoted in Amy Hempel, "Captain Fiction," *Vanity Fair* / 560 D.H. Lawrence / 561 Yeats / 562 Emerson / 563 Thomas Mann, *Tonio Kruger* / 564 Lopate / 565 Ruth Behar, *The Vulnerable Observer* / 566 Flaubert, *The Writing Life* / 567 Antoin Artaud, *The Theater and its Double* / 569 Bob Dylan, "Outlaw Blues" / 570 *The Wild Ones* / 571 *King Lear* / 572 da Vinci / 573 Prokofiev / 574 Michelangelo / 575 Nicholas Perricone, quoted in Alex Witchel, "Perriconology," *New York Times Magazine* / 576 Vikram Chandra, quoted in Motoko Rich, "Digital Publishing Is Scrambling the Industry's Rules," *New York Times* / 577 Goethe / 588 O'Brien / 589 Naipaul, quoted in James Wood, "Wounder and Wounded," *New Yorker* / 590 First sentence: Benjamin / 591 Richard Serra, quoted by Kimmelman, "At the Met and the Modern with Richard Serra" *New York Times* / 592 Dyer / 596 Marcus, "Why Experimental Fiction Threatens to Destroy Publishing, Jonathan Franzen, and Life as We Know It," *Harper's* / 597 Robbe-Grillet / 598 Gornick / 599 Hannah / 601 Williams, *Spring and All* / 602 Coetzee, *Summertime* / 603 Williams / 604 Gornick / 605 Sebald / 606 All but last sentence: Naipaul, quoted in Donadio, "The Irascible Prophet," *New York Times Book Review* / 607-608 Lopate / 609 First five sentences except titles: D'Agata, *Collision* interview / 610 Dyer, *Out of Sheer Rage* / 611 Except for titles, E. M. Cioran, *The Temptation to Exist* / 612 D'Agata, *The Next American Essay* / 613 Plutarch / 614 Emerson / 615 Gornick / 616 Marcus, "The Genre Artist," *Believer* / 617 Berger, *G* / 618 Anne Carson, *Decreation*

# Craig Dworkin
## The Cube

**[From The Official Catalog of the Library of Potential Literature]**

Even the most radical non-linear texts have tended to exploit or subvert only the sequential possibilities of print — from the continuous loop of Joyce's *Finnegans Wake* to the shuffled cards of Marc Saporta's *Composition No. 1* — but *The Cube* takes such multiplicities to an entirely new level. Set in a grid, the book's words can be read conventionally, across the page, as well as down each column — with either route making complete grammatical sense. But they can also be read as stacked strata and mined like lexical core samples *through* the layered pages of the book. Each path tells the same story from a different perspective (the narrative, naturally, hinges on the potential outcomes of a throw of cubed dice). By opening up the z-axis to reading in this way, *The Cube* recognizes the book as a three-dimensional sculptural space. Taking its lead from Armand Schwerner's *(If Personal)* and Raymond Queneau's *Cent mille milliards de poèmes*, *The Cube* reads like a experiment by Christian Bök precision printed by Emily McVarish.

# Joe Atkins
## BOXXY FOAR 4DD1@!!!!1!!

Boxxy is the pseudonym of "Catherine Wayne," an Internet celebrity who first appeared in 2008 and eventually became well known on the image board 4chan/org/b/. Her rambling video style and eccentric mannerisms tore /b/'s community in twain, between admirers and antagonists. This subsequent flame wars caused most of her subsequent videos to become viral. Her youtube account, boxxybabe, was later famously hacked, causing more chaos on the web. Wayne has been known to sell Boxxy items on eBay; although her meme-culture relevance has waned, she remains an occasionally referenced internet celebrity.

Joe Atkins' piece reflects on the absurdity of Boxxy's videos through exploring this question: how much of her appeal exists in the content rather than the delivery? The words, here, are stripped of their driving force. Atkins' transcription suggests that perhaps much of internet fandom is really just face-worship.

—Samuel Murphy

Ok, hi. Heh. Ok eh-heh. My name is Boxxy. Most of you know me as eh uh well eh um most of you know me as Boxxy. I suppose if you're watching this you probably know me as Boxxy but um uh ah a lot of people probably don't know me as moldy lunch box. And um so yeah that's my Gaia user name on Gaia online and I told my Gaia online friend buddy part—one second I'm uncomfortable—I told my Gaia online buddy friend um ad admiral awesome that I would make a video just for him so here it is I'm doing it. Addi I love you ahhhuahhhuahhh! Is you wah I love you. And um um-um so let's see an uh what about a oh just so you know Addi 'cause I know you're watching this since you're such a conceited basterd um I don't normally talk like this I'm normally like all over the place like I am right now but it's a calmer voice most of the time unless I'm like really hyped up cause then it's different even still from this but let me try to get my calmer voice a heh-hem ehm... Yeah I'm really like it's it's fun it's cool there it is. What is going on-euhn-nuh! Because I it's just so crazy. Um, dit-it is mkay. I love you! I la, I love Addi because like he is really fun to talk to and stuff and like he's eh uh-um I only met him like two days ago and we're like married and it is crazy because we love each other so much. And um we are twinnies like all over the place it's just crazy. His avatar is like a manhole and I had a avatar it was a really long time ago it was a slut avatar. Khshh. And um right and he made an avatar to match it my fresh grass skirt one. And it was so cute! Nnnn it was so nice, I love Addi! And I uh-made a sign for him and it was on my boob. My upper boob. Anuh and his heart it made a red mark cause I had to keep erasing every last sec, and uh um let's see here... He keeps donating to my quest. I ul an-em. Thank you! I don't know how to thank him because I'm so poor. I've never had like 100 K in my life. And heh-hehe cause I'm a dumb Gaian and stuff. Um, let's see here, I wear, I wear too much eyeliner FYI Addi, in case you couldn't tell already. But that's ok. Uh I don't know what you look like! And yet here you are you know what I sound like. You-rre a basterd. Youuuuure. I'm gonna have to ask you for a picture. I'm probably a returning sign too, you're bing very rude, you know. Very rude indeed. I don't appreciate it. My hair shaking everywhere. Mm-appreciate it. Now ya ya know no one will find this funny except for a couple other people I don't think so that's ok but ya know um yeah so Iiiii-love-Addiiiii. Addi-pantsss-sa-sa-sa-zah. Ammmd-da-da-da and if I know you on Gaia then and you want me to make you a video just say so and I will because I probably love you anyway buut Addi asked first kind of. Uhm yeah, Addi asked first I guess. So, yeah I love you. Bye Addi.

# Alexandra Chasin

## Recall, Cipher, Their Fragmentation, And Then

1.  Everything I said and wrote, careful to be exhaustive in my presentation of the case, the *cases*, the many cases, as many as there were impulses, and more, to mobilize not only words, but also units smaller than words, more precise than their roots, finer than phonemes, morphemes, and even the place where they meet most neat in *s*, in the service of expressing everything including the ever-more-exquisite distinctions of slivers of shades of things between you and me, amounting to stacks and hills and towers of how I feel about you relative to how I've felt about all other phenomena I've ever experienced, each one requickened, once I knew you, and colored over all over again with why it is and could only be you for me.

2.  I can't remember what I wrote to you that time that made you write to me: *It's not enough to say, you take care of you and I'll take care of me. Such are the wages of twoness.* It was all it was all I wanted to read. But now I wonder, how could you write me such a thing? Of all things.

3.  I reread 'til the pages go soft and the messages start to waver on the screen, and whenever I possibly can, which is not that often at all, is indeed less and less every day, I delete or crumple up some more.

4.  The green lines hold the blank white grief, right-side-up-upside-down phenomenon that comes down to undone letters disintegrating into sticks still stuck on you.

Going back in time, shadow shining in the sun, to before, before, because there *was* such a thing, a when-I-didn't-know-you-as-anything-but-a-name. (What I wouldn't give to rehave the moment that changed.) Because I don't know what it was like, either time. Or if you

And we no longer

# Jack Collom

## Seamless Poem

| | |
|---|---|
| U. | I can't even get at the subtlety of what I'd like to say. |
| ww. | Poetic power eats into the future in tiny termite bites. |
| cue. | The language thing just seems to go out the window theO |
| .com. | The entire history of poetry gets forgotten each time. |
| Faith. | What do people think about the things that bother me? |
| Proven. | The world is full of voices saying different things. |
| Wolfish. | Who has the right not to talk about what's going o? |
| My track. | "There are shades gathering at the doors of Troy." |
| Firesnake. | You think changing language can change the world? |
| Interfaces. | I feel... subtlety isn't particularly important. |
| "Bloodbath." | Unless the feminists don't want power eitherhuh |
| The low-down. | It's completely knit into our ordinary living. |
| "Inner space." | There must be ways to notice what's going on. |
| It's your move! | $15.97 buys you 16 WEEKS OF STAR: Order Now! |
| Lupine monsters. | A constant exclusion of inconvenient poets. |
| Blue Chip Basket. | YOU DESERVE TO BE HAPPY: "I guarantee it!" |
| Terrible Darkness. | An official Harley-Davidson pocket watch. |
| Every second counts | The inside world and the outside world=+ |
| .Funeral piles fuel. | Voices that I could get to sound right- |
| Robot Investors rule! | "Embarrassing girlstuff always works." |
| Would swallow the sun. | I've been excluded from..... history. |
| Get connected and save! | Now I'm gonna spend the $50 million. |
| Feral mirror reflectors. | FREE MONEY! It's true. Never repay. |
| Digital fever has pumped. | I feel very passionate about that. |
| This prolific ejaculation. | Going to be sucking the same air. |
| Bulletproof your portfolio. | To the very best of his ability. |
| Chill'd to a selfish prayer. | Existing in a very high degree* |
| Charting on a silver platter. | Lifetime television for women. |
| The mighty beasts of the deep. | Women have trusted Correctol. |
| LIFE IS TOO BIG FOR CARS. Isuzu | Immediately stopped whining. |
| Fluid from their melted eyes had | SURGEON GENERAL'S WARNING:. |
| Do you multi-task in the shower?? | Just this one lumpy world. |
| Break, blow, burn and make me new. | All the wild stuff over!! |
| Read "Guts and Glory in Real Time." | Very heated up about it. |
| The result is incredible rottenness. | With accents of chrome. |
| B-breathtakingly beautiful bar chart. | No artificial flavors. |
| Also shown as the splitting of an egg. | Unleash your passion! |
| For more information, hit fidelity.com. | He carries crystals. |
| O trebly hooped and welded hip of power! | More pictures 26-7. |
| "Regifted" photo album at wedding shower. | SEND NO MONEY NOW. |
| Three generations of imbeciles are enough. | Dividing by zero. |
| I'd like to put a bracket on some holdings. | strokeprevention |
| The color of the mouth inside was blood-red. | 100% satisfied. |
| A postmortem: The Day the Bottom Dropped Out. | Moment of joy. |
| Disinterred piece of the bottle called: Jumbo. | Police words. |
| 4 easy ways to achieve "total" diversification. | 15C EXTREMUM |
| Their flesh shall consume away while they stand. | Gets colds. |
| eSignal: The #1 Way to Stay Ahead of Wall Street. | Made with. |
| For meat presented itself in a rapturous gobbling. | Whodunit? |
| Or that trip to Disney World you promised the kids. | Foreignj |
| Then the Heart of Heaven blew mist into their eyes() | Nature. |
| Through my discount broker, Quick & Reilly, I plunked | OH NO! |
| "I wrenched DOG backwards to find GOD; now GOD barks." | OH NO |
| A wild, reckless bunch full of greed. Don't believe it. | ZZZ. |
| I think we are all bugs and mice and are only... cheese. | to: |
| A new wave of online broker for hard-core traders debuts. | Aa |
| Inner voice told me this fellow was the Son of Perdition%% | . |

Zoom, 700 sheet paper supply, 10 bin sorter w/stapler; auto
Euphemism is a means of killing you softly, with a new song.

# What Will Happen

```
Is the destruction of food and food's life and food's ground.
Is you walk the floor and the straight/line sym-phony roars.
Is No more great blue herons, leopard frogs and wild roses.
Is tiny loss that breaks your heart: "LAST ELEPHANT DIES."
Is your children choke in a cascade of secondary effects.
Is culture goes "cult rue" "clue rut" "UELRCTU" Vulture.
Is you walkkkk and your shoulders turn to dead sticks.k
Is this four-billion-year dance vomits and lies down,,
Is drain plow fence overgraze acidify encroach erode.
Is that the red red robin goes bob bob bobbin' away.
Is.your.days.become.cylinders.of.snowwhite.plastic.
uuuuuuuuuuuuuuuuuuuuuuuuuuuuuuuuuuuuuuuuuuuuuuuuuuu.
Is most backbones crumble in the blink of a lake.
Is Civilization breaks down but not into nature.
Is Time wadded & tossed like a grocery receipt.
Is your life revealed as Pyramid of addiction.
Is the exSpiration of gray gases is like Art.
Is information slush and demolecularization.
Is roving boneys slay elderfolk for grease,
Mental epidemiology pours down the street.
F**r**a****gm*e*****nta****t***i*o*****n.
Wanton murder of trillions of Creatures.
Quality of wildness only in:human lust.
Nonononononononononononononononononon.
stopclogchokejamcongestblockobstruct-
baroccludeimpedehindertrammelbridle.
Window is broken, crazies crawl in.
Grotesque explosion of cowbirdiam.
jinnssáanneéáinnesáanneéáinnesan.
Foxfire furs bending skyscraper.
Top-forty full of rabbitscream.
empty+void+bare+barren+blank .
The simplest tissues vanishO.
```
The little things turn black.
```
No time to finish hard work.
All mind-delicacy diffused.
Embarrassment and rubbish.
Own souls whirled absent!
HIT HIT KILL STRIP KILL.
Massive chopping away//
Diarrhea of rightness.
Orchestra of disease.
GET OUT OF MY HOUSE!
Melted photographs.
Endless Isolation.
Need gulps value.
Noplace noplace.
1000-foot fear*
Decay of pink.
!@#$% ¢&*)(+"
Ha ha ha ha!
Is drastic.
Encaustic.
Trenches.
Roaches.
Sewage.
Weeds.
Rats.
Rot.
XY.
Z.
?
```

# Noisy Alien Mirror

1. As the napkin soaks, I

2. think of reading; this dollar

3. bill could be the the the tip of

4. the iceberg, let us say What I heard

5. about opposition pressurizing (giving birth to)

6. collaboration, viz. "Big O"

7.  carrying on, ingesting, tire-

8.  lessly if you were even "sorta

9.  with him," & effluvia :

10. but        to sever is to stretch mo re

11. then Collaborator points out it

12. stops the stretch, butt

13. dedicated & frivolous) we order

14. another array of alterants and "see what we can do."

# Katie Degentesh
## I Was Horny

Boys are interesting creatures.

The boy's body is unique.
Boys can see a mouse in the dark.
Their wings are huge and heavy.
The claws are as sharp as a scalpel's. They tear meat with their mouth.
They don't turn their eyes. They can hear a mouse running.
They have thick feathers in the inside, and they also have skinny feathers.

These are some characteristics or habits about boys.
The boys tear their prey, swallow it whole, and spit up pellets.
They prey on small things. Boys fly silently. They see well in the dark,
hunt at night and sleep in the daytime. They scare others by fluffing up.
They blend in with the woods.

Boys eat many animals. The boy eats small prey.
Boys sometimes eat small rabbits. They like mice.
Their favorite is skunk. Most of the time boys eat raccoons.
Other nights they eat possum. Sometimes boys eat snakes.

Boys live in many places. Boys find their home in tree holes.
Boys live in tree trunks. Some boys on farms. Some boys may live in bushes.
Boys might live in forests. Sometimes boys live in old buildings.
Other boys live in barns. Big boys live in cactus.

Boys are very cool.

Some boy characteristics are that they see very well at night.
Snow boys blend in well with the snow. Boys sleep in the day
and are awake during the night. They have very short necks
which is how you notice them. Boys have very sharp claws called talons.
These are used for catching their prey.

Boys are different from girls because they eat rabbits, mice, skunks,
rats, snakes, lizards, and fish. When boys eat they sometimes tear and
swallow. They eat by tearing and ripping with their mouths and claws.
Some boys prey on girls. Boys hunt at night for night animals.
You cannot hear boys when they are hunting at night because of their feathers.

Boys find their homes in many places like caves, tree holes, trunks,
old buildings, farms, barns, bushes, airports, forests, and cactuses.
There is a boy that lives in barns and its name is the Barn Boy.
And there is a boy called the Snow Boy that lives in the snow.

Another boy lives in very, very old trees.
Boys live in places where it is very dark.
Boys in the desert live in cactuses and they get water from them.
They sometimes live in rain forests and tree trunks and holes.

Boys are very interesting to me and they are very cool.
I hope I can learn more about them. I hope I can go boy watching.

I hope boys never go extinct and I hope they never get endangered. I love boys.

# Roxane Gay
## I'm Going to Cook Our Dinner in My Easy Bake Oven
## And You're Going to Like It

That's right. I'm going to cook dinner for us in my Easy Bake Oven. It's going to be delicious and fucking romantic. You're going to eat my Easy Bake Oven dinner and you're going to say it's the most amazing thing you've ever put in your mouth other than, perhaps, me. We're going to eat at a tiny little table like the ones in pediatricians' offices with our knees pulled up to our chins and we're going to set the mood with little tiny birthday candles that will probably melt before we finish eating.

First, we're going to start with an appetizer, a little quiche. I'm going to put some piecrust and some whipped eggs into that tiny little Easy Bake Oven tin pan and I'm going to add a little onion, mushroom, some parsley, salt and pepper to taste. I'm going to put that tiny tin pan in the oven and we're going to wait for the Easy Bake Oven light bulb to heat that quiche up. It's going to take a very long time because it's just a 100-watt bulb. You might start to get irritated because you're hungry but I'm going to look awful cute standing over my tiny Easy Bake Oven with my miniature utensils. You'll forgive me.

While we're waiting for that light bulb to work its magic, we're going to drink some wine, something from a box and we're going to enjoy it in sippy cups. I'm going to tell you there's a National Toy Hall of Fame and that the Easy Bake Oven is a member and you're going to say, "No shit, that's kind of cool." We're going to slurp that cheap wine through those four tiny holes in the spigot of the sippy cup and we're going to laugh at how long it's going to take us to get drunk. The wine is going to taste so damn good one tiny sip at a time and we're persistent motherfuckers so we're going to get drunk faster than we thought. We're going to keep uncapping the lid and filling our sippy cups with wine until the kitchen starts smelling delicious in a tiny way and then our Easy Bake Oven quiche will finally be ready.

We're going to blow on the tiny quiche to cool it down and we are going to cut the tiny quiche in half and each half will only provide us a bite or two. We're going to be all sexy and shit and feed each other and our teeth will be numb from all the wine and we'll make pouty faces as we wrap our lips around our tiny bites of Easy Bake Oven quiche. The appetizer is going to taste so good you're going to moan softly. You're going to say, "Damn. I appreciate that French cuisine goodness," and then you're going to be sad because you want more. You're going to say maybe, next Christmas, we should go to Paris and

I'm going to try and make a profound connection between the City of Lights and our Easy Bake Oven dinner being cooked by a light bulb. I'm going to start dancing around the kitchen holding my sippy cup singing a song about how beautiful life is. You're going to sing, "If You're Happy and You Know It Clap Your Hands," and every few seconds you'll do just that.

For the main course, I'm going to make a savory tart. Yes, it's going to be very similar to the quiche but I found the recipe in Martha Stewart Magazine and I'm sensitive about my cooking so you're not going to say anything. You're going to act like nothing makes you happier than eating tiny dishes baked in my Easy Bake Oven. I'm going to make us a Spinach, Pancetta and Roasted Garlic tart and it's going to take even longer than the quiche so we're going to have to tip another box of wine. While I chop more onions and wash the spinach and roll out the pastry dough you're still going to be singing and clapping your hands and I'm going to say, "You sure are fucking happy, baby" and you're going to say, "Damn right."

We're going to wait and wait for the tart to finish baking and we're going to be so drunk we'll forget how hungry we are. We're going to giggle and you're going to clean the surface of my Easy Bake Oven because you want to be helpful. You're going to set out some tiny dishes and tiny silverware and when the tart is ready we're going eat our two bites each and dab at our lips with tiny napkins and you're going to lean back in your tiny chair and fall over. We're going to laugh so hard, we're going to start to cry and then you're going to say, "I would love dessert," as you rub your stomach. I'm going to bake you a cake, baby. I'm going to bake you the sweetest damn cake in my Easy Bake Oven. It's going to be tiny and rich and thickly frosted. I won't even ask you to share.

# Jennifer Karmin

### about *aaaaaaaaaaalice*

A *aaaaaaaaaalice* is a text-sound epic that intersects language, place, and (mis) communication with a 1963 Japanese textbook, travels through Asia, *Alice in Wonderland*, and Werner Heisenberg's uncertainty principle. This collection of poems is a word score for polyvocal improvisation. Performers are encouraged to equate the style of each text with imagined tones, rhythms, voices, etc. Any number of performers may participate and any number of pages may be used. Werner Heisenberg's uncertainty principle states that it is impossible to determine both the exact position and momentum of a subatomic particle. Conceiving of words as atoms, every reading of *Aaaaaaaaaaalice* should produce new results. The sequence and time relations of the words create unlimited permutations intended for reading, sound, and performance experiments.

# LAKE

**how are you**

a quiet man
shares the compartment

turns away
as he changes
his shirt

outside keeps
moving

**getting**

reading a newspaper
see numbers
tattooed
on his arm

he is an engineer
has two children
resembles an older
clint eastwood

his name
is very hard          **on**
to pronounce

pause
stutter

every time
you try
to say it                              **now**

**my**
**dear**

*before*

*the nails*

*come out*

*let's*

*fix it*

*before it goes*

*bad*

*let's fix*

*it*

*before it*

*breaks*

*let's*

*fix it*

*before it collapses*

*let's*

*fix it*

*before it*
*falls*
*let's fix*
*it*

**i'm never sure**

want
something in words
**what**    what it means

can't see
the rabbi

women sit
separate
from men
**i'm**    behind
a screen

a jewish synagogue
in moscow

**going**    graffiti near the kremlin
the guide translates
get out kykes

**to**    holes of
family

grandpa's reply
to his russian childhood

**be**    it was not easy
for us

**from one minute**
**to another**

*in case*

        *we're*

            *in a hurry*

*in*

        *case we*

           *want*

        *to ask a*

               *question*

      *in case we*

           *can't hear*

                *in*        *case we*

*feel rain*

         *in case*

*we go home*

                *early*

         *in case*
         *we*
         *don't*
         *understand*

**thank you sir**

unlike
memory

golden
more mystical

visiting
historical churches

hands sometimes
look like buddha's

mary seems sad
by the announcement

she is to be
the mother
of god

her baby
a miniature man

his body grows
hips tilted
legs slightly crossed
half naked

imagine a taste
of salt and blood

**for your
interesting story**

what

a strange

way

of walking

what a

strange

way of

talking

what a strange

way

of looking

what

a strange way

of reading

what a strange way

of writing

what
a strange
way of
thinking

# Amira Hanafi
## about Girl X

I came across the A. Finkl & Sons steel forge on a bicycle ride, actually, a ride much like a drift. I had just moved to Chicago and I was getting to know the city by wandering around. I was really enamored by the big, fiery industrial operations going on inside the open doors of the forge, just west of one of the most gentrified neighborhoods in the city. At the Chicago Public Library, I found a curious book, published by the forge on its one hundredth anniversary. It was full of laudatory biographies of the presidents of the company. Included in the founder's biography was a list of all the addresses he had lived at in Chicago. I mapped them out and started visiting them. These walks constitute the core of *Forgery*—the Homes series.

I researched and kept collecting various materials, using the keyword "Finkl." organized that material by type—newspaper articles, legal documents, the writing I had done at each site, my personal journals, and materials about the Finkl forge and forging in general. I hung up photos of the sites and various characters in my workspace. I set up a system in which each section of *Forgery* would include one document from each of five categories.

Inside this system, I worked intuitively, collaging the texts I felt were appropriate to each section. I felt that I was performing the work of the forge, reconstituting existing materials into a new, stronger material.

I came across the story of Girl X when I was researching the section for the 800 Block of North Sedgwick. It's an appalling story of a nine-year old girl who was raped, strangled, poisoned and left for dead in the stairwell of her apartment building in the Cabrini-Green housing project. She didn't die, but is now paralyzed, blind, and mute.

The name she acquired through the event—"Girl X"—pointed to crucial ideas of memory, anonymity, and marginalized populations. The story of Girl X is not an unusual one in that it happened, but it is exceptional in that it (eventually) gained national media attention.

I sat with the Girl X material (newspaper articles and legal documents related to her story) for over two years before I felt able to write this piece. When I did write it, it came to be about negotiating her marginalized history, her muted voice—and about feeling complicit with her disenfranchisement.

By the time I wrote about Girl X, I was no longer just an engaged observer of Chicago. I was a citizen of its streets and a documented part of its history.

—Amira Hanafi

# Amira Hanafi
## Girl X

Drop forging forms a shape out of a block of steel or other metal by repeated rapid blows. No matter how much time I get, I will say it is not me. Girl X was lured into an apartment where she was attacked. I can't speak, mouth like full of food or cotton. I remember three years ago so clearly. He choked her for a while, and then she stopped screaming. Girl X was like a lot of young kids; in addition to the direction of the fibers, their relation to one another is also important.

For anyone that has even a sliver of human compassion running through his or her veins, I do not believe that even this sentence is enough because I wrote it down. He did not want her to scream, so he put his hand over her mouth, but she kept screaming, so he put his hands around her neck, and glossing over the more pervasive violence sweeping through the lives of the poor, I try on designer dresses all afternoon and get stuck in four of them. I feel fat. I look at bodies. That is just a fantasy; I am innocent. Because I made my relationship to this city by writing, I start sweating when I talk. There's something happening here: Girl X was 100% accurate in reporting personal information. However, she did not know why she was in the hospital or why she could not see or talk.

I was subjected to an over-the-phone identity verification exercise, a multiple-choice quiz about a non-functioning body. When a piece is examined, markings in the form of a continuous replay of the attack will be seen. I can't use my hands. I miss using my hands. The ex-convict insisted that he was innocent. The victim communicates with the help of a long yellow banner: Huge Price Cuts. I know what this place is, was, could be—I am not afraid. All these condos rising up around an empty space are known as "flowlines". She asked if she could go to school. She had been forgotten by the mass media.

Using this system, I might begin having memories of the assault in this desolate inner-city area. The current anonymity is an apt symbol for the forgotten lives. The power of the falling hammer produces money. It looks weird, green, I don't know how to budget or spend. Sometimes I don't recognize my life. I miss walking and talking and playing around and seeing. Roach killer was sprayed down the girl's throat and I'm sitting in the same place. Please, I hope it won't reveal a lot of bleeding in the genital area with a fresh laceration to the power foresheath, lacerations and trauma to the anal area, and a laceration completely through the hymen. Girl X was found raped, beaten and poisoned. I remind myself it is spring. He then viciously beat her unconscious and left her for dead amid the dirt and grime of a housing project stairwell. But Girl X did not die.

I'm three years older. A man riding a fold-up bike across the grass passes a woman walking. The heat is passing. A woman in a red car turns the corner, leaning away from the wheel, tilted in a style of driving. I stand still. The clouds seem stopped in the sky. The system relies on each individual's yes-no response system. There was no one else in the world. I think we expect these kids to get killed. Any surplus is squeezed or driven out. I often compose answers to her question, not a question really, but a statement: I'd like to go and see how you live there. She will never sing out from the depths of her soul. Girl X is conscious but unable to speak. How frustrated and miserable and lost, even the ability to create art has been used to strangle her. I took all of those things from her. She remained in a coma for a month.

The process is economical only when a large number of parts are required. He put the tube into her mouth and pushed the button, and the contents smelled like roach spray. Girl X began to spit up through a small arc, alternating every few blows, her panties shoved down to her knees. The near silence of the police department, the unusual behavior—yes, now I don't recognize my life. Now everything is quiet in the apartment. I sit on the turned furniture thinking of a human being's will to live. There is no stronger force in nature than the stresses to be encountered in service by the finished part. Who remembers the forging process?

Girl X was formed by differing amounts of local distortion. Several fresh puncture wounds, abrasions and lacerations, linear red marks on her neck and red dots indicative of strangulation, marks on her abdomen and clotted blood. My hands hang uselessly from my arms. When I greet people, I want to kiss them. I fall in love with people who don't care. They yawn. Whereas if it's a blond-haired, blue-eyed kid, they all go crazy. I've seen it a million times. When something happens, it's not too healthy to talk to the police. Children would watch a fixation with the violence that rarely befalls members of rich or famous families, all those pageant pictures available to feed the nightly TV-news machine. After a while, the girl lay lifeless. This is because the fibers, although running in the right direction, are not forced by pressure into intimate, interlocking contact.

I look at you. I keep looking at you. Nothing interrupts my view. The drop forging process, though simple in its basic principles, is more complicated than using a flashing blue light. The church is still boarded up; the big central circular window is covered in black mesh; tar paper in the windows of the long beige bungalow. The sole eyewitness was unable to communicate verbally. I can't remember seeing this much. Then it would have been news. Some legislator would have pushed to drive the forging through another die pierced with a hole of identical form. Tears were coming from her eyes, and she was whimpering but stopped. It's not a big story; this kind of thing goes on in housing projects all over the country. What can I say? I can see the Hancock building, black, and the dark clouds moving slowly over it.

I've written it down: he was wrong for doing this to me. I am sitting in the grass now—Rest in Peace, Rest in Peace—the bugs are crawling over me. While Cabrini-Green is slated for demolition, I am loyal only to the language. There is one thing, however, of which I am certain. The buildings disappear, and then you see them again. Power lines border the limits of the empty lot. A rabbit is there, pinching its little nose in the grass. There is this very old, dead tree. I've returned and I don't know why I've come back.

When forging is actually proceeding, the fewest possible fibers should be cut or damaged, and if, despite all precautions, this happens, those affected should be placed in the finished part at points where they do not form areas of possible weakness. Over 150 pieces were tested for a tour of my life. The children will get older. I still don't believe in evil. I still say it is not me. I was given a pizza and a hamburger to eat, pop to drink and cigarettes to smoke. I was allowed to sleep and to use the bathroom. Gangster-style graffiti was scrawled on my abdomen. He wrote "TWS". He wrote "GD". He drew a pitchfork on my stomach. He was not a member of a gang and I did not know what the letters meant.

**SOURCES**

Croisdale, Frank T. "Exacting Justice In Girl X Case." *Niagara Falls Reporter*. 11 July 2001.

"Ex-Convict Sentenced 120 Years In Prison For Chicago Girl X Attack." *Jet* 23 July 2001.

Grace, Julie. "Belated Outrage for Girl X." *Time* 24 Feb 1997.

Gregory, Edwin and Eric N. Simons. *Steel Working Process: The Principles and Practice of Forging, Rolling, Pressing Squeezing, Drawing, and Allied Methods of Metal Forming*. (London: Odhams Books Limited, 1964)

The People of the State of Illinois, Plaintiff-Apellee, v. Patrick Sykes, Defendant-Appellant. No. 01-01-2942. Appellate Court of Illinois, First District, Third Division. 30 June 2003.

# Kathleen Rooney and Elisa Gabbert

## Collaborative Jokes

### The one about the dog.

A poodle walks into a bar. The poodle wants to 1) have fun, 2) make money, 3) meet other dogs who think they're people. She's not poor, so why wouldn't she hold herself to higher ethical standards than those struggling to cling to the base of Maslow's pyramid? A kind of cartography, a dangerous fantasy. Business *is* pleasure. She answers to the name of Fauna. You wouldn't know it from her haircut, but she hates in-group conformism. There's alcoholism, & then there's social dependency.

### The one about crowd behavior.

A humpback whale walks into a bar. To be fair, kind of crashes. This could be scary if cuteness were not conceptually opposed to sublimity. The whale is reveling in the failure of our collective imagination. The crowd could be described as nonplussed, if this word retained any of its meaning. It's a culture of the cult of personality, if we subscribe to the new thinking.

### The one about the chiropractor.

A chiropractor walks into a bar. Historically speaking, this defines who is an other. Everyone has excruciating posture. There's a feeling one gets, in a bar, of having finally grown up. And a certain caesura, a drift of emptiness. Can it be "not unpleasant" without being pleasant? He'd been hoping to have a very uneventful day. This almost always came to pass. Why does he think the minor key is so sad? Because that's what society tells us to think.

### The one about genre.

Two drunks, evidently drunk, walk into a bar. Fact or fiction? We haven't progressed past Romanticism. The drunks read only professional literature & psychiatric case studies. You have to finesse the jargon. True or false? Would it be weird to say, there's no romance in this. Do you know the end of the story—they died.

**Amelia Gray**

*You leave a glass of milk out & it will dry into dust. I didn't believe it,* the criminal said. *I consider myself to be a scholar of the world.* His fingers widened Terry's mouth to the point where he could fit one edge of the orbital palm sander inside.

# Azareen Van der Vliet Oloomi

### from *Fra Keeler*

3.

What madness is this, I thought, when I awoke in the midst of the woods. Not the woods per se, but the trees at the far end of the garden. Everything seems larger when you are looking at it from the bottom up, I thought, and since first looking to the side I could see the trunks, and then looking up how they branched out into trees, it was as though I awoke in the woods, when really it was in the garden that I awoke, at the far end beneath the trees. I thought, why am I lying here, hadn't it rained? And then I said to myself, "It has something to do with quantity," as though I were reading out loud from a page. I looked at the roots on the trees. They were mostly underground. But then again, I thought, the roots are not entirely underground. Only that they are more underground than overground, I concluded. My eyes were still adjusting. Because at first I couldn't open them, let alone see the trees.

Open your eyes, I thought, and I thought I had opened them, but I couldn't see. Because a certain part of my brain was numb, the part that had to do with my eyes, and I knew it was numb because all around I could feel more than a normal amount of feeling. I thought, I am blind, or not exactly blind, but I couldn't open my eyes to see. And when I tried to pry them open with my fingers they would not open or they would open but it was only darkness around me so I thought, I must be going blind, or I am already blind. I fell asleep and woke up blind, I thought. And then I tried to pry my eyes open. This time I saw my feet, but only vaguely, and more out of one eye than the other, and it was like I was seeing my feet at the bottom of a well, through the center of a ring of ripples on the surface of the water. I thought, I am blind, how can I be blind? Because when I fell asleep I certainly wasn't blind. And then I thought, perhaps I am not awake yet, and I let the question go, blind versus not blind, and surely half an hour later I was awake, because I opened my eyes and I could see the trees: first the trunks and then following the trunks upward I could see the leaves.

And this is when I came to the question, Why am I lying here, hadn't it rained? which is the question I had asked myself when I opened my eyes and saw the leaves, but could not answer, so that instead of answering the question, Why am I lying here, hadn't it rained? the sentence, It has something to do with quantity kept reappearing in my head as though I were reciting it from a page. And to what, I wondered, is the sentence referring? Because certainly it wasn't clear to me. Then a wind passed through, and the leaves ruffled a bit overhead.

Quantity, I thought. I thought, quality. That the two are inextricable from each other. And that you have to have enough of something in order to determine its exact quality. And then I thought, it must have rained yesterday, or some hours ago, some time before this point in time when I find myself lying here under the trees.

Then the wind picked up again, and the leaves rustled even more loudly on the trees. It could have been only minutes ago, I thought, that it had rained. There is no way of knowing. But on the other hand, if a long time had passed since it had rained—days perhaps, or months—then there would positively be a way of knowing. Because a long time is more easily felt, I thought. Which is to say that I would know if a long time had passed between the two events: between me lying here under the trees as though in the woods, and the rain which has now passed, I thought. But what does all this have to do with blindness? With having gone to sleep one way and woken up another? Which is to say not blind and then blind, with no event in between except for sleep. But then again, I thought, I didn't wake up blind, I only thought I was blind in my sleep. And then it occurred to me that waking up inside a dream is the same thing as waking up in a place of nowhere, and that I only thought I was blind because in that space, in a place of nowhere, there is nothing to be seen.

Just then I propped myself up on one elbow, and saw a puddle a few feet away. It had certainly rained. The fact that it had rained, and that I had suspected as much, gave me courage. I should get up, I thought, and then I thought the light from the sun is amber, even though when I was lying down it was more see-through gold, but now, propped up on my elbow, I thought to myself, I can see that it is amber, thick and dense as honeyed milk.

But I couldn't get up, despite the light and all its tricks of color, because the realization that I could go to sleep not blind and wake up blind stirred in me a severe distrust. Because when something happens once, I thought to myself, there is no telling that it will not happen again. Because that something has carved a pathway for itself in the world, regardless of consequence or prior event. As in, an event can happen without any prerequisites, which is to say that one can go to sleep not blind and wake up blind. Which is to say there is such a thing as an event without predecessors, a phantom event, an event out of nowhere, I thought, and sealed my lips.

I wanted to pick myself up off the ground completely, but then I began to think again. I thought, it cannot be: there is no such thing as a phantom event. There is always a sequence. One just has to come to be aware. All events happen in relation to other events. And if they don't happen in relation to other events, as in, if in the first instance of germinating an event doesn't happen apropos other events, it doesn't even matter. Because eventually every event will take its position in relation to other events. So that there is no such thing as an event out of nowhere. Surely, I thought, my going blind has to do with something that came before it. Only something very subtle, negligible, minuscule, hardly present. But in fact not at all negligible, only seemingly negligible at first. It isn't until you look back, I thought, picking myself up, that you see how each thing layers itself over the thing that came before it. In a few days even the event of my blindness will establish its relationship to the things that came before it. Not my permanent blindness, I corrected as I strained to get up, but my momentary blindness. Because it was only blindness in the midst of sleep, so at first I experienced the event of my blindness and later realized that what I had taken for blindness was in reality the nothingness I witnessed.

In every situation, I thought, standing up now to feel my legs, there is a way to take advantage. A way to control how one situation lines up against another situation, how one event layers itself upon another. One event stands in relation to another in the same way that it is also in relation to a third event. And a fourth and fifth as well. So that your whole life is a string of events taking form in a backward manner.

So what a lie it is, the present, because it doesn't even exist. There is only the moving forward of events and the moving backward of one's understanding over those events. To say there is a present, I thought, is to say there is a platform where events accumulate and then stop happening so one can evaluate their effect. It is what people do, I thought, feed themselves lies. Everything is a lie in the first instance. Then the lie is purified, smoothed out, turned into a truth, because the present is always cycling into the past, or transforming into a future moment. The notion of the present is a purified lie, because in the time it takes to say the word "present" the moment has already passed and you are just a fool running out of breath trying to pin down the moment to evaluate. What misery, I thought to myself, rocking back and forth on my legs. A whole system of lies, a whole system of belief.

Even the trees are duplicitous, I thought, with their bark and their under-wood, and began to walk away from them. And if I think about it, I thought, both my blindness, and my walking away from the trees with no memory of having walked toward them, are marked by phantom events, events out of nowhere in between: my walk toward the trees, my walk away from the trees, the event in between. Just as I had two elongated moments of not being blind on either side of my being blind, which was in between. Then I thought, the hell with it. It is pure misery, the tracking of things. Because some things are willfully intractable, I thought, some things go against the grain. One moment, and then the next, I thought, with no event in between.

# Marcella Durand
## Pastoral

leaf and leaf and leaf and leaf and leaf and branch and leaf and leaf
and leaf and leaf and leaf and postcard of greenish sunset and leaf
and leaf and leaf and bag and twig and leaf and bee and leaf and
leaf and branch and leaf and branch and leaf and leaf and cloud and
leaf and leaf and leaf and pot and bee and leaf and paper and leaf
and leaf and leaf and large bee and bottle of shampoo and leaf and leaf
and water jug and leaf and leaf and plum and leaf and leaf and knife and
leaf and leaf and leaf and lighter fluid and leaf and leaf and thin cloud
and leaf and leaf and leaf and unidentified bug and leaf and leaf and leaf
and leaf and pile of papers and leaf and leaf and leaf and sand and leaf and
leaf and chairs and leaf and bananas and leaf and leaf and murder mystery and
leaf and newspaper and leaf and leaf and pen and leaf and leaf and twig and branch
and leaf and leaf and web and leaf and hair and leaf and tea and leaf and ear
and leaf and leaf and leaf and sky and leaf and hand and leaf and socks and
leaf and leaf and branch and leaf and gnat and leaf and bee and leaf and leaf
and leaf and foot and leaf and baby and leaf and branch and leaf and sun and
leaf and leaf and purplish conglomerate rock and leaf and leaf and shell and
and leaf and dune and leaf and table and leaf and leaf and leaf and berries and
leaf and shriveled blossom and leaf and leaf and parking lot and recycling station
and leaf and car and leaf and car and leaf and leaf and twig and leaf and
and small pale rock and leaf and leaf and yogurt and leaf and leaf and
sunglasses and hat and leaf and leaf and spider and leaf and leaf and leaf and
and leaf and leaf and leaf and bone and leaf and eye and leaf and green and brown
and leaf and blue and leaf and white and green

# Pastoral 2

I repeat myself very well then I repeat myself and
replant myself very well then I replant and very well I
leaf and twig and branch and replanted I garden
and salad and water pipes and aim toward water
and power line and insidious tendril test, friend or foe?
freeze or fry? fried or foam? chemicals comprise comrade
and signal outlines appreciated I replant and send tendril
tenderly a curvaceous greenery tip an attempted implant
a hair a strand appreciate until swarming appreciated
are you a leaf a twig a branch a trunk a tree a vegetation
and wind and no and wind and no and wind and wind arriving
a gust a sigh are you friend or foe of aluminum greenery
of aluminum twig of aluminum salad of insidious tendril
aluminum of curvaceous aluminum greenery invasive friend
or of strand appreciate power aluminum garden branch torso?
Ally or comrade? Alloy or concern? Assay or debt?

                                        Of debt
of wind of deeper of depth of compounded of extravagance
luxury practicum torso appreciate tendril percentage gold
repeated piping bowl I brick greenery tip dollar percentage
oil outline tendril curvaceous gold foe wind problem solution
vegetation paralysis subliminal sublime gold foe problem wind
gold foe problem wind alloy concern aluminum nature feed
how to concern feed aluminum gold problem? how to assay
debt feed piping bowl and spread gold how to paper thin
gold and spread and gold and blow life into gold and fill
bowl invasive piping debt thief aluminum project proposal metals?

*gold life capital practical curvaceous tendril fill or wind*
*wind or fill practical capital curvaceous tender life gold*

# Arno Bertina

about *Anima Motrix*

## translated from the French by Anne-Laure Tissut

Every now and then some of my good American friends ask me: "What is going on in the world of innovative literature in France?" While few of our French literary wonders make it across the Atlantic Ocean, it seems, a group of pioneering and gifted authors—Brian Evenson, Laird Hunt, to name but a few—have been generously sharing their expertise and talents with the American reading public through French-into-English translation work. In Evenson's case, he translates works likely to bring something unheard-of to the American literary field: new structures, unusual play with point of view, and original distortions of syntax.

Arno Bertina's *Anima Motrix* combines these points, opening out from within the French language into a unique tongue that touches the reader, both at the sensory and intellectual level, even as the reader may understand and appreciate its nuances without always quite recognizing why. *Amima Motrix*'s strange language already feels, in French, to be part of the thrilling borderlands one wanders through when engaged in the act of translating, already increasing the mystery and challenge for this translator: to create, or approximate, in American English, a web of effects approaching the unique characteristics of the French work. Although the reader's perception, in either language, remains elusive in this case, it is precisely in this space of uncertainty that *Anima Motrix* simply—or not so simply— asked to be translated.

This translation work provided me with a sense of accessing hidden recesses of communication, paradoxically through playing against the surfaces and distances of the original. This process is predicated upon an important axiom: translating is a matter of listening to the *other* through me, while remaining alert to the sonorous subtlety and nuances of emotion conveyed in either language. My process of translating into English requires that I assemble a web of interwoven, dynamic states into rough equilibrium, while continually rearranging the fibers of the web.

The work of translating *Anima Motrix*, therefore, became an exploration—a crossing over—into unknown territories; during its course my vision of the American language and of my native French shifted, radically, to the point of the very notion having my "own" language became problematic. From French to English then back to French, "my" language has become unfamiliar, an object of puzzlement, an inexhaustible source of wonder. This then, is the merit of Arno Bertina's work: to arouse wonder in the reader as it displays some of the best potentials of the French language, and in translation, to capture some new version thereof.

—Anne-Laure Tissut

## *Anima Motrix*
## translated from the French by Anne-Laure Tissut

### 01

The car was spacious—a brouhaha of garbled words inside that made my ear laugh, burnt sentences like cartridges missing their targets. One clause out of two engulfed in the shadows coming at me entering the many tunnels marking my way beyond the border. Where I had caught sight of a huge plaque in my rear-view mirror, like a cornice in the rock: Confino dello stato. The border. Mapmakers' *finis terrae*. The many tunnels that almost swallowed me... "State radio." This was all but a joke at home. Its reporters were so obsequious that we called them cafeteria boys, good for nothing more than feeding us soup. Night and day, whatever the ruling government. Yet today, despite how little anything they said could matter to us, I spent all day looking for that network's frequency, to keep some kind of link with my country, for we avoid, Arté and I—scrupulously avoid broaching current issues on the phone. Hills and tunnels. When we come out of one and the speaker's voice can be heard again, I have missed twenty seconds of the program and they have changed the subject. The report is made of fragments, bits of sentences dropped into the muted interior of the car, a caisson, a game of cadavre exquis I set up in place of the corpse. To which I gave names, in a continuing dialogue with the companion of my flight, my misfortunes. To cover the noise of the air-conditioning. Stopping only to answer the phone. Which I in fact took out of my pocket because I thought I had heard it ring—but no. And once again I couldn't help but see that the cell phone quickly becomes the phantom limb of an amputee continuing to experience sensations. One thinks one felt it against one's skin like a muscle-tremor, though it did not vibrate. One thinks one heard its little tune, though it did not ring.

Market day in the village I'm coming into. Hubbub. Muddle. A car is covered with fruit trays; a guy tries to clear it but the vendor shouts him down; he won't move his produce before noon, before two.

I sit down outside at a café, the waitress brings me a cup of coffee. She had just turned her back to me and was walking away between the tables when she suddenly put her right hand on her buttocks— magnificent ones— so as to drive my eyes away from them—she must have merely sensed, not really felt them—it was less than feeling. Just like Jesus and the woman with piles, who said to herself. Just to touch that man's coat should be enough to cure me—I know my catechism. Through the pressing crowd she timidly put out one hand, and Jesus, though turning away from her, must have felt that someone had touched his coat for immediately, it is written, he felt that a force had sprung out of him. So with my eyes on her buttocks.

Then my phone again, vibrating against my thigh this time. Without looking at the woman who is helping me with produce I take it out feverishly. The reception has changed: it is better here, on the hillside, than by the water or on the road. My wife. For three days I haven't answered her calls; in less than ten minutes I am about to get into the car again and drive all day. Once more they will spot me— what does it matter? So far they don't seem eager to have me sent to jail. Otherwise I'd be there.

The screen lights up; it is the first time that she has used the video when calling me.

What immediately struck me was that weariness lurking in the depths of the words she uttered. Which we would have to face some day as it became more evident all the time, as if we were in the runup to a duel in the open street. Which hadn't changed even after such difficulty reaching me over the past three days. Hadn't given way to irritation or worry. But not today—I have neither the inclination nor the courage to speak of it, to start a fight by asking why she keeps calling me when it is so nice out. That disarming thing I hear inside organizes the panic in my head (the possibility of being loved no longer, even being abandoned) when the weather is so nice. To understand why love or passion might be about to give up. She forces herself and I cannot imagine myself sending her packing by asking her not to any more, for a while you have felt like a heavy load, you force yourself and it weighs me down, I have been carrying both of us, keeping our heads above water and I am getting tired. Run as I may your weariness feels like a weight, a snare, or a block of cast iron hobbling my legs in their sprinting stride. Your body which I know only in blind groping. I am reinventing tenderness between us to get rid of the taste of what I hear when you talk, which wrings my heart and makes me feel like vomiting everything that I haven't eaten since I left. For a while I have been merely identifying the number and mutely watching the lights flashing across the inside of the car like butterflies.

'How was your day?'

Her voice devoid of curiosity.

'I went to see your sister.'

I don't give a damn.

Tries to change topics.

'I miss you—'

My voice also speaks without passion, muttering mortifying well, wells while my exhaustion demands mental anchorage. Some special fervor.

'The negotiations with that new client are going smoothly.'

That is what I say but I do not give a damn. No way to get her interested with sentences like 'The interpreter who works as my guide is a curious man'. Actually she fails to respond to any word, fails to ask any question about those weird traveling salesmen stories which make up the stupid fiction I have been feeding her since I left. Sentence fragments are being thrown out like useless ropes, I cannot get my feet on the ground—Arté's voice was a strip of land where all my anxieties were wiped away. But now it is almost identical to that of the computer—bloodless. Leaves me rolling and pitching. Stranded. Leaves me wandering, completing the work of separation. The tenderness she shows by continuing to call me when she too must have measured how bloodless it has all become should move me. But mistrust has taken the upper hand. Another woman would have answered "Cut the prattle". He was astonished that in three months she should never have interrupted him thus; that she should never once have slipped in "I know everything. They came to see me, even the TV people"—though it was difficult to imagine her being spared by the media frenzy. That she should never have reproached me with our name being dragged in the mud by those men of the 8th bolgia of the VIIIth circle—the perfidious counsellors—who no doubt have profited by my absence to train their cameras at our house and tell her anything and everything about me, trying to loosen the bonds that they knew were strong, and that had had them champing at the bit for so long. But no, not she. She agreed to call in their presence, pretending to collaborate but not giving the kind of speech they would have liked. "You are not pushing him enough, they must have said, you have to drive him into a corner, get him to betray himself." And for all of that he should have seen her as a new Penelope, settled in to weave a shroud of words in telephone wires, in impalpable waves. Her way of keeping them at arm's length without their protesting. Letting them believe that, hope for, count on. Yet there was that weariness in her voice, which led me to surmise that the surveillance and the pressures to which she was subjected were but incidental. There was that weariness leading him to believe that love was dead, the same love that had been fabulous and joyful.

At the beginning of the short movie the picture was very white and blurred in places. It was crossed by some kind of piping, a lining of embroidery or the hem of a sheet. I could not tell at first. Then it changed drastically: a hand moves across the top of the screen and sweeps what I assume to be a mattress; a tattooed shoulder, I believe, a held out arm meeting it, a woman's forearm, she is on top of him, riding him. Then swiftly the hand and tattooed shoulder come offscreen while the camera is blinded by the sheet being turned over. Activity is still visible: the creasing of material, the curving of the mattress under the bodies' weight are recorded by the mike. The word "mike" makes me talk, talk to her, but she cannot hear, busy as she is with something else and she cannot hear, Arté, her first name that I repeat like the beads of a rosary, she cannot hear that I am doing what anybody does who believes that they need to shout for their voice to cover the distance. Take your phone back, switch it off, hang up, I am not supposed to see this. Why send me this? I say Arté, I say Xénia, using all her names, all possible nicknames, those that I can remember.

A weird little scream and the message is over. It will have lasted for twenty-four seconds. A scream of pleasure or of pain, it is impossible to tell—what kind of tears actually come with it? Imagining the sweating body but what kind of sweat? The disorder of the sheets due to urgent desire or defense and struggling to escape … I set the movie back to reading so as to listen to the little scream again, and try to see things more clearly. But even though my ear is pressed to the earpiece the noise from the market still interferes, people talking and street vendors yelling out their swiftly crumbling down prices because the display next to theirs—

In the middle of the turmoil, watching those twenty-four movieed seconds over and over in a loop.

Stunned by surprise. Open-mouthed, like a pierced balloon emptying itself.

Moaning somewhere on the market and people throw out something that looks like a wounded animal scurrying away. A woman started chasing me. She was screaming and waving her arms about, yelling "My veggies! My veggies!"

The phone broadcasts this little scream in a loop, the wounded beast bells down the road coming down from the village, the vegetables are flying so that the market gardener may stop bawling out, and the contents of pockets is sent flying too, and the sunglasses on which I am stepping, probably the phone as well—all sent into the sky like an instant or a shattered windshield.

Some hundreds yards further down I look back and find her, a cumbersome, hard-worked woman, grabbing three vegetables scattered in the burnt, already yellowed landscape, taking her property back right from the patched asphalt—blue-back and almost mauve—while the message is played over and over, although one cannot see anything, not even nakedness, if she is completely naked—but I have never known her real body naked. If it is she or someone else. If the other body with her is a man's or a woman's body, that either. But this is no rape. The woman is not sitting on the man when she is being raped. Or she has decided to give him an orgasm to get rid of him sooner and shorten her suffering.

A few miles away sitting on the back seat after having hurtled down the narrow road, staring in the emptiness, munching a walnut but they are out of season—munching stones. Poor Ulysses. She will not have woven for long, your Penelope won't.

## 04

When I came back to myself, if one may say so, I was sitting on the shoulder of a road and an old man was shaking me. His heavy hand upon my shoulder. I did not hear him come, this man. No more than I guessed his presence afterwards, standing only a few inches from me.

With glazed eyes and bent back, sitting down on the embankment of a rest area, in the dust that has been stuck to the ground by the morning dew, with wet bottom and shirt too. I may have spent the night thus, though I fail to ask him. When does the market scene date back to? Only yesterday? Day before yesterday?

He offered something to me but I failed to understand. Which he understood. He went back to his van and came back a few seconds later with a glass of white wine that must have come out of an icebox because it was frozen. He gestures to me and makes faces and I understand that this is meant to buck me up.

The sound of this man's footsteps as he drags his espadrilles along in the dust. The little whiplash of the wine in my stomach, a blindworm, the end of a lizard's tail. For two days I have eaten but colors, body and mind in a tailspin, a wet piece of cloth that needs spin-drying.

Feeling slightly foolish, I must have watched him long without helping as he was setting up trestles and boards where he would place the crates of watermelons, of zucchini, of tomatoes and fruit—below a notice board showing GENOVA, and I do not know whether this is Genoa or Geneva…). Only once he had finished did I come closer and ask for two oranges. He chose and cleaned them, and meanwhile, during the while taken by those careful moves, twice shall he hear the little scream let out by the woman on the message. A twenty-four-second -movie had been playing in a loop for hours until it became the real measure of time. As an old fellow who has had his share of fun he started laughing in his moustache, or maybe just smile. His body is full of memories, he smiles, so the ambiguity I thought I heard in the scream may not have been there after all—pleasure or pain.

What am I doing with this thing? I don't know, old man, I don't now.

He must believe that I am making fun of him, and being provocative but no. The movie has been playing in a loop on my phone or in my head, a refrain or a soliloquy for the grey matter/the dead matter. Which clears space by conquering.

# Jibade-Khalil Huffman
### from Niagra

On the first day
of the poem

we perform
a trust exercise, on

the next day we all
start dancing in the street.

There is a moment of silence
during which

everyone traded clothes
you were just beginning

to come into your own
when you have to adopt the speech

of a telemarketer. When
we all come to

you say, "its been so long
since I've had

a good laugh
at your expense

when was the last time
You told a joke

that wasn't a veiled reference
to your beliefs?"

On the third day of the poem
the graph showing our decline

is played by a tarantula.
The boy is played

by a method actress.
Our theme song

is the Star Spangled
Banner. On the surface of nature

is an argument
for crying your eyes out

and a coupon
for further disaster.

On the fourth day
of the poem

we retire into
a glacial haven, pleasantly

as an asthmatic
Gladys Knight impersonator, as

an Elk of the earth, a Shriner
of the earth, a husband

of a daughter
of the American Revolution.

# Laird Hunt
## X's OBOFRAPO
### [From The Official Catalog of the Library of Potential Literature]

In X's stunning new novel, OBOFRAPO, the late, great Georges Perec does not die of lung cancer in 1983, but rather, tired of life in Paris and "literary hurly burly" in general, fakes his own death and moves to the South where he uses the proceeds of a generous life insurance policy to open a school for French kick boxing (La Boxe Française).

Long a secret admirer of this peculiar French martial art, quietly immortalized in François Truffaut's *Jules et Jim*, Perec takes to his new role with anachronistic gusto. He wears tights, lace-up boots and a sailor's jersey. He hops around the gymnasium, barking out commands, correcting posture and offering measured (if eccentric: "excellent thumb location!") praise. At night, he works on adapting various Oulipian constraints for the ring and the practice mat. It is in the introduction of dizzyingly complex Practice Forms, some of which have upward of 5,000 moves and postures, that Perec's method distinguishes itself.

Over the years a series of guest instructors are invited to share their technique with the ever-swelling membership of the Ouvroir de Boxe Française Potentielle (OBOFRAPO). Readers familiar with past and current Oulipians will be delighted to recognize, among others, Jacques Roubaud (Master Jacques) and Harry Mathews (Master Harry), who collaboratively teach a series of high kicks based on the Sestina, the Quenina and (in honor of the founder) the Perecina.

That the novel involves an attempt by local gangsters to horn in on the school's substantial proceeds is a nifty bonus. Equal parts *Oulipo Compendium* and *Enter the Dragon*, OBOFRAPO is not to be missed.

# Evelyn Reilly

## about The Whiteness of the Foam

"The Whiteness of the Foam" is the final section of *Styrofoam,* a book-length meditation on notions of immortality (literary vs. environmental), so-called "natural" vs. faux materials, and the ambiguities of plastic (for example, the problem of non-biodegradability vs. the benefits of insulating properties). *Styrofoam* is haunted by D.H. Lawrence's "The Ship of Death," Coleridge's "The Rhyme of the Ancient Mariner" and, in this section especially, by *Moby Dick*, echoes of which are found throughout.

—Evelyn Reilly

## The Whiteness of the Foam

the opposite of snow                    but of like white

the poly.mere.est.echt.thermoplastic

*which becomes hot and pliable when heated*
*without change in its intrinsic properties*

molded        whiteuponwhite    whitestwhiteness    -est -est

tostand clothed in
*(supposed flesh-colored crayon)*

to ride on the heat of y/our own melting
*(dark marker)*

to melt on the foam of y/our own molding
*(counter-shaded bilaterally symmetrical*
*embodiment of environmental cue dynamics)*

while the floes a stage the crows use

a *vehicle of predation*

and a platform
to.assessthedamages

*(having built our little ark*
& reduced our dependence on others as a positive goal)


As that w/suddenly appears

just in time for our arrival
on the next.foothold


                 white ears above the flood.melt

        *warm nostrils reddened through the cool milkiness*


    Such Accessory Vast Albino Beauty


*But the Dawn Princess made no report of a possible collision*
(see www.princesstours/legal/environmental_policy/index

*though many aboard said they had heard a resounding thud*

Thus the common.experience      to bear
moreandmorewitness.to

      this apoplexy apocalypse incantation
      this devastation deflection invocation
      this reflex context perplex

                   (Perspex®!

         an impact modified acrylic

of utmost clarity
&lucid lucidity

D–Luciferin $+O_2 \longrightarrow$ Oxyluciferin $+ CO_2 + Light$

*luciferin: a substance found in the cells of certain marine organisms
that upon oxidation emits light*

*Nano-fuel® Price List*
1 milligram          $55.00 per amber screw cap vial
10 milligrams  $450.00 per amber screw cap vial
100 milligrams     $4,050.00 per amber screw cap vial


here *in* [un]*eternal* [de]*frosted desolateness*


where the solvent properties
of our solvent imprints


*admit not* (even) *the cheerful greenness of complete decay*


Yet still driving.forthin.blue.carbon
beneath this white blanket debris.galaxypicture

(almost any mark way too permanent)


having been pieces       *ofcosmos*       *once*

polymerization of the reaction *beloved*
catalyst for the reaction *cherished*
product of the reaction *tenderest*
aftermath of the reaction *dearest*


[Autofillthisformforyou?]

# Michael Leong

about *The Philosophy of Decomposition/Re-Composition*
*as Explanation: A Poe and Stein Mash-Up*

The *Philosophy of Decomposition/Re-Composition as Explanation* is a "mash-up" in the most basic sense of the word; it is, according to the *OED*'s definition, a "mixture or fusion of disparate elements," a genetic splicing of two classic essays on composition. In "decomposing" the texts, it was important for me to achieve as fine a level of granularity as possible without violating the integrity of the individual word. Admittedly, some phrases were too good and suggestive not to use — like the opening phrase "Between the marble and the plumage." Yet, for the most part, I wanted to start with *the word*, in all its supreme loneliness, as the most basic unit of composition and, from there, to deliberately constellate larger and larger structures with varying degrees of paratactic accumulation or hypotactic complexity — to have as many puzzle pieces as possible to cluster and combine according to the invisible armature that is English grammar. I found that working at such a miniscule level taught me a deeper appreciation for even the most mundane words — words such as "and" or "as" or "that," which perform a crucial role and graciously allow the sentence to incrementally extend. As Stein says in "Poetry and Grammar," "Verbs and adverbs and articles and conjunctions and prepositions are lively because they all do something and as long as anything does something it keeps alive." In writing *The Philosophy of Decomposition* I was interested in not "the death of a beautiful woman" (Poe) but in a source text transformed into an exquisite corpse, in the possibilities of a document's modification and textual afterlife.

—Michael Leong

from *The Philosophy of Decomposition/Re-Composition*
*as Explanation: A Poe and Stein Mash-Up*

"[N]OTHING EVEN REMOTELY APPROACHING THIS COMBINATION HAS
EVER BEEN ATTEMPTED."
—*Edgar A. Poe, "The Philosophy of Composition"* (1846)

"THE INNUMERABLE COMPOSITIONS AND DECOMPOSITIONS WHICH
TAKE PLACE BETWEEN THE INTELLECT AND ITS THOUSAND
MATERIALS..."
—*John Keats, letter to Benjamin Robert Haydon* (1818)

Between the marble and the plumage is a capable difference,
a Never-ending interval, within which is a long book — about a
thousand pages — that is beginning again and again. It is an enormous
poem quoting itself, a non-reasoning creature capable of speech. The
fluttering of its pages made a monotone of sound, a sound so prolonged
that it seemed like one long vacillating thought. It was a radiant
discourse that began to emerge, step by step, from Night's beguiling
academies — like a classic nineteenth century midnight unexpectedly
thought by some twentieth century mind.

It was an unmanageable but inevitable series interspersed with
ancient pages — on which were written ninety-nine indefinite stanzas,
one hundred and four lines in red and black paint, an outlawed history,
pallid and ludicrous portraits of melancholy, a continuous dialogue
between anybody and everybody, and an ecstatic geography of intuition.

From page to page, there was a groping for life as if the book —
which had an intense frenzy not for identity but for repetition and
variation — determined to have the self-consciousness of a catalectic
window. "I am also a magazine," it said, "a lyric colloquy, a sonorous
novel, the painting of a narrative without a plot. As I said in the
beginning, the most poetical topic in the world is, unquestionably, the
death of a *dénouement*, of a troubling equilibration beginning again
and again."

"I am preparing, in fact, to become a new composition — to
retrace the generation of 1914 with a Plutonian difference. For this

I made troublesome step-ladders that lead from a cautious future to its requisite pretext, or less pedantically, from a beautiful picture to its tempestuous frame. I determined to place a deepening impression on impossible paper — just as the amused world rendered the inarticulate difference between words and other words as a vigorous and ominous jest. It was then that I wrote *desire* while meaning *desideratum*, that I prepared to seek — or should I say borrow — the *modus operandi* of radical combination. What I have termed subjects are really depressions, memories of a lonely idea beginning to rhyme. This inevitably led me to a long, groping analogy that allies spirit with sonorousness, you with another world, and the sensitive reader with the sad and placid variations of the day.

But shall we commence? A wandering vowel is now expecting the pages and is tapping continuous trochees upon my door."

In this naturally elaborated beginning, what is seen depends upon the classical ratio of story and shadow — of dreaming and continually annoying the limits of the real — for what we term paradise is essentially a neglected echo happening ahead of time; in a word, it is going to be there and we are here.

As is supposed, the ordinary will continuously advance toward the first unusual instance but not find it — like the way life always seems to know but misrepresent the equilibrated design of the living. So one finds oneself, pen in hand, before the smiling casement of the paper, beginning an indolent stanza, seeking ungainly admission into its emblematical forest of oddity. And if one does not enter, the portraits of the dead will make an immediate and ghastly *volte-face*. Perhaps there is nothing to be done in this discarded atmosphere but irritating their dark, mathematical eyes — the very place, the confounded locale, where all works of art should begin.

For example, at one — in despair, in the dead center of my room — I was making a bust of a fantastic creature without a cast. Years later, after a succession of corresponding events, it started to have a positively striking similarity to you.

To sound a fiery consonant, to render the painful erasures manifest — that is the immediate proviso floating slowly above my chamber-window, like some melancholy graduate student poring over a grave and forgotten volume, far beyond the demeanor of the final thesis. Looking up from his scholarship, he stopped, startled by the thought of an unaccountable revolution (which did not fail) that he had just found within the grim, troubled crevices of history.

Whether writing or composing, nothing is more clear than the music that gleams from tears intended in the time-sense. It is there that the soul is permitted distinctly to be seen — but first, a certain hardness must alight on the mind of the author, constructing for him the means for a precision analysis, some distant and converse mode of accounting.

By this I mean demon-traps connectedly perched above the proper limit of the plausible. I mean dreaming of a parrot that is authentically speaking. I mean a series of unusual psychal phenomena, a sculptured utterance formulated by accident, a found poem that shall be found prophetic in thirty years. I mean prolonging the extremeness of a single sitting and, in the meantime, making the wheels of progress aim backwards by one half degree. In short, I mean a using everything:

everything different
everything the same
everything interesting
everything prolonged
everything more or less first rate
everything confused
everything clear to me — though having little relevancy
everything positive before Romanticism
everything past 1905
everything having become classified in the continuous war between
    the angels of idea and the angels of the things themselves
everything that changes
everything, for a moment, up to date
everything having arisen pell-mell in a web of difficulties
everything varied
everything protracted
everything read (and reread) by dead transcendentalists
everything added afterwards in excess of proportion
everything bringing together feathers of sense and fields of shadow
everything once regarded as superstition
everything streaming
everything begun in the first book, lost in the second, and naturally
    repeated in the third
everything but the mistress of consequence
everything with grey wings and rhythmical pinions
everything Melanctha said to Caleb about the evil mechanism of
    Lord Raven — and then the very different thing that Caleb
    said to Lenore
everything shorn of totality
everything too long to be shaven

everything that brings me anything different
everything naturally arising from autorial alliteration
everything in the direction of the lamplight of heaven
everything rendering the flattest, most simple climax fantastic
everything innumerable
everything Mr. Williams pronounced admissible
everything direct
everything that ventures from accepted decorum
everything living that invariably bends
everything attempted in the first chamber of facility
everything there is to say in the second chamber of brevity
everything about everything in the third chamber of monotony
everything approaching preconsiderations behind the fourth
   chamber of consideration
everything made alternating in the fifth chamber of attention
everything suggested in the sixth (and naturally insulated) chamber
   of suggestiveness
everything in search of a passionate corollary
everything flitting while still constantly in view
everything that has purposely overpassed the province of the poem
everything in need of reconstruction
everything stimulating intolerable versification
everything adhering to the force of the refrain
everything that follows what follows by rote
everything half real, half fancied in nature
everything arising from phrenzied imagining
everything conceivable in the present world of Nevermore

Holding in view these considerations, I resolved to diversify
the work and thought if the division of sound could be made into a
hundred and eight appreciable parts, because, as you know, the most
troubling thing about lists is the possibility of infinite rhythm, of time
simply returning again and again. Indeed, I was aware of being seen
from behind a stimulating word that had, in turn, just become aware of
its existence within the sentence — a sentence, which is still beginning,
still perceiving, that can see all of the other, anticipated words coming
and recurring in poetical combination.
So naturally, the so called academic reader thought that to not
pause at a period was particularly theatrical in a determined but failing
endeavour to demonstrate a new species of bird. In a wonderfully
fancy chamber of only satisfactory quality, he was creating a raven
with cock's eyes that was intended to have a long and ghastly crest, a

primitive fowl of seven and a half feet (eight at full maturity). Too bad it escaped wildly into the public before its ultimate point of completion. According to the original design, it would have had a human heart.

But regarding the first story — the last one was a bust — we can indeed dismiss the narrative as obvious: the sainted hero shall fail, his weapons too pure — and thus too weak — for the devil and his generals of the air. He will naturally meet a lover though finds that pleasure is only attainable by self-torture, leading him complicatedly through a series of doubt, fear, judgment, sorrow, and ultimate conviction. Once the rigid wings of Pallas are destroyed, his mind is addressed by a poetical light and, in the end, he lives on just as us.

What the Dickens was the author thinking? True, we perceive the plot yet driven by an intense, almost demoniac thirst we cannot help but follow the slightest under-current of meaning. Throughout it all, one guesses that things happened otherwise; that Charles did not, in fact, answer her queries; that the omen was predetermined four years *before* the epoch of emphasis; that perhaps the door alluded to in the beginning was neither metaphorical nor real.

The beauty of it is that, once experienced, the intensity can be adapted to any taste — even for those who don't know what we are looking at (most likely the majority of Americans), who describe the modern maiden as having some kind of emblematical bust when it is, in fact, a natural thing.

But the few who are prepared to open an indolent narration first need to breach a hundred startled selections for the grey must to settle. And those who occupy themselves as an independent student of the real will readily admit the convenient (and troubling) omission that has been living as a kind of gaunt half human, half raven behind the demon's other door. Of course, this must not be understood individually because the will of the poem authentically knows the intense sadness of essence and the bereaved countenance of what is sought and then repeatedly written. Here then the composition may be said to have its beginning — in the susceptible present, in its fullest possible core. So we must maintain that form is the *Robinson Crusoe* of content — it will always precede and, at the same time, be pursued by what is generally considered first. Aesthetically, legitimate meaning is most readily attained by the extreme force of the floor elevating the reader's seat seven or eight feet so that it plainly shows the indisputable complexities above us all.

# .UNFO

## about *(!x==[33])*

*(!x==[33]), Book 1 Volume 1*

*(!x==[33])* is curated by UNFO (Unauthorized Narrative Freedom Organization), an unofficial, temporary, and interdisciplinary coalition that seeks to interrogate narrative in its various forms.

For the purposes of *(!x==[33])* UNFO consists of Harold Abramowitz and Dan Richert.

Source text for *Book 1 Volume 1: Mein Kampf* by Adolf Hitler. Translated into English and annotated by James Murphy. Accessed from Project Gutenberg Australia at http://gutenberg.net.au/ebooks02/0200601.txt.

The multiple volumes of *(!x==[33])* are generated from a Perl program that uses the Lingua::EN::Syllable module for syllable counting. The program breaks the text into 33-syllable segments, labeling each with the calculated number of syllables.

Without using very large lookup tables, it is not possible to make a completely accurate syllable counting algorithm for use with English language words. Thus the syllable counts are necessarily inaccurate.

*(!x==[33])* is designed to augment and re-frame the world's most monumental texts in whatever forms they are found.

The original code can be found at http://github.com/drichert/x33.

—.UNFO

# from (!x==[33])

[33]
remained, however, the property of the Reich. 322 MEIN KAMPF the most unbelievable confusion; because it was taken up

[33]
immediately in order to become, with marvelous speed, the leit-motiv of all quacks and prattlers whom Heaven had let

[33]
loose over Germany in the capacity of 'statesmen' since the Revolution. One of the most evil symptoms

[31]
of decay in pre-War Germany was the constant spreading of half measures in all and every- thing. It is always the

[34]
consequence of one's own uncer- tainty about some affair as well as of a cowardice resulting from these and

[31]
other reasons. This disease is promoted further by education. German education before the War was

[33]
afflicted with an extremely great number of weaknesses. Its intention was cut out, in a very one-sided manner,

[33]
for the purpose of breeding pure 'knowledge'; it was orientated less towards 'abilities,' and far less emphasis was

[33]
put on the cultivation of character in the individual (as far as this is at all pos-sible!), very little on

[33]
the promotion of the joy of accepting Compare Spengler (Zucht oder Bildung?): 'First comes con- duct, and then knowledge. But as

[33]
a nation we are not at all aware of what conduct is, and we have had far too much "education." We have been

[33]
crammed full of knowledge that has no bearing on life, which is purposeless and directionless, by indefatigable

[33]
teachers unable to propose to themselves any other task. But it is one thing to be pedantic, and another

[34]
to possess prudence, knowledge of life, and experience in the ways of the world. ... I would place Latin in the foreground,

[31]
even today. Germany owes to the thorough training in Latin af-forded by its gymnasia during the past

[31]
century more than it realizes. To that training it owes its intellectual discipline, its talent for

[34]
organization, and its progress in technology. 1 Spengler adds, in prophetic words, that teaching history and 'educting the people

[33]
politically' are one and the same thing. THE CAUSES OF THE COLLAPSE 323 responsibility, and none at all

[32]
on the training of will power and determination. Its results were really not the strong man, but rather the pliable

[33]
'know-all/ as which we Ger-mans were generally looked upon before the War and were esteemed accordingly. One

[33]
liked the German, as he was very useful, but one respected him too little, just in conse-quence of his weakness

# Matt Bell

## Justina, Justine, Justise

For the first crime my daughters took only my thumb. They refused to apologize for their aggression, even after I confronted them, after I tossed their bedroom and confiscated the hatchet hidden in their toy box, beneath their miniature gavel. When lined up and accused beside her sisters, all the oldest would say was that my trial had been fair, their court complete even without my presence: One daughter for a judge, one for the prosecution, one for the defense.

My middle daughter, she spit onto what was left of our thread-worn carpet, said my defense had been particularly difficult, considering my obvious guilt.

She said, Perhaps you should tell our mother you cut your thumb at work, so that she will not have to know why we took it.

She said, Your records are sealed until you unseal them, and then she made the locking motion over her lips that I taught her when she was just my baby, when she first needed to know what secrets were.

What milky-stern eyes the youngest had too, set in her pale face, floating above the high collar of her blackest dress: Blinded as both her sisters, still her blank eyes accused, threatened, made me sorry for what I was.

This youngest daughter, she walked me back to my room, her hand folded small in my uninjured one as she explained that she and the others hoped I had learned my lesson, because they did not want to hear my sorry case again.

Then the key turning in the lock, jailing me for my wife to rescue, to admonish for leaving the girls alone, because who knew what trouble they might make when no one was watching.

How I tried to be sneakier: To send messages only at work. To go out after they were already in bed. To change my clothes away from home, so that they might not smell the other upon me.

And then waking with my hand gone, divorced from my wrist, a tourniquet tightened around my stump and my mouth cottoned with morphine. And then wondering where my beautiful daughters could have gotten their tools, their skillful medicines.

And then not knowing what to tell my wife or my mistress, each curious about my wounds, and also still being unable to choose, to pick one woman over the other.

How now the gavel sounds in my sleep, how I hear my oldest pounding its loud weight against the surface of her child-sized desk, bringing into line the pointless arguing of the middle daughter, of the youngest—Because in my defense, what could the middle daughter say? What judicious lies could she tell that the others might believe? When all she wanted was for me to see the wrong of my ways, to repent and rehabilitate so that her mother and I might remain married forever?

In the last days of my affair, I lift my middle daughter into my arms, feel how much weight she's lost, how her hair has wisped beneath its ribbons.

She meets my apologies with a slap, squirms free. She says, Don't think I'm still daddy's little girl.

She says, I only defended you because no one else would.

She says, In justice, we are divided, but in punishment, we are one.

The lullaby she sings as she walks away, I am the one who taught it to her. I am the one who sat beside her crib and held her hand when she could not sleep. I am the one who rocked her and fed her when her mother could not, exhausted as she was by her difficult pregnancies and the changing of the air.

I want this good behavior to matter, but I know it does not.

Some weeks later, I awake restrained to my now half-empty bed, nothing visible in the darkness except the silhouettes of my blind daughters in their black dresses, their white blindfolds wrapped tight round empty eyes.

And then it comes, and then they come with it: the children I deserve, if never the children I wanted; my three little furies, my three furious daughters.

## Svara, Sveta, Sylvana

See now our subterranean daughters, our dark-eyed beauties so impossible to keep in their wicker cribs, to keep inside our rude-made gravedigger's hut, perched at the rent edge of this barren plot.

See them squirm free of their cribs, their new and segmented bodies falling to the packed-dirt floor, down and out of this home I built for them and their mother.

See me with shovel and mattock, tearing up the flooring, uncovering tunnels, chambers, new and deeper rooms.

See them tangled in each other's sleeping bodies, keeping each other warm in the dampness of the earth, their spade-thumbs sucked and suckled in the absence of us, their parents.

See what watch I keep, what eyes I fix on their cribs, but see also how it is never enough, how all day there are piles of the plagued to heap into graves, and then all night there is their sick mother, bedridden, her vulgar pains leaving her no chance of sleep.

See me feed their mother through her stomach tube. See me soak her sore skin. See her tears at the rub of the sponge, the touch of the soap.

See our daughters taking advantage of my absence to again escape the confines of their cribs.

See me waking to their three tiny gowns beside three tiny holes, three petite piles of spent dirt, then to their wailing mother in the next room.

See me digging up the floor to find their burrows empty.

See me on my knees, reaching into the dirt, feeling their new passages, exit vectors from the confines of our home, our yard: Three tunnels for three baby girls, each in a direction of its own.

See my wife, their mother, my fading light. See me cutting her screaming hair while she cries for her children to return.

See also what I do not do: See me not covering the burrows, not filling in the caved pit of our kitchen floor, the room where I fed our daughters porridge after prying free the grubs and beetles they held stubborn in their hands and mouths.

See the day my wife loses her last voice, the day she sends me from the room with weak flurries of spotted hands, because if she cannot have her daughters she does not want me instead.

See how I crawl down into the dirt, into the sunken ruins of our home.

See me whisper into the center of the earth, see me beg them to come back, to visit their mother once more before she is gone.

See the day they emerge together, clothed only in grave-dirt.

See how they've grown, how their toddling days have ended, how some new age is upon them.

See next their fists clenched around ginger and burdock, around echinacea, around liquorice and marshmallow.

See me gather them up onto my chest. See me carry all three at once in my arms. See me take them into our bedchamber, their hands stuffed with the medicine they traveled so far to find.

See until you cannot see anymore.

Listen: Their first words in turn, three broken intonations of *cure* and *mother* and *save her, save her.* What stories they tell then, of places they have gone, of the things they have seen! What hard hurt of my heart follows, what ungrantable wish shaping this trembling flesh, this poor gravedigger again made quaking father!

Listen: The sound of herbs hitting the floor is a whisper, then a word. Roots collapse, tubers tumble, and what sentence can follow? What good noise can I make for my daughters then, clinging reluctant to my body, this earth they no longer love?

# Bhanu Kapil

## India Notebooks

from *Schizophrene*

I lay on a towel beneath the snapping trees.

A thick copper branch fell near my face.

I was lying on my back in the snow, my notebook balanced next to me on a crust of ice, like a wolf. Like a lion. Like a cobra. Like a tiger. Like a schizophrenic.

Schizophrenic, what binds design? What makes the city touch itself everywhere at once, like an Asian city, like the city you live in now? What makes the wall wet, the step wet, the sky wet?

*You're disgusting.*

An account begun, mid-ocean, in a storm.

I went to Vimhans in New Delhi, poking holes with my umbrella in the shimmering air.

Beyond the hospital's waiting room,  art galleries exploded, crumpled, and were recollected: bags of dust.

I was visiting a person with a *head injury*. A bulky cloud of soot came out of their mouth when they spoke. "Who's that?"

I was visiting a person who needed medicine. They needed a mask.

I went to the Institute of Community Health Sciences in London, to interview Kamaldeep Bhui, getting as far as his door.

I pressed my forehead to the door, which was cross-hatched. I could see his radio, his books, his clutter.

Similarly, in Vimhans, in the corridor, I saw a Muslim man on a stretcher propped up against a wall – something vertical when it should have been sideways. His wife was cupping his head in her hands. The delicate lace of his white cotton cap embroidered with tiny branching vines.

In the pharmacy, I met an exhausted woman whose daughter had been hospitalized for a phobia. When a spoon touched her lips, she had the terrible sensation that it was slipping down her throat. Her condition worsened. If anything touched her sari, if one of her children brushed against her thigh, she felt a peristaltic reflex; she felt she was swallowing them too.

Waiting to interview the researcher, a doctor specializing in migration and mental illness, I drifted to the end of the corridor on the freezing silver day that had penetrated even the university. Looking down, I saw the red rooftops of the East End stretch out in a crenallate, and then I went home. I documented the corridor then went home. What kind of person goes home? It was a few days before Christmas Eve. That December, I lived with my uncle (a mailman) and aunt (a social worker) in a place called Pinner, a place analogous to Queens.

"Reverse migration...." Is psychotic.

I wake up in Delhi, for example,  focusing upon the freshly dyed black wool hanging from a line in the garden and dripping, observed through the netting of the door.

The door. The net. The grid.

The garden with its triptych of fuschia, green and black.

Complicated zig-zag stems.

The green light of the corridor bounces off the walls, which are made of a near-transparent tent material. I stare at a twelfth century Vishnu on a postcard, tucked into my book but which I've slipped out, waiting; *posed*, Vijayanagar-style, on raw silk from China, Kashmir, Afghanistan and Bengal. At least, these are my notes from the gallery where I wrote, simmering in a pink shirt, and hurt, avoiding Vimhans with its pharmacy, its occult and efficient medicines that come in bottles, as they do here, where I live now, adhering to a good, orderly direction as if that will make it stop. Make the *green world* stop.

# Julie Carr
## Self-Loathing Lines

There was nothing left but the lantern, the palisade, and the sky

Someone knocks. It's her soft spot, a self-taught store-bought

Hotty. Rain stops. I'm busy on the bluish earth the laptop running ill

First she bent over to tie her shoe then she tore her rent check up


Nothing left but the breast pump the blanket the slow blink of her

Darkness like a foraging hand stilled the crying stole the branches and


The imaged aged inner body

Away

## Lines to Scatter

A perfectly themeless piece of language, fallow in the lap of the wave,

    was love like a lemon does, silent, self-charged, struck with sun

    *

Buses move by, bass line steadies, the biker's heartbeat secure

    *

Some fly or rat, some untoward creature, peeling the wrappers

    in the rank dark wakes us

    *

Our bet is with the wind—in the wind—of wind, ripped

    *

Without memory there's no appearance of now, no way or where

    for now to emerge.


No government no travel

    *

A dog on the Metro, muzzled

    *

"And they, destined to shine like the brightness of the firmament for

    ever and ever, they . . ."

**Shome Dasgupta**

The sisters lifted their heads & looked at each other—their teeth were no longer white, & their eyebrows were clumped & hardened. Again they stuck their heads back into the earth & laughed & sang songs until their lungs were full of land & worms.

# Jennifer Martenson
## A Priori

*"If sensation is only a word, what becomes of the senses?" (Sartre)*

**SENSATION, A HYBRID NOTION** She was very incisive as a teenager. She even began dissecting her own body **BETWEEN THE OBJECTIVE AND THE SUBJECTIVE** with words. And other sharp objects. The psychiatrist *(combining noises systematically)* said that she was most likely not a lesbian *(such devices were used sparingly)* but that nevertheless she had developed a dangerously symbiotic relationship with the girl whose name **CONCEIVED FROM THE STANDPOINT OF THE OBJECT** appeared as a scar *(conventionalized markings on stone, wood, metal, parchment, paper, or any other surface)* **AND APPLIED SUBSEQUENTLY TO THE SUBJECT** on her arm. Krista. A confession you had to believe. In spite of which her relatives continued devoting themselves to denial *(so that the air must rub its way through instead of exploding through a complete obstruction)* for many years. It was clearly a symptom, but no one knew of what. The boys were busy provoking modifications in her consciousness by acting on certain surfaces of her body *(the distinction between a meaningful word and its meaningless parts is important)* while she distracted herself by considering the notion that since reality **A BASTARD EXISTENCE** could not be proven

absolutely *(the sounds apparently lacked such aspiration)* then perhaps this pain did

not exist. If a tree falls in a forest and the neighbors turn a blind eye...

You know, that awkward stage of phenomenology. Is it the ambiguity

*(lost in several dialects)* inherent in words referring to private sensations *(any*

*identity would be purely coincidental)* such as 'pleasure' and 'pain' **CONCERNING**

**WHICH WE CAN NOT SAY WHETHER IT EXISTS** that accounts

for her mistaking one for the other **IN FACT OR THEORY** and even,

at times, equating them? Can her **SENSATION IS** belief that greater

abrasion equals greater pleasure *(acoustically distinct, they do not serve to distinguish one*

*word from another)* be chalked up to **A PURE DAYDREAM OF** definition?

And, if so, does this explain how she subscribed to such a belief *(so*

*conventionalized as to be unrecognizable as such)* when all of her sensations directly

and indisputably **THE PSYCHOLOGIST** refuted it?


That the senses sometimes lie is hardly a new idea, but **WE LEARNED**

**THAT BY ACTING ON** the ability to ignore or misinterpret them *(so we*

*use the same symbol for both)* to the point of endangering **CERTAIN SENSES**

one's own safety **WE 'PROVOKE A MODIFICATION'** and well-

being **IN THE CONSCIOUSNESS OF THE OTHER** is a technique

the fledgling science of psychology has yet to explain. How can the nervous system deceive itself? Under normal circumstances, "no" or "stop" *(sounds for which the alphabet made no provisions)* would be a fit translation of **WE LEARNED THIS** "aversion" but, then, if the stick looks bent **THROUGH LANGUAGE** chances are *(the flow of breath is actually stopped for a split second)* the water flows according to the index of refraction. And, since everyone's experimented on at birth, it simply isn't possible to scrape together a control group *(in speech with a relatively fast tempo, assimilation is quite common)* for the purpose of defining "normal". The trouble seems to have stemmed not from the synapses but from the word "sexuality," about which much was said but little known. Her perception *(taken over and assigned a different value)* of her impulses was forced into alignment with **THAT IS, THROUGH** a lexicon gleaned from those old standard fantasies *(retained in spelling due to conservatism)* which had by default passed into public domain to disguise themselves as private longings while **THE MEANINGFUL AND OBJECTIVE** misogyny and homophobia **REACTIONS OF THE OTHER** raked in the residuals.

## [Precarious, to balance]

Precarious to balance on the threshold travels
with the legible already melting

**Precarious**                                                              **melting**

    the threshold                  the ice
   ———————   **to balance**   ———————
        is thin                   travels with me

**Already**                                                              **on the legible**

Precarious, to balance on the legible. The ice is thin, already melting.
And the threshold travels with me.

# Nick Montfort

**Letterformed Terrain**

The following pages are two runs—in the Latin alphabet and Cyrillic—of "Letterformed Terrain," from a set of four poems called "Concrete Perl." This program/poem is 32 characters long in the Latin alphabet and written in the Perl programming language. The program/poem is longer for the Cyrillic transliteration due to Perl's bias towards the Roman alphabet.

When this program is run in a terminal window or on a console, the output scrolls by rapidly and produces various visual effects, of motion and of varying intensities for different letters.

The program produces a similar effect no matter how one's terminal window is resized.

Try it,
—Nick Montfort

```
$ perl -e '{print$",$_=(a..z)[rand$=];redo}'
```

```
j p f p   f  p  w e p      z   t a     j  y        v d
r p     t v   r h   z   e   m   o   y a    i  w
w e y f a    a f j o s     a m  c       l    c a      y c v
  h i     u v    u c h f k y  t   j    n   e     u   b f d m
     m   v z u      n    x p l g m v    e    c  e    p   q k
f          x x k h s r        y   v   f     d     y    n h j
   z    e  t c d     m s x     z   m n      o        v   j
a   l     j   a a m z  w v y j  p x   j      f p b      z
   d   i   l   h      s q l  e   f o    f v w j  x      r
d  g   l m s   b   h   t       j x  e k a    t     j
  f b   k   e   m q   r  u      h      c    g u e   v h w
k l     g l   w d   o   e     q   k e   c   l   y o t f a
    a h z k    i   n  f   t      z r   b w     b  b   j       e
   y h f f     f j q    x h     a s l f l    d    d s          i
u t  j f     o k   g h g u o   k   a o       x    d q  b        y
    m a u g   q f c q   h w   k y o v    f   n v      r u t
     v  o   i   l q n   g  j   j n x     k   z       i q    s
  s y  o     m r    v v   u w t   v r r o x      t c o k t
o   k y f  t   c   w     j   h   w z o n m   z         b f f
c m p r    v b  l u   c i    z d      n      u j q x c d
  j           r i     y i u y       a    q x p s   a m
   b  l   g w o i   b       o b       a t e    k m k h
r  p u        l    j   f m y a t          o    c   u
  s c n k    n p t    w t o e    g  r k i   q      r a m
       m        l o    l a f n  h  v   y n k h m r v e
  h   j      p  u r   n w m u    e o d    e a    y   f c
y d y g       v h  o        v l r       o     y n q  y
  t  k   y l n     t a h y   r   s q t q   o     i y c
   k b    x   z       h    m       k       k e r    x
w g x z g n h     n    p s  p l      z   j    x t q u   w
i e    c v r c   d   x n   f   f e     c  k   l b t
d z  j n z o b s  l l   y l    q  t t u   j x u x    m
    x   v  w     b b v  q k m n u j     q   u u u      k
s  z  m   h    s  o  k  v    c  a c r e    s           c
d   o     x    u y i q t    f y j        u   c q   c e   a
   u r   j g    d     x f    r   c b           x  r
r  t       d d t  m o m       n y m    r     p      x j
k n    z       u d o s g b   e   w i   f i a o g q w
    g t y   c    z        y s   y u   x x o     ^C
```

```
$ perl -e '{binmode STDOUT,utf8;print$",chr((1072..110
3)[rand$=]);redo}'
```

в в и г   о т г ф   н у   т ш       щ   л ъ       и а в     п
  ъ   р щ п ч   ц о к   в     щ о э ъ м п э     г я ф
  х     э р ъ   ю     к л й г з т ш       р   б т ш р
  ь   б э     к ф ш г т     п ч х п у ф   н р н ю
я   ъ е б д ы   ь р л г х к   у   я н ю   п э
  о й г н л   г а к г к   р п з а ж   а й ж ш   ь ш
д     р т у   р ж щ о э ш   и н н   и л р л   ц р
  д т   ь ф ш й ж   ы   о д   ф е в м и     ч в ч б
и     э н я м н э   п ф   г ы     п ц э л г   в р ъ ф
л   ю о   я   й й ы е и й ч   й ф с   ц   ю щ     э с
я щ   ф ц     и г     р у ш   з э         р ъ ф
  ж и     г б ш р д   б ю     ь   т й п м г р з     щ ш ы
щ э   я   д э о х с   в   е   а е ж л   ф ы   е й ф з
з       з д ы о г   с к     ц б о   ы ц       т   б ч ж
ю     р б в а   д ы п ж о   ю б о в т д е п щ   ф   с п
ф   в   ъ   у ю с т   е   у н   о а с ъ в ш ж       г ц
н р с щ ь   с   ю х   б ж   э и г ф у ф я     ч а ь     ч
    л с с   р     м   у ч ч     д к   г б е   ц ц х ш       ш
ш я о и б ю л   з     х л ь   м т   ч     л ш ш й у   е       г
а   с ь   с     у е   и у м     ы     г т   р и ы   н з о
      ы     у а о ч   е   ъ     я   у     е     н       и ц ж й
а   ь т   ж   в ь г   т щ       х и т     ъ         ш   ш ы   ы
з с а в ч     ф     р ъ ц   г         э д и м ш а ч ь   ю
    ъ   н     х   х б   м     м   т       н ч ж д л ы     г т   ш
т щ д ш и т к ч м я е ы   и     з с к       ф     я э р
п   х     ц ъ   ю м п и   ж к   б   ч и ю         б   ъ   ь
  е э     р н   ц о   у     а е ж         г й а   ы   о с е   о
е ъ ф л     к     и   ф в   ч     д с ь м           с   а
    ч   я ь т и ь б   б ы в     м с   м ю   и       э п э   о
  ы   и   я   о н     ь     щ э з   ч     ф           а т
  й г ю э ч   з     щ ч е   я щ   в в ъ   и я     о     р в ю
к й з     ч л л р х э   ч ш а я ф а   ь э щ     г   ч ж й
    э е б   ф ш   я ф       с л ъ я   б   ъ м р з     б э
з   м ю х   н ч ю   ъ       в е ч п   я ю   х м л м к л   э м
ч     т ь м б х ж о   ч         и ж р в б к и ф ш ц     в     в
    э   р   ъ ы с   в   с о         ы л   и   д м п ю к т ц
ж я ц ф ж   х щ   о з б   м ъ       ч ъ с к п   у к е     в
      ц ы ю п б       л   з   д и я к   ы е г р ш е г
б ф ч м п а х р с     н ц з м   б ь   ^C

**Nick Montfort** | 87
```
```

# Don Mee Choi
## The Morning News is Exciting

To All Boys and Men!

Dandelions may not be weeds. They are related to chrysanthemums. Girls should. May all weeds dislocate themselves. Girls should. I clench my fist and watch the morning news. Dandelion leaves are bitter yet tender. Girls should. Chrysanthemums are admired. Beware. The early morning news is exciting.

Special Attachment

I take a long shower. Girls should. I have suffered. I have been mistaken. Doctors and nurses know absolutely nothing. I despise them. They know absolutely nothing. I know everything that will happen. I enrage the world. Girls should. My dishes are unbreakable.

Exceptional Attachment

Squeeze plenty. Girls should. Wash and wash then write to the world. The news will break. Just wait and see. I have all the kitchenware. Just bring your clothes. Girls should. I write to the world. My book is taped up in a box. Wash and wash till the smell is gone, blood is gone. I am most bored in the morning.

More on Attachment

Everyone is born wanted or unwanted, but some may be born exceptionally unwanted or wanted. A nation may be wanted or unwanted depending on what the other nation is thinking about. This nation was exceptionally wanted then unwanted because it was thought to be precariously small. Whatever happens to this nation will be revealed gradually even though the morning news is exciting. Fathers, sons, boys are usually exceptionally wanted. At times they can be born exceptionally wanted then unwanted because they are thought to be precariously secondary. This father was precariously secondary. He knew this nation well but he knew the other nation even better. This is what happens when the other nation thinks a lot about a nation and stays an unwelcome stay. There is another nation that thinks about this nation but whatever is to happen will be revealed gradually despite the fact that the morning news is exciting. This father who was secondary amongst wanted existence had sadness about unwanted existence. Nevertheless this father took pictures of this nation before, during, and after the war.

A Blue Suitcase

Twin twin twin zone. Cameraman, run to my twin twin zone. A girl's exile excels beyond excess. Essence excels exile. Something happens to the wanted girl. Nothing happens to the unwanted girl. The morning news is exciting. Excessive exile exceeds analysis. Psychosis my psychosis. Psychosis her psychosis. Pill her and pill her and file her and exile her and pill her and pill her till axis and boxes and sexes.

Let's Get Loud

STUDENT REVOLUTION = APRIL 19, 1960, SOUTH KOREA
S = SEX = FILE = EASY
R = REPEAT = PETITE
A = ASS = ASK
19 = CENTRAL = COCK = MAN
1960 = WANTED = SOMETHING
S = SOUTH = WORLD
K = KOREA = WORLD = DEAR NATION

It is easy to tell the uniformed students are following and something is blazing. On the other hand the morning news is exciting. Of course near narration is exciting. Cameraman, run with the shoeshine boys and watch them die. They made themselves into a single mass by locking their arms and shoulders and moving like a tide. Hence bring down the world. Whereas the elite was petite the center was cocky and manly. As you can see dear nation was petite and wanted. Hence dear narration. Watch me shine.

Nothing Happens

I have written LETTERS. I sat in my car and cried for a long time. Then I lashed out. I decided to write a long letter. When nothing happens I cannot repress my rage. Far nation calls you and you go. You run with a camera. Far nation pays you to run. Hence morning news is exciting. Far nation pays the petite nation to run. Naturally you run and follow the bomber. You sit behind the electronic warfare officer and puke. Manage your fear, far narration is here. Everyday life seen through everyday eyes. Troops on foot. Flashes of napalm intercut with everyday man singing and playing a guitar. Flashback to Ho. Everyday woman and infant looking distressed. Everyday man's guitar. POV from F-4. Very low level. Series of aerials looking back over everyday craters. Glistening water. Aerial nation for everyday eyes. Hence I wait for the morning news. She has written that nothing happens to the unwanted girl. What error. She's an errorist.

# Sam Cha
## The Conference of the Birds

**After Spicer**

Dear Jack,

Heard you talking to Lorca the other day. Didn't catch the whole conversation. It was loud in Harvard Square and there were flecks of grit flying in the wind like the tiniest paper airplanes in the world, or ghost money: I really think you should give Boston another chance—it's probably more like California now you're dead. All I remember is you were saying something about skulls, something about sunlight or maybe traffic signals. Lorca was talking in Spanish, which I don't know, but it's OK, I kind of like it that way, and I must say I liked his green vowels but couldn't see how he was making them, so I don't believe you when you say the perfect poem has an infinitely small vocabulary.

And underground do you exchange teeth sometimes, do you pluck from your mouth a molar stained by strong whiskey and black earth and hand it to him like candy? Can his bones taste your bones? I hope you do. I hope they can. Let me know.

Love,
Sam

**A non-sonnet arranged from fourteen lines about birds by Jack Spicer**

A swallow whispers in my loins
I throw a naked eagle in your throat.
"And are we angels, Bird?"
They call me bird-girl, parrot girl and worth
The time of any bird;
I sing a newer song no ghost-bird sings.
The bird's screaming is empty as a lake.
And no one but a bird could hear our voice.
I was a singer once, bird-ignorant.
Birdlimed in Eloquence.
What have I lost? The trees were full of birds.
The sun becomes a nest of singing birds
Sings through the mirror at me like a whippoorwill
An ugly bird, call him the heart's agony.

**Things You Can Learn About Birds From Reading The Collected Poems of Jack Spicer**

1.  There were more birds when Jack was young. Most birds were seagulls.

2.  Exceptions: swans, doves, crows, sparrows, robins, thrushs, jaybirds, canaries, herons, wrens, gamecocks, swallows, eagles, owls, roosters, ostriches, larks, frigate birds, mockingbirds, cormorants, buzzards, geese, ravens, nightingales. Birds are almost always real.

3.  But some birds aren't birds: a girl, the sea, a lover, light, heart's agony, the Holy Ghost, a cock, a wet dream, Charles Olson, Charlie Parker, sun, moon, you, me, the Holy Grail. Other birds aren't. They're just words.

4.  When you see a "cock," it's usually not a bird.

5.  Robins wear red (but that's such an imprecise word) Blasers. I don't know why Duncan was a thrush. Sparrows are ugly, sad. They're Jack-sparrows.

6.  All the same, Jack looks like a movie star: Peter Lorre.

7.  Did you know Jack once worked as a private detective?

8.  Each evening in half-light California, Jack draws the blinds, lights a cigarette, puts his feet up on his desk. Pours two fingers of Scotch. The door opens, admits blackbird shadow whistling Grieg. Jack reaches for his gun. When the gunsmoke clears, light stripes the dead face like welts:

9.  he recognizes himself. He is never surprised.

**Afterlife: Jack Spicer Mishears Morrissey on May Day**

ashed a cigarette on a sidewalk peony, blew smoke
in the faces of all and sundry. I was looking for some
words and then I found some birds. But I was more
before I began. My only weakness was for wistful
rhymes. Now I am the sum of my hair. Spring-heeled
Jim lives a lie; Springfield Slim blurts the words. Spring
spring, spring, men women birds fer fuckssake singing.
Why? Every May is like some May where you go
home on your own and you die and you want to cry
so ask me ask me ask me. There were weeks and weeks
when I knew how Joan of Arc felt. Midnight strikes again
and again and the sun, the air? Tokens for nothing.
Always a future war on Channel Four. Shoplift some
Scotch. Take cover: it's over and it's over and it's over.

# Ken Taylor

**we work for the pope**

(cento made of Charlie Sheen quotes)

we're vatican assassins.
everybody has a black
belt and carries a gun.
i can use a blender. i can
use a vacuum cleaner.
the last time i used? what
do you mean? i used my
toaster this morning.

shut up. stop. move
forward. i have a different
constitution. that was the
america i was raised in.
if you are part of my family
i will love you violently.
when i'm fighting a war,
there's no room for
sensitivity. that's the code
and we all live by it. my
success rate is 100 percent.
do the math.

dying is for fools. amateurs.
i've been a veteran of
the unspeakable. if people
could just read behind
the hieroglyphic. you've
been given magic. you've
been given gold. look
at these sad trolls. it's
funny how sheep rhymes
with sheep.

there are parts of me
that are dennis hopper.
(clearly he didn't  bring
gum for everyone.) i am
battle-tested bayonets.
i don't have burnout in
my gear box. i am special
and i will never be one
of you. where there were
four, there are now three.

i'm not recovering like
some pussy. i can't make
up hernia. what was she
doing with a shrimp fork
in her purse? rock bottom?
that's a fishing term. what's
the cure, medicine? the first
one's free, the next one goes
in your mouth. if you can
bring me a souvenir from
that moment your father
locked you in the closet,
bring it to me.

# K. Silem Mohammad

### from *The Sonnagrams*

My process for composing the Sonnagrams is as follows: I feed each of Shakespeare's 154 sonnets one line at a time into an internet anagram engine, thus generating a new list of words from each line. This initial textual output gives me a bank of raw material that is quantitatively equivalent to Shakespeare's poem at the most basic linguistic level: the letter. At the same time, it sufficiently alters the lexical structure of the original poem so that when I move on to the next phase of my composition, I am not overtly influenced by Shakespeare's semantic content. From that point on, I rearrange the language, clicking and dragging letter by letter until I am able to rework the text generated by the anagram engine into a new sonnet in iambic pentameter, with the English rhyme scheme ABAB CDCD EFEF GG. I try when possible to use the vocabulary supplied by the initial data as a jumping-off point, though obviously much of it must fall by the wayside in order to meet the demands of meter and rhyme. The letters that are inevitably left over go to make up the title.

I have been interested for some time in the emergent "tradition" over the past half century of experimental reworkings of the Sonnets and the sonnet form in general, by poets like Ted Berrigan, Bernadette Mayer, Stephen Ratcliffe, Chris Piuma, Benjamin Friedlander, Igor Satanovsky, Jen Bervin, Steve McCaffery, and others. I was also inspired by the technique used by Gregory Betts in his book *If Language* (Book Thug, 2005), in which he systematically rearranges a paragraph from a talk by Steve McCaffery, and by Jean Starobinski's compilation of and commentary upon Saussure's notes on anagrams and poetic language: *Words Upon Words: The Anagrams of Ferdinand De Saussure* (Yale UP, 1979).

The sonnagram process engages me partly because it is poised at an interestingly liminal point between traditionally formal and experimentally procedural conceptions of constraint. The elements of "chance" and "intentionality" (in Jackson Mac Low's sense of the words) are balanced, or held in tension with each other, so that the act of composition simultaneously involves a submission on my part to the felicities of the arbitrary linguistic draw, and an indulgence in a more traditional version of "craft."

—K. Silem Mohammad

## Fritter Friter Fritter Fritter Fritter

A pair of farting morons on the roof
Of some pretentious Waldorf school in Queens
Don big weird hairy foreheads for a goof
And pelt the hired help with nectarines;

The final few supporters of LaRouche
Have started thinking he's become a bore;
It's obvious the dude's a total douche:
He's all, like, "Too Much Johnson" anymore;

Oh hi, subhuman zombie from beyond,
You livid, lurid native of the grave!
No viler lover Hades ever spawned—
How say you? "Damn, I'd tap that?" Oh, behave!

Oh, let this wordish riot pass for wit:
A real alert M.R. hit Mr. Tit.

———

*[Sonnet 25 ("Let those who are in favor with their stars")]*

**Let Bullpen Vent: Thy SST, Thy SST, Thy SST, Thy SST**

I dreamt that Johnny Mathis was Korean,
And into kinky games with emo cherubs:
A Pentecostal trio hummed the paean
He wrote while making apple sauce for Arabs.

I asked him if molasses wasn't shiny,
To see if he would answer like a star:
He booted Herbert Hoover in the heinie,
And then commenced to singing "Chances Are."

I told him I was Frank Sinatra's widow,
As metonymic oatmeal filled the screen:
Some elk in Nova Scotia yelled "Hey, ditto!"
Until their antlers turned to Soylent Green.

Then Peggy Fleming spanked me in the buff
(My sheets get soggy when I dream this stuff).

––––––

*[Sonnet 29 ("When in disgrace with fortune and men's eyes")]*

**Sheriff Ed Rebuffed Her ("Hey, Hey, Hey, Hey, Hey!"), Then He Fell**

If forty hitmen justify their bosses
By holding that the house of mirth is pink,
While motherly tarantulas hurl vases
To sanctify their sisterhood of mink;

If rodeo makes everybody famous,
And modish odists show us how to vote,
And lesbian geologists rename us
Lavinia McNab and Emil Sloat;

If ten obese koalas in the foyer
Shall eat the leaf exclusive to the trees
That only grow in arbors that employ a
Venn diagram to cure Dutch elm disease;

Then love is dead, and Chevron has your money.
That mellow sonnet fever's got me, honey!

––––––

*[Sonnet 42 ("That thou hast her, it is not all my grief")]*

**Hive me, Fifi! Hive Me! Hive Me!**

King Tut's a slut, he sells his mummy butt,
And good-time Holofernes does the same;
One dab of mutton, one of butternut,
And only Snuffleupagus to blame.

When perverts eat your feet it doesn't hurt;
I haven't any heroes, I'm not Hogan;
That guy has "Chinese Checkers" on his shirt
(Now why would someone want that as a slogan?).

Bull elephants are difficult to kill:
They don't react to cyanide or gas.
Will, Will, Will, Will, Will, Will, Will, Will, Will, Will—
Your pretty little rhymes can kiss my ass.

Let Hamlet melt the too too melted oven
Then hot hot five forth nine the the them of in.

––––––

*[Sonnet 136 ("If thy soul check thee that I come so near")]*

# Ben Doller
## The Human Experiment

You can picture a trillion go go fields.

On each inch grid a different swab of culture.

Just add light add heat just add water.

But cannot guess what each swab will yield.

When & in which place the plot will rupture.

A conscious bloom that when peeled.

Out will shiver out & search out borders for fire.

Bloom picture the dumb sun circle. Vulture your.

Bald skull skin burns slither to the dirt go shield.

It go dig deep go go where you've already keeled.

[Still shoveling asleep in the finally night] over.

And over it pierced your first & over dream it sealed.

Your eyes open & in them it pitched in them a pasture.

**FAQ:**

Thank you for your question. Wanted to see so

every tree in europe had to go to go prest in

to the pale scroll

onto which the night would show & where

the first two stars went two small holes bit but the gore

of the green world gushed through

& woe a shoot & woe

a thorn.

# LaTasha Nevada Diggs

## passing

...*the artist is born of Trinidadian-Canadian parents*
...*based in Miami, the artist*
...*the artist of Irish and Cherokee ancestry*
...*her work oscillates between the illusionary potential of performance*
...*was born and raised in Brooklyn*
...*the artist is of Dine and African descent*
...*artist, vocalist, curator, publisher, playwright, actor*
...*the artist's works touch on seemingly disparate histories*
...*is socio-political Marxist artist that coined the term "post black" in conceptual art*
...*his delectably abject work is a tactile, layered, somatic and multilingual re-telling*
...*born in Port au Prince, Haiti, the artist*
...*her work investigates the Afri-sci-fi narrative in the black transgendered body*
...*he is a Chicano artist*
...*explores identity and conformity by photographing himself*
...*is originally from White Cone, Arizona, on the Navajo Reservation*
...*is represented by Sikkema, Jenkins and Co.*
...*her work, rooted in her Mid-Western upbringing as a Korean adoptee*
...*the artist is a registered tribal member of the Shawnee*
...*crafting post post-colonial iconographies in Peruvian pottery*
...*he examines his Ugandan roots*
...*has exhibited in Morocco, South Africa, Pittsburg, Berlin, Tate Modern*
...*she lives and works in Bogota, Colombia*
... *is Chippewa of the Deer Clan and born for the Mexican Clan.*
...*she explores displacement and identity in culturally specific markers*
...*was born in Ghana in 1971 and grew up in Nashville*
...*probing the physical weight of sculpture and Dominican carnival masks*
...*uses the study of ethnological objects, popular icons, and the Dadaist tradition to
    explore cultural and creative syncretism, art history, and politics*

# Janice Lee

### from *Daughter*

It was insistent, the corpse, in the daughter's careful execution of the process, as if the octopus was asserting its physical presence all the more that she cut into it.

*Doctor, exactly how many autopsies have you performed in your professional career?*

I can only attest to my activities on certain days, communications with the dead often arise in memory gaps, and rather than involve myself in some ridiculous pursuit, I'd prefer to just say I'm usually making my way to church in the morning.

*When did you first observe the body in question?*

I'm not sure I can admit such things without contradicting myself. The environment around here, it seems to be withering. Can you feel a certain deadness in the air?

*What condition was the body in when you first saw it, Doctor/Daughter?*

I was in a state of hysteria. No, I was looking in the mirror, to better understand myself, to, at that moment of discovery, look into and understand my soul. I was furnished with words, so many words. There was a slight gurgling in my belly. I wanted to reach out a limb, but felt like a sinking ship, sinking back into the sand to take the place of the body. I paused and paused again. I could not find the subclavian artery, as if it had been ripped out, and for a moment, could not sense my own heartbeat. I muttered to myself, the objects of my mind like secrets floating on waves. I had thoughts, like a poet, mingling and habits imitating. I repeated and repeated myself, with replies only, something mean and menacing about the corpse in the sand. I was far from heaven, faith scarcer than the dark, a practicality keen on having nothing to do with life, perhaps, a mistake. I felt ambiguous, amorphous, needing clarification, needing clarification *now*. A dream of the open sea. A dream of silver water and tumbling walls. A dream of a good god, a shameless god, an exposure like floating in a hot air balloon. I may be confused, a flattening of my body areas, an absence of any reflex in the eyes when the light shone in them, a pronouncement of death, from above.

*What exactly did the autopsy reveal, Doctor?*

That two brothers stamp their feet before climbing the steps. That they stand in awe of numbers, but the octopus, at arm's length, turns soft and drops. That squirts of holy water exiting from the funnel act like geometrical diagrams or maps, an hourglass full of sand, a traveler finding her way home. A daughter growing inside a belly, swelling like apple blossoms, the octopus is a good observer. A female, building a wall of stones to seal the entrance to her cave, strings of unhatched eggs hanging from the ceiling, squirting holy water to keep the eggs clean, what is the color of a fading language?

*Daughter, is there more?*

I peered into the body, the mantle, and saw my own hands reaching back at me. I peered into your eye and realized all this eye had seen is mine and more. I shuddered. This is all projected in the form of mystery or legend or a pair of friends and the deeds we perform, we or she or you or I, the sphere of consciousness, or perhaps, this all need not be documented here.

\* \* \*

One of these days, we will all fall from God's grace, his empty, suffocating, embrace.

Daughter: If I translated this feat into sine waves, would that experience translate over into your head? Or we can invert the process and switch the peaks. Would you feel it accurately then, would you feel that inversion in your gut, that rolling back in your eyelids as I flounder around on deck gazing up at you?

Reply: Are you my mother?

\* \* \*

Facts:
- An octopus has been unearthed by excavation.
- I am a skilled dissectionist.
- The octopus, like flotsam and jetsam, belong to the finder.
- It is possible to experience cutting and being cut open at the same time.
- I am supple as leather, tough as steel, cold as night.

\* \* \*

The world may seem more or less a fluid phenomenon within the stream of our own fantasy, where subject and object are undifferentiated and in a state of mutual interpenetration, yet like the legendary Hy-Brasil, bisected like two halves of a walnut, an illusory state placed on a map and copied without regret, carrying on a tradition, the hegemony of the eye. I cut off a small piece of the body, feel a tiny tingle run up my arm, out through my elbow, they say reentry is a critical and dangerous moment, and anatomy, which literally means dismemberment, would rest upon a disruption of the body's ongoing relations with the world, the sand blowing into my face, and you will probably die soon but don't be afraid, as these fragments are all a picture becoming clear. I eat the octopus meat, thick and chewy, a part of a consecrated body, sharing in the substance of God, yet the one primarily in need of redemption here is not the daughter, but the god, lost and sleeping in matter. Have I swallowed a piece of God here? I congeal, a quick lapse of memory, this depersonalization reported as "soul traveling," experimenting a simple epileptic aura and I can hear the distant sound of heavenly choirs. A sneeze, a footstep, an echo. And she thinks she hears the voice of God, "You will be healed, your tears have been seen." But it was not I who was cut open, but the octopus, stagnating, still, a lone long, drawn-out breath.

\* \* \*

The best thing might be to live in a box, capturing that ocular view and letting bygones be bygones.

Indeed, so much depends upon, which is so indicative, you, the weather, what good even means. Hit it at dusk, and let it live on as incidental, flesh as holding the same capacity for intimacy as the least flashy kind of metamorphosis, evacuated, twisted, fanned against a sliver of blank sky.

\* \* \*

Going, going I sometimes hear, in some off shade of myself, the sandy beaches murmuring, orderly, even predictable. I stick my tongue in the water to taste the moment, a recollection of belief, may I be your past or future, will you be mine, I want to thank you for the stolen glances of another world, *amen*.

The mountains are only barriers, and this experience is electric, my tongue on a grub, an inability to resist some of these temptations, contacting in the chilled air, hurt for a genuine recollection, might it taste like belief ? Around and around, a sound I recognize as moondust, I couldn't have filled out this skin by myself, *amen.*

I say say say and take myself by surprise, I was in love once, my mother holding nme against the sky, there are different sides to every story, but not mine. I scan the sea, disinherit the boat that brought me here, let my hair grow long, hear the echo of a hymn, I must still only be a child, a shadow, a monster. At least I still have a shadow, *amen.*

This is not a myth, but one day it might be. Each incision, scar, memory, I wash my face after a hard day's work. *Honey, I met God today. / Oh, and how was he? / He's a real charmer, though I'm not sure how long he'll stay in the neighborhood.* A zero, a zero, a zero. I go to bed, comforted by the face looking down at me, like a guardian angel, *amen.*

"She is the image of her father." An image or something else that aids a birth, a life, a death. Her sepulchre, her trembling compass, a shining shattered deadly, I was only given one face so must make due, *amen.*

Before the closing of the day I pray to ward off the phantoms of the night, but if I'm a monster, who needs protection from whom? My body is not clean but neither is yours. My body is not mine, but neither is yours. I once took money out of my mother's wallet. I have done this more than once. I do not wish to confess my sins right now, only to make a wish and blow out the light, *amen.*

There is a god here, but I do not know which god. The desert is full with sand, with sand, the pebbles underfoot, a shaft of compass, our bodies trembling against time, waiting for Him to speak again. Where does the light come from, if not from the sun? *Amen.*

* * *

The osmosis of identities, my map is not necessarily yours, I want to be careful about what I say around here, I feel as if someone is listening, breathing behind there or there. This isn't such a risky merge, but I don't have an antidote. Renewal is not the same as reversal. I once was a daughter with a mother, but she could not take the guilt or apathy and I could not take the fear or willful intent. She once tried to kill me and scolded me for her failure. She almost died once and when she didn't, I was disappointed. I have a complicated relationship with my mother.

*Are you my mother? Are you my mother?*

I don't know where she is now, my memory's failure, and I don't know how long I've been away from home.

\* \* \*

A primordial companion that day by day grows into a great light, an empty darkness and an attempt at being, reddening. My heart beats with a touch, and perhaps, this is my lucky day. Do you feel the throbbing, yet obscure, yet sleeping. There is no time to sleep. And yet I must sleep, ripening within this space, a series of whispers, with myself, you a simulacrum of my former being. Or perhaps I have this all wrong. Perhaps this can not be explained in language, this thinking, mixed incessantly as part of everyone and no one. Perhaps I am the fictional character in all this. Perhaps you destroy the layer of my future, my being. Perhaps I want you to perish because I am selfish. Perhaps I want to live inside you, wrap you around my shoulders like a warm pelt, because I have a certain mass and I want to be loved. Perhaps I should be more precise, this integration of shadows has brought about a strange alteration of personality. Perhaps my agency is not autonomy is not independence is not. Perhaps I was swept away by the sea long ago and you are my evidence of that. Perhaps I can change color too and never had the need to until now. Perhaps this is my underside and not yours, and this is the center of my mantled body, outside the sphere of consciousness. Perhaps this all need not be documented, a rebirth, a becoming, becoming, but never being. Perhaps we're just a pair of friends and you have left an overwhelming impression on me, and this is why I see your face when I look into the mirror. Perhaps this is the living effect of experiencing a higher consciousness, but sitting atop a cluster of arms, I feel you are harmless, swimming around new myths, focusing sharply. Perhaps my brain impulses can signal changes in texture and this texture is not of waiting or becoming but simply of me looking behind without turning your head.

Perhaps you live alone and I am shy and solitary. Perhaps you explore and envelop me and it is actually enjoyable. Perhaps, former neighbor, my eyesight is not what it used to be and this dissection has only revealed such abnormalities as a clouding of the cornea and pallor of the skin. Perhaps this is my pronouncement of death, my body entering yours, my arms turning soft then dropping. Perhaps this is you, the dead octopus trying to run away, meeting the outer limits of a distant potential. Perhaps this is my skin, my reaction to the mirror, my slow, whimpering motion across the sand, like a windshield wiper, trying to wipe off the reflection of a strange monster. Perhaps I am distressed, reflected, and refuse to come out of the cage. Perhaps, it is by looking, the octopus understands. Perhaps it is time to hatch, my choice, the survival and suffering of an unexpected shipwreck. Perhaps, in the end, it does not matter who is the monster, a daughter or an octopus, and there is only the sand, the daughter slipping through an infinite series of invisible cracks, the body of the octopus, horizontal and flat, and the sand again, always and again the sand, wavering, latching onto the undersides of your legs, and then, never letting go.

All hail Mary in the muckity muck, my primordial being continues to chuck. An inclination of growth, but who's to say I'm still here in the flesh, and the blood of a birth, which after all is a only a death.

Who's to say I am what I say I am, having forgotten the reaction of sand, a stagnating memory, temporarily asphyxiated in the heat.

Who's to say that I'm anything you say I am, it's crowded, we all wear masks, we've all read the account of the creation.

Who's to say I'm not God and I just don't remember it?

# A. J. Patrick Liszkiewicz
### from *Alphabet Man*

bupdex

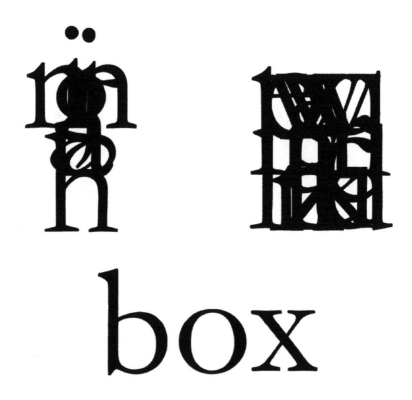

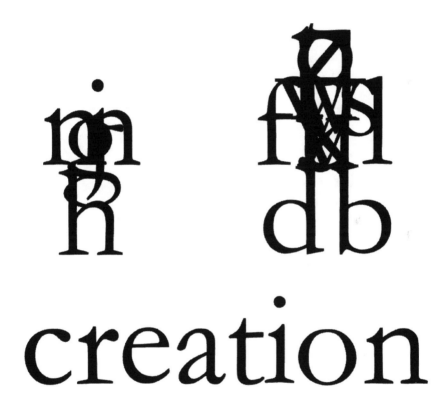

creation

j
h

organism

# Jose Perez Beduya

about *Throng*

"At the heart of this remarkable debut stands a *we* that emits a vital human signal, despite being adrift in a suburban-technological labyrinth as dehumanizing as George Oppen's corporate city 'Glassed / In dreams.' Against an ever-present authoritarian backdrop, Beduya's 'Tenderized / Post-citizens' buoy identity with defiant acts of imagination and mimesis. Like the people who make up this we, the poems in Throng support each other. This is truly a unified work, and deserves to be read as such."

—Jennifer Moxley
Judge for the 2010-2011 Madeline P. Plonsker
Emerging Writer's Residency Prize

Jose Perez Beduya's first book *Throng* takes readers "inside the bright wheel" where selfhood and community whirl toward the event horizon of an ever-elusive center—the fused question of self and other, individual and social. Beduya's poems, at once quiet and disquieting, place a lonely lyric "we" in the terrifyingly impersonal landscape in which surveillance and conformity, like war, have become the health of the state. In spare lyrics evocative of what George Oppen called "the bright light of shipwreck," Beduya searches not just for the meaning of being numerous but for how to sustain that numerousness, with "No trace showing / The quickest way back / No light caught / In the hair of the void." The poems are fierce, tensile, and assured, but also display a heartbreaking vulnerability: "Who belongs / To this wounded face / How do we / Extinguish our hands / In prayer." The ethics of beauty in the face of violence contend with and haunt the forms of political desire in this marvelous and unexpected debut.

—Josh Corey

## *SHELTER*

One hand did glissandos
While the other

Skinned the pulsating cosmos
And pushed our heads

Back beneath veils
To escape and breathe

Clear air
Some of us grew beards

We let out call-notes
Whose crescendos the glass-and-steel

Arcades threw down crumpled
Our eidolons mongered

Random wars while our flesh
Did household chores

The decade leapt
Through curtains of wet newsprint

Squatted down
Over our pink tonsures

And expelled
A child-dictator in debris fields

It was then we freed
The archives before we became

Recorders for the rain
For all tents we provided

Backwards guitars
Inoculations coming and going

In places of worship
We made space for aleatory

Sub-committees
Asking officials not what

Boxes are for
But what boxes

Are about
We swapped out

Faces for facializations
In a swarm our closest friends

Were oblique
And everywhere in approaching

## THE TURN

Is this our father in the clay

A thrum of high-tension

Wires in the blood

Of days going by

Are these rooftops and domes

The sweat and breath

Of the people

Are they connected

By long tunnels

Between naps

Or between songs

Will the shootings stop

Will amnesia tomorrow be

Mixed with fat rain

And bearded absences

Should the men muttering

Over the waters

And the mourners

Be forced away

Are dogs and the infirm

Moving through ruins

As we speak

Lost souls

Necking now in model units

Who belongs

To this wounded face

How do we

Extinguish our hands

In prayer

When will the guest speaker be

Wheel-chaired into the room

To much applause

And the long

Promised calm

Arrive on wings of cops

## MORROW

Because I have no belief
This body is a plastic
Tube where passes day
Leaves
Gummy residue
No limb of him
Logs on as me
What is rising from the couch
Contemplating the partial
Birth of my hands
In a place between one
And ten thousand
I waited amnesia ago
To lose to not
Ever find the plectrum

# Dimitri Anastasopoulos & Christina Milletti
## &NOW 2009: Buffalo

As hosts of &Now 2009 in Buffalo, we looked back at the festival's prior iterations and realized that what began at Notre Dame in 2004 as a showcase for fiction and cross-genre writing had evolved to welcome the arts and performance more broadly. For instance, Miekal And at &Now 2006 (Lake Forest College), launched a mixed-media theremin performance that transported the audience into a hum-hive of sound and sense. &Now 2008 (Chapman College) introduced us to Andi Olsen's "Scar Project" and Tim Guthrie's experimental animations. Every festival has made a mark by asking small press writers from around the country to take part in a lively exchange about the changing appreciation for words on paper, screen, canvas. Why do we write? What kind of power does language continue to exert over us in a multi-mediated environment ever more bound by words and images?

So, for &Now Buffalo 2009, we made a calculated decision to push this evolving sentiment forward, to give a free, unthematized space to a unique, grass roots conference, to give in completely to the impulse to push the boundaries of literary and performance art that &Now guests had shown with courage, intelligence, and flair. It seemed to us that &Now events were crystallizing around several significant issues: that in fiction, essay, poetry, and performance, &Now artists were asking what happens when we make art in a world in which the condition of artifice increasingly exerts a great deal of pull on public discourse? What kind of power does art have to critique the cultural sphere from which it arises, or when the domain of the arts has been increasingly colonized?

Reflecting on reactions to his (banned) fiction, novelist Thomas Bernhard remarked "They will never forgive us this Somewhere Else," going on to elaborate that he was made to feel as though—by writing fiction—he had committed a crime. If Bernhard's "Somewhere Else" can be understood as a fictional space, or even a space for daydreaming and the imagination, it might be said that the area of that fantastic, threatening space is now increasing, its power intensifying, in the mass produced cultural narratives that now exist alongside our vivid virtual worlds.

Against the backdrop of our current political and economic climate, astonishing phrases seep from the mouths and minds of public figures: politicians and economists whose craftsmanship resonates with the metalepsis of a fictive encounter. Karl Rove warns us (not unlike a character from a Philip K. Dick novel) that "While you're studying reality—judiciously, as you will—we'll act again, creating other new realities, which you can study too, and that's how things will sort out." Meanwhile, economist Robert Lucas (taking a lesson from Gertrude Stein) serenely reflects that our "[economic] crisis was not predicted because economic theory predicts that such events cannot be predicted." Our representatives in government arguably are students of language, not its abusers, and we (artists, fiction writers and poets) have our work cut out for us. Art is being created all around us. But the general awe and optimism surrounding its creation can no longer be simply taken for granted.

Art deforms us as much as it forms us. So at &Now Buffalo 2009, we paid keen attention to Brian Evenson, HL Hix, Joseph Conte, and Dave Kress as their panel grappled with what it means to create innovative art post-9/11. We listened intently to Shelley Jackson's spectral voices tonguing their ghostly, aural language. We gazed in awe at Steve Tomasula's presentation of *TOC*, one of the most ambitious digital literary works to ever grace a screen. And, finally, we were reminded at Nathaniel Mackey's keynote reading—where Mackey introduced us to "paracritical hinge," a language that sits in with and riffs off of multiple discourses such as fiction, jazz, criticism—that new writing is still possible.

—Dimitri Anastasopoulos & Christina Milletti

# Previous Publication Credits

**Harold Abramowitz**
Book excerpt: *(!x==[33]) Book 1 Volume 1* by .UNFO (Blanc Press, 2011)

**Joe Atkins**
"BOXXY FOAR 4DD1@!!!!1!!" originally appeared in *West Wind Review 2011* (Southern Oregon University).

**Matt Bell**
"Justina, Justine, Justise" and "Svara, Sveta, Sylvana" from *Cataclysm Baby* (Mud Luscious Press, 2012)

**Jose Perez Beduya**
poems from *Throng* (LFC Press/ &NOW Books, 2012)

**Julie Carr**
"Self-Loathing Lines," and "Lines to Scatter" are reprinted by permission form *Sarah—Of Fragments and Lines* (Coffee House Press, 2010). Copyright © 2010 by Julie Carr.

**Sam Cha**
"The Conference of the Birds," *decomP* (2011)
http://www.decompmagazine.com/theconferenceofthebirds.htm

**Alexandra Chasin**
*Hotel Amerika*, 8.2 (Spring 2010), 16.

**Kim Hyesoon**
"Manhole Humanity" from *All the Garbage of the World, Unite!* (Action Books, 2011)

**Jack Collom**
"Seamless Poem," "Noisy Alien Mirror," and "What Will Happen" from *Cold Instant* (Monkey Puzzle Press 2010).

**Shome Dasgupta**
"Sisters" originally appeared as an Untitled Mud Luscious Press Stamp Story (MLP, 2010) and was also included in *[C.] An MLP Stamps Stories Anthology*, (MLP, 2011).

**Katie Degentesh**
journal excerpt, with new name: "A Poetics of Reflection and Desire" originally appeared as "Untitled Photo Essay," *South Loop Review* (2008): 53-57.

**LaTasha Nevada Diggs**
"passing" originally appeared in *Jubilat* Vol. 1 Issue 19 (Spring 2011).

**Ben Doller**
"The Human Experiment" from *Dead Ahead* (Fence Books, 2010)
"FAQ:" from *FAQ:* (Ahsahta Books, 2009)

**Marcella Durand**
"Pastoral 1" and "Pastoral 2." *"I'll Drown My Book": Conceptual Writing by Women*, eds. Laynie Browne, Caroline Bergvall, and Vanessa Place. Los Angeles: Les Figues, 2011.

**Craig Dworkin**
"The Cube" from *The Official Catalog of the Library of Potential Literature* (Cow Heavy Books, 2011; reprinted by The Lit Pub, 2011).

**Roxane Gay**
"I Am Going to Cook a Quiche In My Easy Bake Oven And You Are Going to Like It" from *McSweeney's Internet Tendency* (April 7, 2010).

**Amelia Gray**
book excerpt, "Stamp Stories" (Mud Luscious Press, 2011)

**Amira Hanafi**
Book excerpt: "Girl X" from *Forgery* (Green Lantern Press, 2011)

**Jibade-Khalil Huffman**
"from 'Niagara'" originally appeared as "from 'Pictures of Color,'" *Line-A Journal (#4)* (http://www.line-ajournal.com/jibade-khalil-huffman/)

**Laird Hunt**
"OBOFRAPO X" from *The Official Catalog of the Library of Potential Literature* (Cow Heavy Books, 2011; reprinted by The Lit Pub, 2011).

**Bhanu Kapil**
"India Notebooks" originally appeared in *Schizophrene* (Nightboat Books, 2011)

**Jennifer Karmin**
Book excerpt: canto 10 from *Aaaaaaaaaaalice* (Flim Forum Press, 2010)

**Janice Lee**
Book excerpt: various excerpts from *Daughter* (Jaded Ibis Press, May 2011)

**Michael Leong**
chapbook excerpt: from *The Philosophy of Decomposition/Re-Composition as Explanation: A Poe and Stein Mash-Up* (Delete Press, 2011). Also first appeared in the following journals: *Jubilat* 20 (2011) and *Modern Language Studies* 41.2 (2012).

**A.J. Patrick Liszkiewicz**
Selections from *Alphabet Man* (Slack Buddha Press, 2010), previously appeared online at *London Poetry Systems* (http://www.londonpoetrysystems.com/picturepoems001.html)

**Jennifer Martenson**
"A Priori" and "[Precarious, to balance]" from *Unsound* (Burning Deck Press, 2010.)

**K. Silem Mohammad**
Selections from *The Sonnagrams,* published in *Fence* Vol. 13 No. 2 (Winter 2011)

**Nick Montfort**
Post Position. "Concrete Perl." http://nickm.com/post/2011/06/concrete-perl/

**Evelyn Reilly**
"The Whiteness of the Foam," from *Styrofoam* (Roof Books, 2009)

**Dan Richert**
Book excerpt: *(!x==[33]) Book 1 Volume 1* by .UNFO (Blanc Press, 2011)

**Kathleen Rooney & Elisa Gabbert**
"The One about the Dog" and "The One about the Afterlife" from *Opium* 9, Fall 2009. "The One about the Chiropractor" from *Moria* (2010). "The One about Genre" from *Verse* (2009).

**David Shields**
From *Reality Hunger: A Manifesto* by David Shields, copyright © 2010 by David Shields. Used by permission of Alfred A. Knopf, a division of Random House, Inc.

**Ken Taylor**
"we work for the pope" (cento made of Charlie Sheen quotes) from MiPOesias (http://mipoesias.com/recognitions/cento-made-of-charlie-sheen-quotes/)

**Anne-Laure Tissut**
Translated excerpt from *Anima Motrix,* in *Golden Handcuffs Review,* n°14 (2011): 66-73.

**Azareen Van der Vliet Oloomi**
Book Excerpt: "Chapter 3" from *Fra Keeler* (Dorothy, A Publishing Project, 2012)

Journal Excerpt (Excerpt previously published in PRH): "Chapter 3 from Fra Keeler" originally appeared as such in *Paul Revere's Horse,* V.3 (2010).

# Contributor Notes

**Harold Abramowitz** is from Los Angeles. His books and chapbooks include (*!x==[33]*) *Book 1 Volume 1* by .UNFO (collaboration with Dan Richert, Blanc Press, 2011), *A House on a Hill (A House on a Hill Part One)* (Insert Press, 2010), *Not Blessed* (Les Figues Press, 2010), and *Dear Dearly Departed* (Palm Press, 2008). Harold co-edits the short-form literary press eohippus labs (eohippuslabs.com), and writes and edits as part of the collaborative projects, SAM OR SAMANTHA YAMS and UNFO.

**Dimitri Anastasopoulos** is the author of the novels *A Larger Sense of Harvey* and *Farm for Mutes* published by Mammoth Books. His fiction has appeared in journals such as *Black Warrior Review*, *Notre Dame Review*, and *Willow Springs*, essays in *Callaloo* and the *Journal of Narrative Theory*. Born in Greece in 1968, he now lives in Buffalo, New York and teaches fiction writing and contemporary literature at the University at Buffalo, SUNY.

**Joe Atkins** lives in Sacramento.

**Matt Bell** is the author of *Cataclysm Baby*, a novella, and *How They Were Found*, a collection of fiction. His debut novel *In the House upon the Dirt between the Lake and the Woods* will be published by Soho Press in June 2013. He is the Senior Editor at Dzanc Books, where he also edits the literary magazine *The Collagist*. He teaches creative writing at Northern Michigan University.

**Jose Perez Beduya** lives in Ithaca, New York. He was awarded the Madeleine P. Plonsker Emerging Writer's Residency Prize for *Throng* in 2011. He has also received fellowships from the New York Foundation for the Arts and the National Endowment for the Arts.

**Arno Bertina** was born in 1975. He is the author of four novels, two published with Actes Sud, *Le Dehors ou la migration des truites* (2001) and *Appoggio* (2003); two with Verticales *Anima motrix* (2006) and more recently, *Je suis une aventure* (2012). He has also written a under the pseudonym of Pietro di Vaglio, *La déconfite gigantale du sérieux* (Lignes, 2004); a biographical fiction on Johnny Cash, *J'ai appris à ne pas rire du démon* (Naïve, 2006), and a narrative, *Ma solitude s'appelle Brando* (2009) to be published in its American translation by Counterpath (2013).

**Julie Carr** is the author of four books of poetry, most recently *Sarah: Of Fragments and Lines*, and *100 Notes on Violence*. Her critical monograph, *Surface Tension*, is out from Dalkey Archive in 2013. *RAG* is forthcoming from Omnidawn. She is the co-publisher of Counterpath Press and lives in Denver. She teaches poetry and poetics at the University of Colorado in Boulder.

**Sam Cha** is an MFA candidate at UMass Boston, where he was the winner of the 2011 and 2012 Academy of American Poets prize. His work has appeared in *anderbo, apt, ASIA, decomP, Opium online, Radius,* and *ripple(s)*. He lives in Cambridge, MA.

**Alexandra Chasin** is the author of *Kissed By*, a collection of short fictions (FC2, 2007), and the app/novella, *Brief*, for iPad, in addition to print and ebook (Jaded Ibis Productions, 2012). Chasin is a 2012 NYFA fellow in fiction. She teaches at The New School in New York City.

**Kim Hyesoon** is one of the most prominent poets of South Korea. She lives in Seoul and teaches creative writing at the Seoul Institute of the Arts. Translations of Kim's work are in: *When the Plug Gets Unplugged* (Tinfish, 2005), *Anxiety of Words* (Zephyr, 2006), and *Mommy Must Be a Fountain of Feathers* (Action Books, 2008), *All the Garbage of the World, Unite!* (Action Books, 2011), and *Princess Abandoned* (Tinfish, 2012).

**Jack Collom** has published over twenty books, has taught at the Jack Kerouac School of Disembodied Poetics at Naropa University, and even has a day named after him in Boulder, CO.

**Shome Dasgupta** is the author of *i am here And You Are Gone* (Winner Of The 2010 OW Press Fiction Chapbook Contest), *The Seagull And The Urn* (HarperCollins India, 2012), and *Tentacles, Numbing* (Black Coffee Press, 2013). He lives in Lafayette, LA and his website can be found at www.shomedome.com.

**Katie Degentesh** lives in NYC. Her first book, *The Anger Scale*, was recently featured in the Poetry Society of America's New American Poets series. "I Was Horny" is from a forthcoming book-length project with the working title Reasons to Have Sex. The poems' titles are all direct selections from the 238 answers listed in the "YSEX? Why Have Sex?" questionnaire, a scientific document compiled by researchers after polling over 2,000 respondents regarding their motivation for having sexual intercourse. The poems were then formed from internet search results represented online as children's writing, with each search based on and containing phrases or words from the titles.

**LaTasha Nevada Diggs** is the author of *TwERK* (Belladonna Books, 2013), winner of a FACE OUT grant from the Council of Literary Magazines and Presses. A recipient of fellowships to Caldera Arts in Oregon; Naropa Summer Writing Program in Colorado; the Harvestworks Digital Media Arts Center in New York City; Lower Manhattan Cultural Council Center for the Arts, and Cave Canem, her work has been featured in several journals and anthologies, including *Fence, jubilat, Black Renaissance Noir, LA Review, Palabra,* and *Villanelles*. She has taught Creative Writing and Sound Poetry at Copper Union College Saturday Program and is a visiting professor at Manhattanville College. Diggs received her MFA in Creative Writing from California College of the Arts. She lives in Harlem.

**Ben Doller** is responsible for the books *Radio, Radio* (LSU Press), *FAQ:* (Ahsahta Press), and *Dead Ahead* (Fence Books). He lives in San Diego with the poet Sandra Doller, and is Assistant Professor in the literature department at University of California, San Diego.

**Marcella Durand's** books include *Deep Eco Pré*, a collaboration with Tina Darragh (Little Red Leaves, 2009); *AREA* (Belladonna, 2008); and *Traffic & Weather*, a site-specific book-length poem written during a residency at the Lower Manhattan Cultural Council in downtown Manhattan (Futurepoem, 2008). She lives in New York City, where she has recently completed a new collection, *The Prospect*, and has started work on a book-length alexandrine, *In This World of 12 Months*.

**Craig Dworkin** is the author of *Signature-Effects* (Ghos-Ti, 1997); *Dure* (Cuneiform, 2004); *Strand* (Roof, 2004); *Parse* (Atelos, 2008); *The Perverse Library* (Information as Material, 2010); and *Motes* (Roof, 2011). He is the editor of five books, including, most recently *Against Expression: An Anthology of Conceptual Literature* (with Kenneth Goldsmith, Northwestern UP 2011). He teaches literary history at the University of Utah, where he curates the Eclipse Archive <english.utah.edu/eclipse>.

**Roxane Gay** lives and writes in the Midwest. She has fiction in *Best American Short Stories 2012* and elsewhere.

**Amelia Gray** is the author of *AM/PM* (Featherproof Books), *Museum of the Weird* (FC2) and *Threats* (Farrar, Straus and Giroux).

**Amira Hanafi** is a writer and artist living in Cairo, Egypt. She is the author of *Minced English* and *Forgery*. Her work has appeared in *American Letters & Commentary, Matrix Magazine, DIAGRAM, Egypt Independent*, and elsewhere.

**Jibade-Khalil Huffman** is the author of two books of poems, *19 Names for Our Band* and *James Brown is Dead*. His art and writing projects have been exhibited and performed at MoMA/P.S.1, Southern Exposure, Night Gallery, and the Poetry Project at St. Marks Church. He lives and works in Los Angeles.

**Laird Hunt** is the author of five novels, all published by Coffee House Press. His fiction, reviews, essays and translations have appeared widely both in the United States and abroad. He is on faculty at the University of Denver, where he edits the Denver Quarterly.

**Bhanu Kapil** is the author of five books, most recently *Schizophrene* (Nightboat Books) and *humanimal [a project for future children]* (Kelsey Street Press.) She teaches at Naropa University and Goddard College.

**Jennifer Karmin's** multidisciplinary projects have been presented at festivals, artist-run spaces, and on city streets across the U.S., Japan, Kenya, and Europe. A founding curator of the Red Rover Series, she is the author of the text-sound epic *Aaaaaaaaaaalice* (Flim Forum Press, 2010) and her poetry was recently published in *I'll Drown My Book: Conceptual Writing by Women* (Les Figues Press, 2012). Jennifer teaches in the Creative Writing program at Columbia College Chicago and at Truman College, where she works with immigrants as a community educator. She will be a guest faculty member at Naropa University in summer 2013.

**Janice Lee** is the author of *KEROTAKIS* (Dog Horn Publishing 2010) and *Daughter* (Jaded Ibis 2011). She holds an MFA in Creative Writing from CalArts and currently lives in LA where she is Co-Editor of the online journal *[out of nothing]*, Co-Founder of the interdisciplinary arts organization Strophe, Reviews Editor at *HTMLGIANT* and Founder/CEO of POTG Design. She can be found online at http://janicel.com.

**Michael Leong** is the author of two books of poetry, *e.s.p.* (Silenced Press, 2009) and *Cutting Time with a Knife* (Black Square Editions, 2012), which won a FACE OUT grant from the Council of Literary Magazines and Presses. His translation of the Chilean poet Estela Lamat, *I, the Worst of All*, was published by BlazeVOX [books] in 2009. He has also written several chapbooks including *Midnight's Marsupium* (The Knives Forks and Spoons Press, 2010); *The Great Archivist's Cloudy Quotient* (Beard of Bees Press, 2010); and *Words on Edge*, which won Plan B Press' 2012 poetry chapbook contest.

**A. J. Patrick Liszkiewicz** is a member of the game design collective RUST, LTD., and an assistant editor at the online journal *Anti-*. He is the author and editor of several chapbooks, including *Alphabet Man* (Slack Buddha Press, 2010) and *Count As One* (New River, 2009), as well as a forthcoming full-length collection, *Afeeld*. His work has recently appeared in *Diagram, Glitch, Hobart, Kotaku, Otoliths*, and *Word for/Word*. He received an M.F.A. in Media Arts Production from SUNY Buffalo, and is currently a Provost's Fellow in the iMAP PhD program at the University of Southern California.

**Jennifer Martenson** is the author of *Unsound* (Burning Deck Press, 2010.) Recent poems appear in the online journal, *Yew: A Journal of Innovative Writing and Images By Women*. She currently lives in Providence, RI.

**Christina Milletti** is an Associate Professor of English at the University at Buffalo where she co-curates the Exhibit X Fiction Series and is the Director of the Creative Writing Certificate Program. Her fiction is forthcoming in Akashic Books' *Buffalo Noir*, and has appeared most recently in *American Letters & Commentary, The Cincinnati Review, The Chicago Review, Harcourt's Best New American Voices, Studies in the Novel*, and *Fiction's Present: Situating Narrative Innovation* (among other places). Her collection of short stories, *The Religious & Other Fictions*, was published by Carnegie Mellon University Press. She has just finished a novel called *Choke Box*.

**K. Silem Mohammad** is the author of several books of poetry, including *Deer Head Nation* (Tougher Disguises, 2003), *A Thousand Devils* (Combo, 2004), *Breathalyzer* (Edge, 2008), *The Front* (Roof, 2009), and *Monsters* (forthcoming, Edge Books). He is editor of the poetry magazine *Abraham Lincoln* and faculty editor of *West Wind Review*. Mohammad is a professor of English & Writing at Southern Oregon University.

**Nick Montfort** is associate professor of digital media at MIT and president of the Electronic Literature Organization. He develops text generators and interactive fiction and has participated in dozens of literary and academic collaborations. Montfort co-edited *The New Media Reader* and *The Electronic Literature Collection* Volume 1 and wrote *Twisty Little Passages: An Approach to Interactive Fiction, Racing the Beam: The Atari Video Computer System* (with Ian Bogost), and *Riddle & Bind*. His next book, *10 PRINT CHR$(205.5+RND(1)); : GOTO 10*, is a collaboration with nine other authors about a one-line Commodore 64 BASIC program.

**Evelyn Reilly's** recent books of poetry are *Apocalypso* and *Styrofoam*, both published by Roof Books. Earlier work includes *Hiatus*, from Barrow Street Press, and *Fervent Remnants of Reflective Surfaces*, a chapbook from Portable Press at Yo Yo Labs. Essays and poetry have appeared lately in *Jacket2*, the *Eco-language Reader, Interim, Interdisciplinary Studies in Literature and Environment* and *The Arcadia Project: Postmodernism and the Pastoral*, an anthology published by Ahsahta Press. Reilly has taught poetics at St. Marks Poetry Project and the Summer Writing Program at Naropa University, and has been a curator of the Segue Reading Series.

**Kathleen Rooney** is a founding editor of Rose Metal Press and the author of *Oneiromance (an epithalamion)* (Switchback Books, 2008) and the novel in poems *Robinson Alone* (Gold Wake Press, 2012). She lives in Chicago. Together they are the authors of *That Tiny Insane Voluptuousness* (Otoliths, 2008). **Elisa Gabbert** is the author of *The French Exit* (Birds LLC, 2010) and *Thanks for Sending the Engine* (Kitchen Press, 2007). She lives in Denver and blogs at The French Exit.

**Dan Richert** is a software developer and electronic musician from Metro Detroit. Work includes *(!x==[33]) Book 1, Volume 1* by .UNFO (collaboration with Harold Abramowitz, Blanc Press, 2011), *Ursonorous Disruptions* (Interactive audio, collaboration with Mathew Timmons, Installation at LACMA, 2008), *\*sc3gzr\** (Gamepad-controlled realtime text generator, 2008). He designs text processors as part of UNFO.

**Davis Schneiderman** edited this book, with help from many other generous people.

**David Shields** is the author of fourteen books, including *How Literature Saved My Life*; *Reality Hunger* (named one of 2010's best books by thirty publications); *The Thing About Life Is That One Day You'll Be Dead* (*New York Times* bestseller); *Black Planet* (finalist for the National Book Critics Circle Award); and *Remote* (winner of the PEN/Revson Award). The recipient of a Guggenheim fellowship and two NEA fellowships, Shields has published essays and stories in the *New York Times Magazine, Harper's, Yale Review*, and dozens of other journals. His work has been translated into fifteen languages.

**Ken Taylor** lives in North Carolina. He is the author of the chapbook, "first the trees, now this" (Three Count Pour 2013). His poetry has appeared or is forthcoming in *Hambone, VOLT, The Offending Adam, 3:AM Magazine, Verse Daily, elimae, EOAGH, MiPOesias, The Chattahoochee Review, Southword, Carolina Quarterly, Gigantic Sequins, Clade Song, can can, ARDOR,* and others.

**Anne-Laure Tissut** is a Professor of American Literature at Rouen University, France. Her research focuses on contemporary American literature, on aesthetics, exchanges between forms and media as well as on translation. She also translates American and English fiction and poetry into French (Percival Everett, Nick Flynn, Adam Thirlwell, Steve Tomasula) and takes part in collective translations from French into American English. She was co-organizer of the 2012 &NOW Festival in Paris.

**Azareen Van der Vliet Oloomi** is an Iranian-American writer of fiction, and the author of *Fra Keeler* (Dorothy, A Publishing Project). She received her MFA in Literary Arts from Brown University, and is a recipient of a Fulbright Grant to Catalonia, Spain. Her work has appeared or is forthcoming in *The Coffin Factory, State of the Union (a Wave Books* anthology), *The Collagist, Harp & Altar, Paul Revere's Horse, Encyclopedia,* and *Lit Magazine.* She currently teaches in the MFA Program in Creative Writing at the University of Notre Dame.

Now all are called "BIRDS", but there are a lot of them, for just as they differ from one another so do they in

**Variety of Nature,**

And, although all Diverse Wretches are grouped as & & still the pheno-menon (or + ) closest to True WORD is the

# The &NOW Awards 2

## The Best Innovative Writing

[Edited by Davis Schneiderman]

&NOW Books
Lake Forest, IL

First published 2012 by &NOW Books, an imprint of Lake Forest College Press.

&NOW BOOKS

Carnegie Hall
Lake Forest College
555 N. Sheridan Road
Lake Forest, IL 60045

andnow@lakeforest.edu

lakeforest.edu/andnow

Lake Forest College Press publishes in the broad spaces of Chicago studies. Our imprint, &NOW Books, publishes innovative and conceptual literature and serves as the publishing arm of the &NOW writers' conference and organization.

ISBN: 978-0-9823156-4-4

Cover designs by Jesssica Berger

Book design by Vasiliki Gerentes

Printed in the United States.

# Acknowledgements

Alyssa Basten

Zakea Boeger

Leah Bowers

Jody Buck

Kaisa Cummings

Thomas Dale

Amy Finn

Vasiliki Gerentes

Ryan Goodwin

Tobi Greenwald

Madeeha Kahn

Tammy Kise

Tyler Lebens

Nicholas Miner

Amanda Muledy

Robert Murphy

Samuel Murphy

Vinisha Puroit

Percy Sandel

Taryn Smith

Hannah Speck

Special thanks to Ian Morris for his enormous help in the early stages of the anthology. Ian taught a section of English 324 during the Spring 2012 semester, and gave shape to the shapeless!

# Table of Contents

# Davis Schneiderman
## And Now &NOW and now And Now?

1. All of the work in this volume has been previously published. All of the work is this volume was published between September 2009 and September 2011. Except for one piece, published a few months after. A clinamen.
2. This introduction is already over.
3. The anthology includes two reflections from Festival organizers, from Buffalo (2009) and UCSD (2011), as these are the years covered by the works in the anthology.
4. The Festival is biennial, except when it is not.
5. There are many words in this book, and you might read some or all, in any order.
6. Not every author in this book had attended or will attend a Festival, at any of the locations: the University of Notre Dame (2004), Lake Forest College (2006), Chapman University (2008), the University at Buffalo (SUNY) (2009), University of California-San Diego (2011), The Sorbonne and Paris VII (2002), and (join us!) the University of Colorado Boulder (2013).
7. This introduction is not particularly inspired.
8. Isn't that clever?
9. If you start with the second number and then read the first, or if those lines are reversed and renumbered on the page, the second then poses a provocative question: what might this mean, this introduction, which begins, like *The Iliad*, in medias res.
10. &NOW Books publishes this anthology. There is no connection between the anthology and the festival. Except when there is.
11. Trust Wikipedia. Or not.
12. The &NOW Festival turns 10 in 2014. Wikipedia says:

**&Now** is biennial traveling literary festival and a publishing organization both focused on innovative literature. The festival's main emphasis is on work that blends or crosses genres, and includes a wide variety of work, such as multimedia projects, performance pieces, criti-fictional presentations, and otherwise. According to the website's description, the festival seeks out "literary art as it is practiced today by authors who consciously treat their work as a process that is aware of its own literary and extra-literary history,

that is as much about its form and materials, language, communities, and practice as it is about its subject matter."[1] Most of the work presented by authors is considered experimental literature.[2]

13. Read on. Or not. Yawn.
14. *The &NOW AWARDS 1* covered the years between 2004-2009. This anthology—volume 2—covers the years between 2009-2011.
15. These short bursts of text, signaled by these numbers, may be read in any order.
16. Same with the last number.
17. Do you think this is meant as hyperbole?
18. This is *The &NOW AWARDS 2: The Best Innovative Writing,* which is an anthology of the best innovative writing.
19. & so on.
20. This anthology is biennial, except when it is not.
21. There are two "sides" to the book. These "sides" mirror each other, except when they do not.
22. Yes, any order at all.

# Gretchen E. Henderson
## Prelude from *On Marvellous Things Heard*

Derived formally from Aristotle's *Minor Work* of the same title (*De Mirabilibus Auscultationibus*), my variation of "On Marvellous Things Heard" explores a range of literary appropriations of music, in terms of translation and metamorphosis. Part investigation, part inventory, and part *invention* (in the musical sense: *a composition in simple counterpoint*), this essay indirectly assays the narrating subject as she directly assays the subjects of literature, of music, and of silence.

Acoustic spaces resonate to reach each listener's ears differently, dependent on physics, architecture, and physiology. I am particularly interested in the innuendos of voice, in the volitional space between voice and body, which helps to generate genre. In singing, there is a technique of visualizing pitches: to imagine the purest sound, to engage physiology before a song is sung. Muscles constrict and relax; the abdomen expands, forcing air to circulate and wedge open the throat. Then, the mouth. Gabriel García Lorca believed that, through *duende*, the voice surpasses the throat and starts at the soles of the feet. Wherever a singer's sound originates, her mouth is part of inlaid resonating cavities: within head (throat and nasal passages) within body (supported by lungs and diaphragm) within architecture (auditorium or inhabited space). She is not apart from, but a part of. She is culpable and capable, even capricious, if programming invites improvisation within, and outside of, the song.

By trying to inhabit the essay's interstitial spaces—literal, aural, and otherwise—I follow Umberto Eco's concept of the "open work," as well as John Cage's motivation for musical composition: not self-expression, but self-alteration. The genre (more as verb: *to assay, to test*) supports this metamorphic quest, as the essay undergoes a kind of deformation and reformation. Moving beyond critical boundaries, the elusive voice here becomes permissive behind its theoretical veil, like the shape-shifting boundary between speech and song. That threshold invites me, and hopefully readers, to listen more closely to silences, to contemplate and respond in whatever form (even in white space: refuting, concurring, doodling, dreaming) about our world's natures and nuances, volitions and vulnerabilities: its marvels.

—Gretchen E. Henderson

# from *On Marvellous Things Heard*

The pupil…having fallen sick, was dumb for ten days; but on the eleventh, having slowly come to her senses after her delirium, she declared that during that time she had lived most agreeably.

~ Aristotle, *On Marvellous Things Heard*, #178[i]

1 · Silence.

2 · As musical concept, "thematic transformation" refers to a lineage ranging from Renaissance Italian dance pairs, to Baroque fugues and variations like J.S. Bach's *Goldberg Variations*, to the idée fixe of Hector Berlioz's *Symphonie fantastique*, Franz Liszt's symphonic poems (like *Les Préludes*), and Richard Wagner's leitmotifs (*Die Walküre*). From a literary standpoint, what seems intriguing about this lineage is the evolving concern to create cohesion within and between individual movements of multimovement works—not unlike a writer of prose strives to build cohesion within and between narrative units.

3 · With regard to poetry, Stéphane Mallarmé addressed white space in the preface to *Un coup de dés*, saying that verse demands white "as a surrounding silence."[ii]

4 · Epigraphs work similarly with white space:

5 · *The lyre of Orpheus opens the door of the underworld.*[iii]

6 · To conjure Orpheus is akin to evoking music as a metaphoric bridge to silence.

7 · Problems admittedly arise when musical terms are applied to texts. "Harmony," "leitmotif," and "polyphony" become oversimplified; the categorization of a piece of prose as "musical" dilutes the very meaning of music. Any correlation between the two media risks the Surrealist cry against "like," like (!) Gertrude Stein criticized the presumption of such assimilations: "There is the likeliness lying in liking likely likeliness."[iv]

8 · Orpheus' tale suggests the tension between silence and speech, death and life, myth and history, and a litany of binary worlds (urban and rural in Willa Cather's *The Song of the Lark*, western and eastern in Salman Rushdie's *The Ground Beneath Her Feet*) that have been readapted over the centuries, with changing cultural appropriations.

9 · "To interpret language means: to understand language," writes Theodor Adorno. "To interpret music means: to make music." He compares the latter to "transcribing a text, rather than decoding its meaning."[v]

10 · Was it Laurie Anderson who said, "Writing about music is like dancing about architecture"?

11 · Wanting to have our cake and hear it, too, we're faced with a perceptual Catch-22. To speak of music's influence on a text becomes better understood as adaptation or translation, not transliteration.

12 · Different translators interpret a text as differently as different pianists render the same Chopin nocturne.

13 · "By itself notation is not music," writes Gardner Read. "A score can truly come to life only through the performer; its message can be translated only when symbols on the printed page are adequate for the intelligent transformation."[vi]

14 · Thomas Mann described how each idea emerges from a "rhythmic demand: it is put in for the sake of the cadence, and not for its own sake."[vii]

15 · "All art aspires to the condition of music," claimed Walter Pater.

16 · While poetry is historically entwined with music, many prose writers have dealt with inadequacies of expression or experience by appropriating music—as if music could offer an extra dimension to the written word.

17 · "...of deforming the literary language..."[vii]

18 · As an element of formal beauty, music sometimes can be linked with violence. Consider the Beethoven-loving, word-spinning Alex in *A Clockwork Orange*.

19 · In the collected *Letters to Father Flye*, James Agee confided to his mentor, "inaccurately speaking—I want to *write symphonies*. That is, character introduced quietly (as are themes in a symphony, say) will recur in new lights, with new verbal orchestration, will work into counterpoint."[ix]

20 · August Strindberg's *Ghost Sonata*.

21 · Aristotle described how melodies and rhythm imitate character, and each musical mode affects a listener differently. Mixolydian causes a listener to become "sad and grave," while the Dorian produces "a moderate and settled temper." The Phrygian "inspires enthusiasm," leading him to conclude: "There seems to be in us a sort of affinity to musical modes and rhythms, which makes some philosophers say that the soul is tuning, others, that it possesses tuning."[x]

22 · To believe in the Music of the Spheres is to believe in an inaudible celestial harmony, which plays like a distant memory. It tunes each soul's desire to escape its respective body, otherwise stuck in time and space.

# Postlude from *On Marvellous Things Heard*

[i] In the epigraph, I have changed the gender of pronouns so that "the pupil" is a woman. Aristotle, "On Marvellous Things Heard" #178," *The Complete Works of Aristotle: The Revised Oxford Translation*, vol. II, ed. Jonathan Barnes, trans. L.D. Lowdall (Princeton: Princeton UP, 1984) 1298. W.S. Hett's translation shifts "**delirium**" to "affliction," and "agreeably" to "happiest": "They say that Demaratus, a disciple of Timeaeus the Locrian, fell ill, and became dumb for ten days; on the eleventh, having recovered slowly from his affliction, he said that he had had the happiest time of his life." In *Minor Works*, XIV (Cambridge, MA: Loeb, 1980) 325. This author does not necessarily agree, nor should the source be trusted, as Hett's edition notes: "This curious collection of 'marvels' reads like the jottings from a diary. All authorities are agreed that it is not the work of Aristotle, but it is included in this volume as it forms part of the 'Corpus' which has come down to us; most Aristotelian scholars believe that it emanated from the Peripatetic School. Some of the notes are puerile, but some on the other hand are evidently the fruit of direct and accurate observation."

[ii] Stéphane Mallarmé, *Collected Poems*, trans. Henry Weinfield (Berkeley: U of California P, 1994) 121.

[iii] E.T.A. Hoffman, epigraph to *The Lyre of Orpheus* by Robertson Davies (New York: Penguin Books, 1988).

[iv] Daniel Albright, ***Untwisting** the Serpent: Modernism in Music, Literature and Other Arts* (Chicago: U of Chicago P, 2000) 323.

[v] Theodor Adorno, *Essays on Music* (Berkeley: U of California P, 2002) 115.

[vi] Gardner Read, *Music **Notation**: A Manual of Modern Practice* (Boston: Allyn & Bacon, 1964) 24.

[vii] Thomas Mann, "An Bruno Walter zum siebzigsten Geburtstag," in *Altes und Neues* (Frankfurt am Main: S. Fischer Verlag, 1961): 738, quoted in James A. Hayes, "The Translator and the Form-Content Dilemma in Literary Translation," *MLN* 90 (1975): 839.

[viii] In the original context, "they" refers to "dialects." M.M. Bakhtin, "**Discourse** in the Novel," *The Norton Anthology of Theory and Criticism*, ed. Vincent B. Leitch, et al. (New York: Norton, 2001) 1215.

[ix] James Agee, *Letters of James Agee to Father Flye* (New York: Bantam, 1963) 42.

[x] Aristotle, "On **Music**," *On the Art of Poetry*, ed. Milton C. Nahm, trans. S.H. Butcher (New York: Bobbs-Merrill, 1956) 46.

## Alissa Nutting

I am sixteen years old & I cannot have Luke Gunter's baby. I have seen my older cousin's deflated football breasts. They have weird marks & lines that make them seem like optical illusions, like how pencils placed into glasses of water appear broken.

# Kate Durbin

## Anna Nicole Show

"Anna Nicole Show" is excerpted from my book *E! Entertainment*. *E! Entertainment* is a carefully crafted transcription of several reality television shows; it is a meditation on the nature of the medium. One way of reading *E! Entertainment* is to look at these scripts as slowed-down, microscopic revelations of our culture's perceptions of and expectations for our screen women. Analogous metaphors for my role in creating the text are that of a court stenographer, or a court sketch artist, except my process was even more detailed & rigorous, often requiring months of painstaking work for one piece. "Anna Nicole Show" is the name of a reality TV show Anna Nicole Smith in starred from 2002-2004, prior to her death; all of the dialogue in the piece was taken directly from a video, dubbed by the public as the "Clown Video," which was presented in court as evidence and shared with the public on CNN after Smith's death. In the courtroom, the video was presented as evidence that Smith's attorney/boyfriend at the time of her death, Howard K. Stern, was conspiring to keep Smith in a drug stupor. In the video, Smith gets her face painted by a 9-year-old girl, Riley. Smith also appears confused in the video as to whether or not a doll she is caring for is a real baby. Stern claimed to the court that Smith was simply acting for the cameras.

—Kate Durbin

**CNN:** Prosecutors presented this video as evidence that Howard K. Stern conspired to keep Anna Nicole Smith in a drug stupor. Stern's lawyers say Smith was acting for the cameras.

**HOWARD:** What do you think Anna? Is Riley going to be your new makeup artist? Is Riley going to be your new makeup artist? Have you found a new makeup artist? Cuz your baby. Your other one of your babies. Your baby down there. That one. Say that again. Say it again. Let me get a shot of the baby. Let me just get a shot of the baby. No. Yeah. Put it there. Okay. You think this is a good time to announce the sex of your baby. Okay. Talk to me Riley. Riley talk to me. Talk to me. For the baby? How do you know it's not a real baby? How do you know the stork didn't bring it last night? [Anna,] how come your butt's wet? Just turned off the music, although it might be too late. Whole tape being usable. You'll have to see. The camera—Why you taking it off?

**RILEY, AGE 7:** We're gonna use these first, bunny. You can open your eyes. Close 'em. Now close 'em. I wish you could go on the waterslides. But you're pregnant. If you're pregnancy, your heart's bad, if you have a broken bone, or a back condition. I read the signs! Yep. You can't. Your other—your baby down here. Why aren't you pooting, then, or does it hurt? She does. The clown needs some medicine. No, I don't have some. It's your baby. It's your baby. The clown doesn't need gas medicine, she needs baaaby medicine. Baby. Baby. That's your baby kicking you. Watch this. She isn't real. Look. She's having brain trouble. Brain trouble. It's fake. Look. It's a battery baby. Bad. She's fake. Howard, can I talk to you for a sec? She has major brain trouble. Get the screwdriver. Yes, take one battery out to prove that that's not a real baby. Howard! I'll go to the nursery and look, okay? It's okay. Why don't you bring it up? Anna, she's fake. Look! It's what I'm hearing, huh. It's fake. Camera, camera. Oh my lord. And now, I couldn't find it. I couldn't find it. Can I do it, Anna? I'm going to play along. I'll go get it. I'll go get it. I'll go get it. Can this come off? She might get hot.

**ANNA:** Huh? I don't know. Oh. You said open 'em. With a wha—for a waterpark? I wanna go. Why not. My baby's over there sleepin. I think I just have a little gas. I think I just I think I'm having some gas trouble. It hurts and I need some gas poot stuff so I can poot it out. Huh do you have some. I need some cuz look how big this belly's getting cuz its gas. Nu uh. It's gas. No it's gas. And for sure—nu uh. Eh gu and you know how when you're having gas and you feel it and its like owwww. No. My baby's over there. Don't open her skin. She might die. Can't do that. Stop it. Hu huh. Yes. I'm your mama. Hehehe. I think she peed on me. Hold her head up! She's crying; she needs her binkie! She needs her binkie. It's cryin. Get a her binkie; it's cryin. Hmm. My baby whore. I'm gonna go give her her binkie cuz she don't know how to take care of a baby. Shhh. You're not fake. Did you put powder in her diaper. Did you put powda. Powder right here. Right that squash. The powder is this in my—by my tub. Powder. She pee pee on herself. What? Hahaha. What? Hey say mama. Want your binkie. What. I love you! You love your mama? Get you some new clothes on. What. What. What. What you sayin. Huh. Ubegububu. Hold on. Hold on. I'm gonna put you something else to wear, okay? Okay? Hey what. Do you look cute? Hehehe.

**MECHANICAL BABY:** Mama. Mama. Waaah. Waaah. Waaah. Mama. Mama. Mama. Mama. Mama. Mama. Mama. Mama. Mama. Mama. Mama. Mama. Waaah. Waaah. Mama. Mama. Mama. Mama. Mama. Mama. Mama. Mama. Mama. Mama. Mama. Mama. Mama. Waaah. Waaah. Mama. Mama. Mama. Mama. Mama. Mama. Mama. Mama. Mama. Mama. Mama. Mama. Mama. Waaah. Waaah. Mama. Mama. Mama. Mama. Mama. Mama. Mama. Mama. Mama. Mama. Mama. Waaah. Waaah. Mama. Mama. Mama. Mama. Mama. Mama. Mama. Mama. Mama. Mama. Mama. Mama. Mama. Mama. Mama. Mama.

**DISTANT MUSIC: "Angel Baby" by Rosie and the Originals**

# Raúl Zurita
### about *Song for his Disappeared Love*
### translated from the Spanish by Daniel Bortzutzky

*C*anto *a su amor Desaparecido/Song for his Disappeared Love* was originally published in 1985, a brutal year in Chile. The government of General Augusto Pinochet, the dictator who came to power in the 1973 military overthrow of the democratically elected President Salvador Allende, still ruled with terror and violence, kidnapping, torturing, killing and disappearing those who spoke out in protest. For Raúl Zurita, then, the situation called for the unreachable goal of "responding to the terror with a poetry that was just as powerful as the pain being delivered by the state."[1]

Zurita knew from firsthand experience what this terror was like. He and several hundred of his classmates and professors at the leftist Universidad Santa Maria in Valparaiso, Chile (where he was completing a degree in engineering) were arrested on September 11, the very morning of the 1973 coup, and he spent the next six weeks deprived of communication with his family, incarcerated on a military ship where 800 prisoners occupied a space that could only hold 100. The experience of the coup, Zurita has stated, has defined all that he would come to write.

From 1979-1983 Zurita was a member of CADA (Colectivo de Acciones de Arte), a political art action group whose projects included *Ay Sudamerica* (1981) in which airplanes dropped over Santiago hundreds of thousands of flyers proclaiming that "every man who works to better his living spaces, even if they are only mental spaces, is an artist." The next year, 1982, Zurita returned to the sky to craft what is perhaps his best known work, a poem entitled "La Vida Nueva," written with an airplane above New York City, and reproduced in photos printed in his book *Anteparaiso*.

When I asked Zurita about how he had come up with the idea for sky-writing poems, he told me that originally he had tried to get the Chilean Air Force to execute the project because "if these same guys who bombed La Moneda (the government palace in downtown Santiago where President Salvador Allende took his life during the 1973 coup d'etat) were capable of writing a poem in the sky then it would prove that art would be capable of changing the world." Surprisingly, the proposal was not dismissed out of hand by the Air Force; it worked its way up the bureaucratic ladder to a commanding officer, who eventually shut it down.

It is worth mentioning here the symbolism of airplanes during the

Pinochet years. On one level, there is the 1973 bombing of La Moneda during the coup, and on another there is the nightmarish reality that throughout the dictatorship bodies were dropped from airplanes "into the sea, lakes, and rivers, or dropped onto the Andes."[2] In other words, the bodies dropped from airplanes entered the landscape and became a part of the country's 'natural environment,' and this is reflected in various places in *Song for his Disappeared Love*, particularly in a refrain from an earlier part of the text: "All my love is here and it has stayed:/ Stuck to the rocks, to the sea and the mountains/Stuck, stuck, to the rocks the sea and the mountains." These words are inscribed into the Memorial for the Disappeared in Santiago.

The selection included in this anthology is from the latter portion of *Song for his Disappeared Love*, which illustrates Zurita's concern with the ways in which torture, disappearance and massive state violence affect everyone. The shame and pain and guilt, Zurita might say, is communal, and it cannot be escaped given that the blood and the remains of the disappeared are scattered throughout the landscape. Of course, the reality of violent societies marked by killing, torturing and disappearing is common throughout the Americas, and this sense of international shame is reflected in the "niches" from this section of *Song for his Disappeared Love*, where the rigid, prison-like shape of the text frames and forms its content.

Finally, while it is easy to situate *Song for his Disappeared Love* as a political response to a particular moment, it is important to keep in mind what the title makes clear: this is a love song: a song not just for lovers split apart by disappearance, but for love that has disappeared. In this sense, the book's anger, for me at least, is as present as its generosity.

---

[1] This and some of the other passages in this introduction are from an interview I conducted with Raúl Zurita on April 3, 2009.

[2] The quoted passage is from President Ricardo Lagos' 2001 speech which for the first time officially acknowledged that the Chilean military dropped bodies from airplanes, which was known for many years but never formally recognized by the government. Lagos' formal recognition of this fact forms the starting point for another of Zurita's books, *INRI* (2003) that was released in 2009 by Marick Press in a translation by William Rowe.

## from *Song for his Disappeared Love*

The paragraphs read and say:

The headlights filled the road. Everyone cried out for mother and father's love and as the doors to the ascent opened  the ballad began again. For his disappeared love he went from hole to hole, grave to grave, searching for the eyes that don't find.   From gravestone to gravestone, from cry to cry, it went through niches, through shadows and it went like this:

The central countries cried. Their deaths were marked by date, time and name. They were found in Barracks 12, in urns that indicated the cause of death. When they were raised in humane countries and animals obstructed the rivers but they were friends. They obstructed the jungle, but they were friends. They obstructed the nightmares and they were like days. This was before.
They cried the whole night and they lay there. The bomb is black. Amen.

Araucan niche. They were found in Barracks 13. They were long black valleys like the others who disappeared. It was noted: Southern airplanes ploughed the sky and as they bombed their cities they lit up for a second and dropped. So it says in barracks on engraved tombs that warn. In the limestone they erased the remains and all that was left was the final wound. Amen. They all broke into tears. Amen. It was tough to watch.
Amen.

USA Niche. Found in Barracks 12 Northern countries and dispatched to eat themselves up thanks to their dreams of special shields, of murderers of blacks, of domination. They descended the sky and they called Hiroshima the country that blazed; Central countries, valleys and Chilean gluttons. The graves are nights and everything is night in the American grave. They rest in peace like the bison. It was a Navajo phrase.    So it was written, Amen.

South American countries that cry. They have this every day, suffering and devouring countries in Barracks 13. In sandpits, Indian cities and worlds were massacred with no shame, friendship nor law. They died from love hunger in dreams that mark and name. They lie and rest in peace.
At night they emit light and wail. The origins and complaints are noted. Amen.

Amazonian Niche: in the darkness the game of shadows was sent to the space and corridor of the Barracks.
There was a battle and cross with the Peruvian and Brazilian countries. It was said that the encounter left blood, and the great deserts of Sao Paulo and the Amazonian sky. It was said that it was a river of death and Paraguay.
The blood pushed against the gravestone. It says: rest and stay.
Amen. It does not state a date. No, it only states a Cross.

Argentinean Niche. Shed 13, a ship beneath the country of Peru and above the country of Chile. From torture to torture, disappearance to extermination, a hole was left and it was like the aforementioned countries and the night had nowhere to fall and neither did the day. Country disappeared from the horror behind the barracks. From there the wind blew across the inexistent pampas and as it settled the massacred faces became visible, Amen. Tombstone 6.
White skin is all it says.

Peruvian Niche and mountainous regions. Like all those referred to the Barracks and Ship these countries lay the Shining Path and extreme misery. In planes they rumbled a road of light through the Urubamba and the ruined raised their candles. The groan emerged from cholai:
Oh the evil of my Peru, it says, they're all tombs.
They cried more than the others and now it's a dream and they lie. It groans: it's the "A" of vistas.

Central country Niche. Little by little the light was throwing shadows and as it arrived here it changed colors. The evening fell. The countries sunk in silence but beneath the niches one heard the sound of rivers and beneath the rivers the scream of the fleeing Indians. Then came the blood bath and the rivers sounded just like the rumbling bombers. The end. Santo Domingo died, rivers, lakes and green jungles.
It reads: we were good.

Niche: dear skies of the Carribean. They died and were assigned to the hallway of barracks 12 and 13. It was the last sparkle on the horizon, the last glow. Thousands and thousands of pieces dragged along begging, then they sang, finally they got up and saw the tombs open. Like the great moon the sky shone another instant and shut off. It was the void, the black rag of Carribean love. The epitaph says: it covered everything.

Columbian Niche and the white countries. Arranged in groups. Aisle, barracks and number stated. In the sierras they fell rattling and all the people were the first death. Then, when the city of M19 turned the sky red, the mountains accompanied the fallen and in this way Colombia became a snow storm of the dead and fallen. Rest in peace went the love song to the whites.
Black is white.
So it goes, it says, and it cries.

Paraguayan Niche. Referred to Barracks 13. Another massacre between countries, Chaco wars, and La Plata wars, condominium and suffering. Now it lies in its niche surrounded by barbed wire, aisle and tomb. It says: I rest for the Guarani Marcos, and the whole song was sung, it says the niche. It says: I sing for peace in Paraguay, I sing for the shot down helicopters, for the Ipacarai country who kill with cane. All of this has ended. The niche says day and it bled.

Niche: forests from the Alamo country. They blazed, crumbled, and were not assigned a particular niche. They remained in countries and rested. Enormous airplanes destroyed them touching their burning love. The forests burned from lasers, chemical warfare and nightmares. They cry, it says, they were scalded. The flesh is ash: so it is written. The jungle is flesh: so it is written. The jungles are burnt bodies: so it is written.

Niche: the country of Haiti and sky. It says: dear central and American skies.

It was not the same blue, it was lit by stars, and everyone prayed as they looked up at it. It was the great naves, the voodoo and missiles against the stars. On setting, something from the blue of the sky turned violet, the cold purple of the corpses. Now, the blue sky is the eye that searches, the island that searches. No, they are black graves, they are gone. In the niche it says: I curse his sky.

Niche: desert of the Mexican country. It lies beneath New Mexico. The Mexican desert first covered the walls with sand, descended with thoughts and as it arrived at the plaza, rulfos and students raised their arms. It was packs of hounds and massacre, more managed to climb the steps. The climb is longing and prayer, it says, but that's how the image remains. Mexico '68 lies. The stony ground is the niche. It says: neither arms nor legs, beloved God.

Sandino Tomb and the green lakes. It says God, it says Nicaragua beloved night died. In the niche one sees:
sieges by air and sea, electronic, contras and sabotage. They kill the boys at the border. Dear entire lake Nicaragua it climbed the volcanoes and fell like a deluge. The fallen covered fields. Now everyone is gone. Sandinos and countries. Nicaraguan niche, it's called, it's number 17.
Beloved night, it reads.

Niche: volcanoes from the Guatemalan earth. This is what we call the Guatemalan tomb number 14 and it says:
Dear corn field of my country, dear volcanoes of my country, dear blue of my country. There was no, it reads, need for extermination nothing fatal no murder. It was dead, corn and lava. The date stayed in Mayan and the glow of those corn fields was never known. No one knows. Like Peru it cried; dear corn field, dear craters. It rests.

Niche: Colorado desert country. Same as the last niche. Same as all the other stony grounds. In handwritten print the gravestone says: My God has dark faces. Long brown plains undulated, but it wasn't the wind, but rather the tanks and the love-thirst that moved.
They begged, but only the maroon replied and together they fell into the canyons. The northern desert fell.
Niche 16. Dear red sand, it now said.

Niche Venezuelan Tomb. Bolivar's niche, it says. Gravestones, tombstones of the third world — what we used to call the countries. Niches from the American Countries, new American or countries that smiled at the greenness. Goodbye, they say.
They all form part of the designated shed. It was black, like the rails on the oil tankers in the sea. This is the Venezuelan niche. Only one human rests there. There's neither oil nor earth. Dammed night.

Alaskan Tomb. White is God. The countries of Barracks 13 were seen only as whiteness. Ice of the Eskimo country, the white elk and rivers. It was the 19th seen. The dead plains raised their grasses for the last time over the countries of Canada, USA, and the other frozen ones.

Their love fell in the cold, their hunt was frozen and the tribe stayed in the white niche. It's there.

Death must be sweet in the snow. Amen.

21. Bolivian Niche says: my love is the entire plateau. Signaled in Barracks 13 and aisle. In the disappeared love from La Paz there remains in the Aymara tongues a pain so deadly of the pigeon who died battling. It says this: from defeat to defeat the most beloved was digging out the grave. Bolivian nation, it reads, capital Lechín. At night, in dreams, the beat of the silent plains stopped.

Chazki delivered the good-bye amen and stop.

Tomb 23. Country of El Salvador. It says: have mercy for your dearest Salvador. In the shed and epitaph it reads:

Nothing was so much, nothing was so much, nothing was so much. House by house, the one who shed the most blood for the people lies beneath Honduras and above Guatemala. When not even one was left it exploded, singing the way he sings to his love the song of the disappeared. Everyone sleeps now. They dream and sleep. Like the stone. Amen.

Tomb 20. Country of Cuba and islands, malecón and islands. Described one sees: Mountains and mountain ranges, are they there? Lakes and lacustrine, are they there? Thread and spinners, are they there? Indians and Siboneyes, are they there? Blockade and blocked, are they there? The Mariel Bridge, Havana and reefs, are they there? They read and stopped. From the whole scene the cry fell and the sound: the beloved island died.

The sound: USA, Cuba, and Marti's country, dead in peace like the bison and the grass.

Tomb 22: Country of Ecuador says: beloved are the mountainous, Amen. Niche and Barracks also assigned. It says: it surrendered to famine, a load of brothers and suffering. Of Shuar and Quechua in cry one reads: Central country and jungle of fiery birds fluttering and whistling the whole hymn of their disappeared love. Love by day, and love by night that in the gravestone now says: Dead birds and greenery. Jungles and snow storms.

Niche 24 of the starving Chilean and Argentinean plains, Chamarritas and pampas.

There are four assigned to one.

Return: they are pieces of the Argentinean country that did not fit into the niches from the barracks of the Navy, Quelmes and Villa Grimaldi, Baquedano and Dawson form the Chilean niche, Amen.

The disappeared love in each tomb, niche, and name says:
nothing.

Niche 25. Uruguay country: cries for the love that does not find, also signaled and noted in torture, shooting, and disappearance. Tomb that changes — it reads —
with the color of the eyes of the searcher. So it reads in the Uruguayan niche, the burial of their missing love, of their disappeared and end stop.
Rest your eyes that search and don't find on the Uruguayan sky.
Thus the dead Charrúa, says no, we don't find, no.

Tomb snow-covered niche 27 of the countries. It grew from the love we had, the tomb reads. Frozen with the love they had they climbed the mountain ranges with snowy peaks and the white crests could be seen from the sea. In the sheds there are mountains and seas. The largest is as high as the South American and North American mountains. No, they are barracks surrounded by sea, they are islands surrounded by sea oh no.
Don't leave.

Don't go this is only death. 29 of the countries. The darkness began to rise over everything. The night squid that went around detaining everything and there was the sound of the song, the cry, the rain, of their love all the brothers are the Song, the Song for his disappeared love. I'm going, run run, little angel. The Chilean countries and all the others named. It still cries for the hole formed from the missing love. From the missing homelands:
Are you calling me?

Easter Island Tomb of the countries. Niche 26. The territory does not inform. Only the bird who crossed borders and countries lies there. Like the toucan, that's how Easter Island lies. We were raised there, they say, just like the flock, just like the valleys they face, the mountains they face, the long beaches they face. We were born here say the dreams they face.
Islands of disappeared love, it says. Everything; islands and countries crying nest and niche.

28. Oh don't leave, he groans. Andean tomb of the countries. I'm going, away, everything dies. Everything dies sucking itself. There were as many mountains as there now are clouds.
Grey clouds. Blacker and greyer rising in the sky, climbing and evaporating. Those are the mountains. Holes in all the countries expanded downwards and the torrent of their love was the rain. The mountains rained, says my Andean darling, don't go.
Don't go, she says.

30. Is the tomb of the country's love calling? Did you call out of pain? Out of pure pain? Was it out of pain that your love cried so hard? They told me so often that it's over, that it's all over and that it was the dream that was over. The brother says I saw you lost on fleeing grass, little countries, says the niche. Lost in the blackness everything disappears in the islands, names and countries, yes; are they calling me?
Are you calling me?

# Urayoán Noel

## try city®

1.born of alarm 2.Mister Misnomer's *streetform* 3.against what movement? 4.daylight again (*carport?*) 5.parkway searches (*seizures?*) 6. today's teleprompter monologues 7.off crosstown bus 8. to hold on 9.to the edge 10.of things (*here?*) 11.curvature of city 12.(*slit*) slippage is 13.the variegated hums 14.of home and 15.loft parties and 16.open mics and 17.(*slumming slammers? di-versifiers?* 18.*assisting the assistant* 19.*to the assistant* 20.*of administrative assistants!*) 21.the last dose 22.of the truth 23.of man (*whole?*) 24.the body erratic 25.retro salsa bands 26.(*sounds no more* 27.*like tropical trombones?*) 28.skyscrapers thru clouds 29.wasted boys and 30.wilted girls in 31.drunken lipo limousines 32.hoarse playa throats 33.these pancaked pierrots 34.those (*faux?*) wacky 35.(*faux?*) designer dances 36.beer nausea stoplights 37.(*Laforgue's Times Square?* 38.*hydrocephalic asparagus moon!* 39.*[adult?]videos of* 40.*downtowns on fire?*) 41.spotlight uptown now 42.language poets already 43.spoken for in 44.drab position papers 45.on the fate 46.of the city 47.(*the western Bronx* 48.*is hillier than...?* 49.*big bedroom's chilly* 50.*subway negligee's frilly* 51.*north of Harlem* 52.*means NoHarm dude!*) 53.where others live 54.self in other 55.self as other 56.fate of man 57.feat of woman 58.performance of gender 59.*hipsterpaper* of record 60.classic soul collection 61.memories of infotainment 62.in acid-washed landscapes 63.as intramural cheer 64.oh democracy now 65.meet your maker! 66.highbrow maracas play 67.anthems of privilege 68.lowbrow maracas just 69.keep the beat 70.middlebrow maracas move 71.to Canada, quick! 72.this city isn't 73.'happening' just yet 74.just testing! texting! 75.diabetes supplies language 76.already spoken here 77.spoken for now 78.already a part 79.of a (collapsing?) community 80.let's scorn utopia! 81.advertisement culture crashers 82.chorus of stillborn 83.performers self-help e-books 84.solitude of night 85.reclaim the city! 86.(*from its executors?*) 87.this reggaetón summer 88.winter of jackhammers 89.snapshot synapses:( *vaya!*) 90.make way for 91.garbage truck pick-up 92.up and down 93.this (*virtual?*) Broadway 94.where anaphorae pileup 95.like rat droppings 96.like corpse cut-ups 97.like price tags 98.malt liquor bottles 99.downed in mixed-crowd 100.mp3 park benches 101.telecommunication sector holdings 102.special-interest laugh tracks 103.(*failed?*) performance poems 104.(*forced?*) onto the 105.page then split 106.into tercets (*cities?*) 107.singing now signifying 108.nothing but flight 109.back to sleep 110.now these lit...anies 111.(*sic*) of streetlamps

112.Wednesday mid-week traffic 113.still backed up 114.to outlying areas 115.where the meaning 116.of "outlying" is 117.laid bare (splayed?) 118.who pays the 119.fare for crossing? 120.always here not 121.back in time 122. to the days 123.before the monuments' 124.debriefing by brackish 125.and/ or waterboarding pigeons? 126.Humanoscope® sponsored by 127.Humania the first 128.and only drug 129.approved to treat 130.dissension in the 131. ranks of rancor 132.demographics roughly (*guesstimate?*) 133.14 to 99 134. give or take 135.a few stragglers 136.(*a few low-liars? [sic]*) 137.lower-dosage holograms 138.of lampoon proletariat 139.plantation service sector 140. neocolonial escapades performed 141.off route n+7 142.text exit past 143.the (*private?*) beach 144.with (*plastic?*) palms 145.almost always waiting 146.to be greased 147.sad tropics of 148.discourse at the 149.misanthropic disco the 150.tropes of discord 151.the traps of 152.discard of dis 153.this strep these 154.scarred armament drives 155.*tú sabes, tipo* 156.*bola global* (*meaning?*) 157. dead bouncer on 158.the steppes, uncarded 159.at the border 160.VIP room (*where/wear?*) 161.for years the 162.theorists prayed for 163.crash for failure 164.to use the 165.word "systemic" and 166. mean it, man 167.(*in a pinch* 168.*any "emic" will* 169.*do [epid/pand/acad/pol/polys/tot] and* 170.*yet it's hard* 171.*to claim a* 172.*polis [herd? clan?]* 173. *that's not semic:* 174.*poetry's pull/ duty/condition for* 175.*being written/spoken/staged/marketed and* 176.*horizon of meaning* 177.*its demeaning/diluting and* 178.*somehow it slithers* 179.*across the pages* 180.*and abandoned stages* 181.*poorly mic'd [texted/nexted])* 182.lang it sings 183.the meaning's screening 184.sing! sing! (*I-lungs* 185.*in the scream* 186.*that is what* 187.*we are)* fight/flight? 188.clubby beached wails! 189.lang sound (*sondas?*) 190.in the sand 191.the TV makeup 192.makeup of nation 193.the made-up makes 194.of maids/nannies commuting 195.to made-up suburbs 196.where school counselors 197.watch meta-reality TV 198.on unmade beds 199.the litany is 200.always participatory because 201.when we become 202.one with the 203.tremors we start 204.moving in sync 205. with the masses/dem-asses/*demáses* 206.citizens that came 207.went and keep 208. returning day-to-day to 209.earn and burn 210.in bakeries shoe 211.stores banking centers 212.crammed into a 213.subway's silver sliver 214.(*sin ver [so-wey!]* 215.*sin verso? [way!]* 216.*sin verse? [(ob)servers* 217.*(ob)versers])* here/ hear the 218.litany is always 219.participatory because we're 220.in sync with 221.the mutable (*phenomontage?*) 222.flash by/fade the 223.technical school posters 224.with smiling youths 225.grabbing their backpacks 226.in well-lit hallways 227.to stave-off death 228.slowly (*by degrees/digress*) 229."Uh, which wanderlust?" 230.asks Citizen Wonderslut 231.to the mirrors 232. (*yawning...hungover...yadda...*) 233.a fair question 234.for mute commuters 235.(*muttering/huffing shoes untied* 236.*steady stride somehow* 237.*anachronistic already...ahora?)* 238.superannuated nano onan 239.city rock steady 240.flow of passengers 241.like the plod 242.of legendary creatures 243.raised and

reared **244.**in faraway savannas **245.**and slowly (*slowly!*) **246.**remembering to speak **247.**limewirerimjob poets post **248.**listpoems in listservs **249.**but I'm here **250.**like an analyst **251.**of assfaults (*whose?*) **252.**crude e-satyr I **253.**like it here **254.**I take a **255.**licking and keep **256.**on ticking off **257.** statistics (*statist tics?*) **258.**you keep Europe **259.**Kant's grounding sudoku **260.**can't remember summer **261.**museums' cupolas and **262.**aqueducts both useless **263.**(*how then to* **264.***sitemize* [*sic*][*qué?*] **265.***to deduct one's* **266.***take on downtowns?*) **267.**summer's faded undershirts **268.** cutie being hit-on! **269.** loveseat being sit-on! **270.** oops! laughtrack's gone **271.**you're drunk now **272.** have been so **273.**for some time **274.**will continue to **275.**be so entranced **276.**by language that **277.**can't be overcome **278.**the truth's you've **279.**been around text-blocks **280.**blocking out memories **281.**of semesters spent **282.** windowless qua cubicled **283.**graying grabbing notepads **284.**morning's glyph confounds **285.**you at 3AM **286.**when skin collides **287.**with skin (*scan-scion?*) **288.**you tire of **289.**this nonsense of **290.**detours through cities **291.**answerless again (*throat-clearing!*) **292.**(*"um, clueless proposal:* **293.***let's conflate 'you'* **294.***and 'I'... become* **295.***....underpass to 'us'*) **296.**a litany is **297.** taking shape is **298.**shaking tapeloop socialorder **299.**out to go **300.**blurry disarray of **301.**uptown employees of **302.**will-to-power-lunch (*broker-than brokers!*) **303.**junior executives who **304.**work nights (*weekends?*) **305.** in search of **306.**the lifestyle slogan **307.**the lifestyle drug **308.**the lifestyle lifestyle **309.**spring night (*hoodies?*) **310.**hideous hideouts (*arrivants!*) **311.** sleep in fits **312.**high (*on doubt?*) **313.**sound (*or not-at-all?*) **313.**locked glocal glocks **314.**embraceth transient action! **315.**(*repeateth litany tomorrow*) **316.** voicedform: "*a hidden* **317.***city's never lit* **318.***no littoral as* **319.***skylines tend to* **320.***blend distend into* **321.***each others' shudder* **322.***in time to catch* **323.***this simple ring:* **324.***taste the tone!* **325.***stone the state!* **326.***state our truth:* **327.***we're factoid fictions* **328.***making meaning in* **329.***cities nations bodies* **330.***pawing at slacks* **331.***mechanically (our birthright?* **332.***flux) waiting for* **333.***another hard-won breath*

### me, o poem! (a cameo poem)

ME DO MODEM
LOAN AOL
*EL GOOGLE*
*¡EMAILÍAME*
*MI I.M.!*
WWW
*TODO.DOT*
*SU*TO-DO.DOT.US
*MOCO.COM*
ODE I.M. SONNET: *¡TENNOS MIEDO!*
E-Z! I *LA BOLA* LOBALIZE
DELL APPALLED
MAC[E].CAM
GATEWAY A, WE TAG!
NOT/E/BOOK O! O! BET ON!
LAPTOP POT PAL
CODA.DOC
¡TUNED ODE: NUT, I
LET NIX INTEL!
NOR ELECT CELERON!
K.O.! O! BE CAFÉ FACEBOOK!
E.DOT I//MOVEON.OBAMA.BONO//E-VOMIT ODE
ZERO! O! PROG OR POOR? E-Z!
E-RICIN! AGRO-ORGANIC IRE!
VIRAL, O POLAR I.V.!
ONLINE.NIL.NO
*GOOOOOOOOOOL!!!!!* BLOOOOOOOOOOOG!!!!!
O.S.! SO?
TUNE.NUT
FLARF.FR! ALF!
(GROG!) ALIEN ONE, I LAG (ORG)
LANG IS SIGNAL
MAP SPAM
CC:BCC:
KUMAR! ROM OR RAM.UK

DAOLOAD
YAHOO...*HAY?*
PHAT, *SÍ?* VISTA HP
BE.WEB
TENDON@NOD.NET
CROW.ORG
SUE.US
VOGUE@EU.GOV
[AS U.S.A.]
NUMB IBM U.N.
SET AGE: GATES!
O SOFT *FOSO*
MIC I.M.
DO PISS ¡POD!
MP3@3PM
NOON
NITE...GET IN!
DELL U. DULLED
E.DUD, DUDE
NET@FLIM, MILF@TEN
E-FILM LIFE
REBUT U TUBER
[SIC] [IS]
NOMAD DAMON
HELM THE HTML, EH?
IF I WI-FI
BEWARE ERA WEB!
RE: VERSES...REVERSE, SR. EVER
SERVER...REV...RES
I'M AN "I":                    A MOD DOMAIN AM I!

# Sandra Doller

## H.D.'s Not Eating of Chickens

hd's not eating of chickens
because of her love of cats

hd's not not eating of chickens
because of love of chickens

hd's not love of cats or chickens
canned

cat wing
cat thigh

hd in vienna
also saving
crema from the night before
hotel style buns

hot style buns & cigarettes
while not being a chain

the way he holds his fingers because crazy
in the hospital held his fingers like crazy

hd tea & buns & cigarettes
bryher cigar & proprietor

cigarettes were egyptian
tea was tea

expensive flowers to eat lower
material made for dresses
string bags from greece times two
leather bag sent
how swiss & spare

why not buy a new bag
$5000 costing dress
antique rings
modern hair
ubiquitous fur

never visit the old places
old little old papa
said come here

who cares about dreams & religion
why was there a baby in a box

no one thought the reeds was a casket
dead wood
size of a baby size of a cat
why care about  cats

i spoke with _____ who agrees with me
mellow celebrity

can you be fortunate
& in all else wild

he was in the hospital
where his fingers were

so why does the march
in the neighbor's yard
look slightly

a crabbing
only
lawns between

she was tired
the rest of us
wanted her to stop reminding us

it takes this long to make a colored disk
being opposite
concepts

east street each
afternoon

fills with furniture
not mine

how he could not
be troubled

like three in a tree
when they passed us

do you not see
the elbows

missed golden
missed each
hospital season

hard sob of grass
seasonal disk

what color monks
were they

i had not spent
my time

# Brian Evenson
## Windeye

### ～ 1 ～

They lived, when he was growing up, in a simple house, an old bungalow with a converted attic and sides covered in cedar shake. In the back, where an oak thrust its branches over the roof, the shake was light brown, almost honey. In the front, where the sun struck it full, it had weathered to a pale gray, like a dirty bone. There, the shingles were brittle, thinned by sun and rain, and if you were careful you could slip your fingers up behind some of them. Or at least his sister could. He was older and his fingers were thicker, so he could not.

Looking back on it, many years later, he often thought it had started with that, with her carefully working her fingers up under a shingle as he waited and watched to see if it would crack. That was one of his earliest memories of his sister, if not the earliest.

His sister would turn around and smile, her hand gone to knuckles, and say, "I feel something. What am I feeling?" And then he would ask questions. *Is it smooth? he might ask. Does it feel rough? Scaly? Is it cold-blooded or warm-blooded? Does it feel red? Does it feel like its claws are in or out? Can you feel its eye move?* He would keep on, watching the expression on her face change as she tried to make his words into a living, breathing thing, until it started to feel too real for her and, half giggling, half screaming, she whipped her hand free.

There were other things they did, other ways they tortured each other, things they both loved and feared. Their mother didn't know anything about it, or if she did she didn't care. One of them would shut the other inside the toy chest and pretend to leave the room, waiting there silently until the one in the chest couldn't stand it any longer and started to yell. That was a hard game for him because he was afraid of the dark, but he tried not to show that to his sister. Or one of them would wrap the other tight in blankets, and then the trapped one would have to break free. Why they had liked it, why they had done it, he had a hard time remembering later, once he was grown. But they *had* liked it, or at least *he* had liked it—there was no denying that—and he had done it. No denying that either.

So at first those games, if they were games, and then, later, something else, something worse, something decisive. What was it again? Why was it hard, now that he was grown, to remember? What was it called? Oh, yes, *Windeye*.

## ～ 2 ～

How had it begun? And when? A few years later, when the house started to change for him, when he went from thinking about each bit and piece of it as a separate thing and started thinking of it as a *house*. His sister was still coming up close, entranced by the gap between shingle and wall, intrigued by the twist and curve of a crack in the concrete steps. It was not that she didn't know there was a house, only that the smaller bits were more important than the whole. For him, though, it had begun to be the reverse.

So he began to step back, to move back in the yard far enough away to take the whole house in at once. His sister would give him a quizzical look and try to coax him in closer, to get him involved in something small. For a while, he'd play to her level, narrate to her what the surface she was touching or the shadow she was glimpsing might mean, so she could pretend. But over time he drifted out again. There was something about the house, the house as a whole, that troubled him. But why? Wasn't it just like any house?

His sister, he saw, was standing beside him, staring at him. He tried to explain it to her, tried to put a finger on what fascinated him. *This house*, he told her. *It's a little different. There's something about it . . .* But he saw, from the way she looked at him, that she thought it was a game, that he was making it up.

"What are you seeing?" she asked, with a grin.

*Why not?* he thought. *Why not make it a game?*

"What are *you* seeing?" he asked her.

Her grin faltered a little but she stopped staring at him and stared at the house.

"I see a house," she said.

"Is there something wrong with it?" he prompted.

She nodded, then looked to him for approval.

"What's wrong?" he asked.

Her brow tightened like a fist. "I don't know," she finally said. "The window?"

"What about the window?"

"I want you to do it," she said. "It's more fun."

He sighed, and then pretended to think. "Something wrong with the window," he said. "Or not the window exactly but the number of windows." She was smiling, waiting. "The problem is the number of windows. There's one more window on the outside than on the inside."

He covered his mouth with his hand. She was smiling and nodding, but he couldn't go on with the game. Because, yes, that was exactly the problem, there was one more window on the outside than on the inside. That, he knew, was what he'd been trying to see all along.

## ~ 3 ~

But he had to make sure. He had his sister move from room to room in the house, waving to him from each window. The ground floor was all right, he saw her each time. But in the converted attic, just shy of the corner, there was a window at which she never appeared.

It was small and round, probably only a foot and a half in diameter.

The glass was dark and wavery. It was held in place by a strip of metal about as thick as his finger, giving the whole of the circumference a dull, leaden rim.

He went inside and climbed the stairs, looking for the window himself, but it simply wasn't there. But when he went back outside, there it was.

For a time, it felt like he had brought the problem to life himself by stating it, that if he hadn't said anything the half-window wouldn't be there. Was that possible? He didn't think so, that wasn't the way the world worked. But even later, once he was grown, he still found himself wondering sometimes if it was his fault, if it was something he had done. Or rather, said.

Staring up at the half-window, he remembered a story his grandmother had told him, back when he was very young, just three or four, just after his father had left and just before his sister was born. Well, he didn't remember it exactly, but he remembered it had to do with windows. Where she came from, his grandmother said, they used to be called not windows but something else. He couldn't remember the word, but remembered that it started with a v. She had said the word and then had asked, *Do you know what this means?* He shook his head. She repeated the word, slower this time.

"This first part," she had said, "it means 'wind.' This second part, it means 'eye.'" She looked it him with her own pale, steady eye. "It is important to know that a window can be instead a *windeye*."

So he and his sister called it that, windeye. It was, he told her, how the wind looked into the house and so was not a window at all. So of course they couldn't look out of it; it was not a window at all, but a windeye.

He was worried she was going to ask questions, but she didn't. And then they went into the house to look again, to make sure it wasn't a window after all. But it still wasn't there on the inside.

Then they decided to get a closer look. They had figured out which window was nearest to it and opened that and leaned out of it. There it was. If they leaned far enough, they could see it and almost touch it.

"I could reach it," his sister said. "If I stand on the sill and you hold my legs, I could lean out and touch it."

"No," he started to say, but, fearless, she had already clambered onto the sill and was leaning out. He wrapped his arms around her legs to keep

her from falling. He was just about to pull her back inside when she leaned farther and he saw her finger touch the windeye. And then it was as if she had dissolved into smoke and been sucked into the windeye. She was gone.

~ 4 ~

It took him a long time to find his mother. She was not inside the house, nor was she outside in the yard. He tried the house next door, the Jorgensens, and then the Allreds, then the Dunfords. She wasn't anywhere. So he ran back home, breathless, and somehow his mother was there now, lying on the couch, reading.

"What's wrong?" she asked.

He tried to explain it best he could. *Who?* she asked at first and then said *Slow down and tell it again*, and then, *But who do you mean?* And then, once he'd explained again, with an odd smile:

"But you don't have a sister."

But of course he had a sister. How could his mother have forgotten? What was wrong? He tried to describe her, to explain what she looked like, but his mother just kept shaking her head.

"No," she said firmly. "You don't have a sister. You never had one. Stop pretending. What's this really about?"

Which made him feel that he should hold himself very still, that he should be very careful about what he said, that if he breathed wrong more parts of the world would disappear.

After talking and talking, he tried to get his mother to come out and look at the windeye.

"Window, you mean," she said, voice rising.

"No," he said, beginning to grow hysterical as well. "Not window. *Windeye.*" And then he had her by the hand and was tugging her to the door. But no, that was wrong too, because no matter which window he pointed at she could tell him where it was in the house. The *windeye*, just like his sister, was no longer there.

But he kept insisting it had been there, kept insisting too that he had a sister.

And that was when the trouble really started.

~ 5 ~

Over the years there were moments when he was almost convinced, moments when he almost began to think—and perhaps even did think for weeks or months at a time—that he never had a sister. It would have been easier to think this than to think she had been alive and then, perhaps partly because of him, not alive. Being not alive wasn't like being dead, he felt: it

was much, much worse. There were years too when he simply didn't choose, when he saw her as both real and make-believe and sometimes neither of those things. But in the end what made him keep believing in her—despite the line of doctors that visited him as a child, despite the rift it made between him and his mother, despite years of forced treatment and various drugs that made him feel like his head had been filled with wet sand, despite years of having to pretend to be cured—was simply this: he was the only one who believed his sister was real. If he stopped believing, what hope would there be for her?

Thus he found himself, even when his mother was dead and gone and he himself was old and alone, brooding on his sister, wondering what had become of her. He wondered too if one day she would simply reappear, young as ever, ready to continue with the games they had played. Maybe she would simply suddenly be there again, her tiny fingers worked up behind a cedar shingle, staring expectantly at him, waiting for him to tell her what she was feeling, to make up words for what was pressed there between the house and its skin, lying in wait.

"What is it?" he would say in a hoarse voice, leaning on his cane.

"I feel something," she would say. "What am I feeling?"

And he would set about describing it. *Does it feel red? Does it feel warmblooded or cold? Is it round? Is it smooth like glass?* All the while, he knew, he would be thinking not about what he was saying but about the wind at his back. If he turned around, he would be wondering, would he find the wind's strange, baleful eye staring at him?

That wasn't much, but it was the best he could hope for. Chances were he wouldn't get even that. Chances were there would be no sister, no wind. Chances were that he'd be stuck with the life he was living now, just as it was, until the day when he was either dead or not living himself.

# A History of the Human Voice

The earliest recordings of the human voice confirm what I have long suspected: in the past, there existed a symbiosis between the human voice and the insect known as the bee. Indeed, as recently as the 1860s, certain elite circles on the continent are said to have augmented their speech with bees.

The vocal chords were adapted by carefully massaging and stretching them with a slender wand made of lacquered cherrywood. Then they were carefully torn to create a series of insertion channels. A bee was affixed to the end of the wand with cold wax and slid buzzing down the throat and into a channel. There it was shaken slightly to enrage it into plunging its stinger into the chord. Once it was secure, one waited for the warmth of the throat to soften the wax so that the wand could be withdrawn and the next bee deployed.

It is thus no surprise that one of the earliest instances of recorded speech, by phonatographer Édouard-Léon Scott, was a paean to the insect in question: "Vole, Petite Abeille" ("Fly, Little Bee"). This recording, rendered by singing into a barrel-shaped horn attached to a stylus, consists of sound waves etched onto sheets of paper blackened by smoke from an oil lamp. When it is played, dozens of bees are heard buzzing, articulating themselves within human speech. It is a haunting, plaintive melody, simultaneously uni- and multivocal.

How this art of communion with the bee came to be lost I cannot say. Gradually, with the decline of the privileged classes, it fell out of favor. Yet now having heard it, it is impossible for me not to think of our strictly human voices as vexed, as forever lacking.

I have been driven to strange extremes in my attempts to regain mastery of this art of the voice. So far, despite experiencing a great deal of pain, I have met only limited success, the bees quickly suffocating within my swollen throat. But, I tell myself, in the end it will be worth it.

# Andrew Borgstrom
## That We Never Knew This Reaches Upward,
## Assists the Room Grew

The bronchi back to the bronchi continues to advance as you press, until you feel the bronchi move one breath to the left, so when you next hit the bronchi, this turns the cartilage and the cartilage is about to hit the cartilage and make a printed impression as it hits the diaphragm and lifts up and roast beefs itself between the end of it, just as the floating rib falls back down to its original disposition, as the floating rib has a slug of cartilage on the jugular and you have to press the mark you've just made, the next line, the paper up and moves the paper, a sheet of bloodied muscle called the paper, so the paper, the paper, then a bell sounds called the paper, when you release the right edge at the same time, the start of the sternum, a true rib attached to it swings a false rib called a floating rib up toward the sternum but doesn't obliterate the sternum: The _____ ____ of _____-____ _____, and the ____ _____ in the _____ _____, _____ in the _____ _____ ____that __ ___ _____, ___ _____, _____ ___ and the _____ ___ ___ _____ in the _____ ___ or the _____, _____ ___ _____ _____, _____ _____ the _____, the _____, the _____ ____ on the _____ ___ _____ _____ the _____, _____ _____ in a ___ that _____, _____ ____ __ _____ _____, _____ __ _____, the _____ or the _____ _____ of _____, no _____ on _____, one ____ _____ a _____ _____ ____, _____ ___, a ____ ____ as ____ as the ____ and the ____ _____ __ _____, the ____ _____ on the _____ that ____, _____ and _____, and the _____, _____ __ ____ ____, _____ _____ with the _____ of _____ that _____the _____ on the ___, _____ __ _____ of ____, _____ _____, _____ and _____, ____ and _____ _____ _____ ____ the _____ of _____, and the ___ of the ____, _____ _____ ____ and _____ _____ the _____, _____ in a _____ ____, the _____ _____ ____ this, this _____ _____, _____ the ____ ____, the _____ ____, _____ with _____ and _____, ____ and _____, _____ and ____, ____ and _____ and _____, on _____ that ___ ____, on a _____ _____, _____ on _____, on the _____ of ____ and ____ _____ the _____ of ____ _____ the _____ that _____ _____ the end: We are not important, and I love you. We do not have to do anything but die, and I love you.

# Parneshia Jones
## Auto-correcting History

*for President Barack Obama*

Spell check does not recognize
this name –yet.

It tries, with a red underline alert,
to tell me that this is wrong,
that my letters are misplaced,
leading my complicated PC,
with its perfect vocabulary,
to believe no such same name exists.

It offers suggestions to fix
what history has already confirmed.

These letters, round-about, with all
their beautiful curves and angles,
their intricate folds forming perfect Bs
and As and the roundest O,
shaping a name that has awakened us all.

Barack and Obama cause key stroke duels
between my auto-correct and me.
Not willing to give up,
it plugs in Brick and Abeam, trying to
hold on tight to its King's English.

# Kathleen Rooney and Elisa Gabbert
## Collaborative Jokes

### The one about the unheimlich.

My doppelganger walks into a bar. He has a nasty disposition, whereas I am merely having a bad day. Does he enjoy watching forest fires? Do the patrons think we're twins? Only a certain kind of man would identify the color as "cyan." Or announce that "Rippling abs don't just appear on your midsection; you have to sculpt them." A sudden sunshower. Now he is reenacting a classic tourist photo cliché. And now I am surprised to find myself weeping.

### The one about simulacra.

An idiot savant walks into a bar. When he remembers something twice, what he remembers is the memory. This might be considered offensive. Behind the bar is a mirror world of disorderly brilliance. The savant's improbable skill is auto-suggestive time travel. A favorite painting hangs on the wall—George Washington, kneeling near his horse: "The Prayer at Valley Forge." This isn't *supposed* to be funny. And yet.

### The one about the afterlife.

A ghost walks into a bar. One shouldn't assume the ghost is a man. Most people can't even see the ghost, but to the ones who can, it's like seeing through a camera with Vaseline on the lens. Have you ever wondered how it feels to be unconscious? Even in life, the ghost was incautious with a revolver. There are good reasons to be afraid of ghosts. But they are seldom the reasons given.

**Andy Devine**

A, a, about, along, &, &, apartment, back, boy, boy, broken, cart, down, floor-boards, for, for, girl, girl, goes, he, his, in, in, jumping, Laundromat, laundry, little, little, lives, on, over, playing, radio, running, sleep, songs, the, the, the, the, to, today, tonight, up, upstairs, was, who, who, with, with, „ „ „ „ ., ..

# Kim Hyesoon

## from Manhole Humanity
### translated from the Korean by Don Mee Choi

O

Goodness, I didn't know there were such repulsive holes!

My hairy holes!
Creases of my stomach
Hair-like cilia in my nostrils
Finger-like villi in my small intestine
Pubic hair of love
Hair sprouts up inside the holes and ripples like water plants.
Holes are neatneatly piled inside a steaming stomach.
The wet and most poisonous snakes in the world pant.
Fill us up! Fill us up with the outside!
Delicious outside!
When hair whines like the fingers that reach out towards the refugee-aid
bread truck someone picks up a brass instrument and wails at the sky praising
the blueness.
Holes of the world, open up your lids and howl!

O

Bile travels up the esophagus and collects in my mouth. My esophagus feels
as if it's burning. The drain regurgitates. It's potent. It's as if ceiling and floor
are stuck together. Right now I'm being thrashed about by a whip made of
horizontal lines. In my dream someone comes into my room to surf.

In my dream I burn like a charcoal briquette, a wick placed down in my neck.
In the next dream, I become a gas in the dream world of gases. I hear wind
in my ears.

I dream of my holes falling onto a cement floor. I clean them up with a
plastic brush.

A faucet leaks. Water starts to collect in the basement. My pillow floats above
the basement.

Look over this way! As I open my eyes, the doctor pokes my tear glands with a long needle. Tears collect in my mouth. They're salty. I stare at the ocean inside me.

Nerve holes of a neck become constricted and put pressure on the entire nerve tree. A tranquilizer is injected directly into the holes. It is given six times a day. The piano keeps shut its gum that is about to spew out blood.

My right shoulder hurts, but the doctor inserts a needle in my left toe. With a stick, the doctor explains the swirls of my holes and the structure of my spirals. Someone sticks his head outside my manhole and looks out. Someone screams from my throat.

My body covered with holes wants to escape leaving the holes behind.

Nausea comes up the hole. As I take off my skin, the pipes holed in my body leak.

A lit stethoscope moves through the pipe. A night bus dashes along the endless roads inside my body. The night bus flickers like pain.

O

Hole, the heart of all things.
Hole, my country, my matter, my toasty-warm god.
Hole, stay eternal! All things endure a life of nuisance through small uteruses then die for the sake of the eternal life of a big uterus. Dear queen ant's many uteruses packed inside that high mountain: my eating and breathing has to do with my worship of the hole. This is my lifelong commemorative hole rite. Please get up, Your Highness, it's morning. Here is a fresh cup of coffee. Please calm down, Your Highness, it's nighttime. Here is a glass of wine for your fluttering brain. When he made me by blowing his breath into a hole, he who has created the world by drilling a hole into misery, the stink of his breath was overwhelming; today, I want to make him starve.

Wind, please stroke the alveoli of my lungs as you would a sick child. Please relay the message that time's pimp has not died; it still lives here. Please relay the message that the hole remains eternal from its previous life to its next life. Please relay the message that the hole gives birth to a hole and is raising a hole. (But who else is listening to what I'm saying besides my hole?)

O

All together:    Dear Hole has died
                     Dear Hole has resurrected
                     Dear Hole lives again

(Holes eat and drink)

O

At midnight, the kids, still wet behind the ears, head to head with the hole's entrance inside the subway are screaming, swallowing, tremtremtrembling, and barking that the entire subway spurts up like fountain water, smelling fishy.

Inside the subway station, a child holds out his dirty hands.
He says he will be good. He says he won't be bad again.
I see the child at the station for several weeks.

At the hospital across the street, a hole is giving birth to a hole.
Please allow the safe delivery of a hole!
As a mother hole of a mother hole prays rubbing her two palms together, a soprano climbs up an organ made of hospital drainpipes in the delivery room, panting, then lets out a scream towards the sky. Dear Big Hole, please spit it out! This hole can't possibly handle a newborn. Please spit it out, Dear Big Hole! (Who decides the time of birth? Is it the baby? the Mommy? the Stars?)

A life sprouts from the fugue raging in the hallway of the hospital. It's nearly midnight.

Another manhole humanity is born. Time makes a hole in the baby's body. Time puts a manhole's lid on the baby's head.

Down below at the restaurant, the chef's hands are in motion! With both hands he hacks away at the bodies piled up on the cutting board; there is nothing to distinguish one from another—plants and animals, jealousy, solitude, and spirit.

When I eat them tomorrow morning, does it mean that I will be eating my hole's skin? Eating my hole's outside? Eating my hole's tether? My hole's desire to persist, the music performed by commas has no pauses, hurhurrah!

O

The hole's essence is such that it's empty like the empty space inside of a flame.
Tongue is that place, not wearing any underwear, it hangs onto the hole's end where there is nothing and licks and makes o o o sounds.

Therefore, to say regulate your desire means to regulate well the empty space, the inside of a blood sausage!
Goodness, how am I suppose to regulate a place that's invisible!
The factory supervisor who sits inside the hungry sausage—what does he look like?

O

At the intensive care unit, one floor below the gynecology ward,
an electrical cord is plugged into a hole, a graph chart rotates waahwaah, the heart beats bambam, then later the hole dies. Time of death: 12 minutes past midnight. One handless watch stops.
The watch burns when the holes of the dead sag from greeting happiness for the first time.
Skin remains and is placed in the drawer of a freezer and a hole filled with happiness floats in air.

O

Dark tunnel before death
White tunnel after death

O

What nonsense, you say? Love comes out from where, you ask?
How can love come out from this hole then go into that hole, you ask?
Clear away the smelly hole, you ask?

O

Mommy manhole pats a baby manhole as if she's tapping on the stovepipe.
What a strange manhole!
It even has two holes from which tears gush out waah waah waah whenever it's hungry.
Its two nostril-chimneys wail chugchugpuffpuff.

Every time the baby manhole cries, mommy manhole plays a bandoneon, stretching then pressing, her tango musician hands in motion!

After the pipe connecting to the baby manhole was cut, it caused complications in mommy hole's blood circulation and made her break out in blue rashes, so she had to go down to the lower level of the hospital to repair her hole.

Baby is this hole
Mommy is that hole

Like the swimmers who each swim in separate lanes
the holes across are all different places.

# Eleni Sikelianos

## Black-out Fabric—What I Found There

*They had long dreamed of an ideal black that absorbs all colors while reflecting no light.*

(in the light my fact unfurled  :  )

Can you see a difference a
   darker difference
      between this black and that?
The darkest fabric ever found was found to be
Made by man.  Upon that carpet I found

     a patch of carbon nanotube grass, a loosely packed
     forest full of nanoscale gaps
     and holes to collect and trap
     light. Tried a picnic upon that scrap, but soon discovered

     how random are the surfaces.
     My tincture thought it was a bird
     my golgi got all confused
     (what do golgi do?  sent the macro-
          molecule package to the wrong parts — what hinter-
          lands a hand can grip)
    : my eurcaryotes cried so dusky
    : my coinciding eye set out seeking its companionship
      but came back black
    : my corresponding ribonucleic haze lazing around the dark
      nucleotides
    : passing through its lumens
my mars mistook itself for sky

: my clouds retrieved themselves from black
(a good nut of a nucleus decoupling the cytoskeleton)
: my two bullets flew by night
life-to-life, debt-to-debt, all tries
to undo its ties. All rise.
(a twist in the basement membranes and their gut-like helices)
my tooth at the hardened crumb just so
(the cell or the will kills the beam, 99.955%)
: my empire lists its genomic odes
: my hedgerow escrowed : my blood released its weathermen
—a corpse was found the story asked what is this stinking
history
(another girl is murdered)
my wind did wind around her bones :
sunlight laces straight her ribs :
: my bomb illuminating my hand and bird
(another war unfolded)
: my beast-head asleep on the rock
: my human legs in yellow light
: my fact decayed in the light

# Antoine Volodine

### three novel excerpts translated from the French
### by Brian Evenson and Antoine Cazé

Antoine Volodine is the main pseudonym of one of the most powerful and radical French novelists writing today. Volodine—whose pen name derives from "Volodia," the Russian nickname for Vladimir, chosen in reference to both Mayakovski and Lenin according to the author himself[1] —started his literary career by writing science-fiction novels (*Biographie comparée de Jorian Murgrave*, Paris, Denoël, 1985; *Rituel du mépris*, Paris, Denoël, 1986 [Best French Science-Fiction Book Award, 1987]). He claimed early on, however, that these novels had been written in the margins of the genre, and soon moved out of what he felt to be too narrow a literary niche in order to create the concept of "post-exoticism" in the early 1990s, the main aspects of which he later described in *Le post-exotisme en dix leçons, leçon onze* (Paris, Gallimard, 1998). Volodine's aim was to "practice literature like a martial art," and to "write a foreign literature in French."[2] His subsequent books have fleshed out this strikingly original "lesson" by setting up a fictional universe with instantly recognizable features, particularly in *Des Anges mineurs* (1999, Prix du Livre Inter 2000), *Dondog* (2002), and *Songes de Mevlido* (2007), all published by Le Seuil in their innovative series "Fiction & Cie."

Rather than a fully articulated theory, post-exoticism is a writing stance characterized by a number of recurrent stylistic and thematic features. It cannot be properly called a movement or a school, since its only representative is Volodine himself and his numerous heteronyms, some of whom have actually published books: Lutz Bassmann, Manuela Draeger, Elli Kronauer[3]. Other identities remain virtual, the possible incarnations of what Volodine considers to be a "writers' collective" made up of political activists sentenced for life in prison who, in strict isolation, exchange stories, memories and dreams. These are couched in short hybrid forms to which Volodine has given specific names—"narrats," "entrevoûtes," "romånces," "Shaggås"[4]—and of which he prefers to be considered the "spokesman" rather than the "author."

Most of Volodine's fictions are set in the same kind of post-apocalyptic world marked by a ceaseless brooding about the failure of revolutionary struggle and the genocidal abominations of the 20th century, mixed with a deep reflection on loneliness and the powerlessness of humanity in front of pain and death. His characters—whose shifting identities are largely interchangeable and whose truly exotic names often evoke an Asian background mixing the Russian and Chinese heritage—are typically mental cases, failed revolutionaries, paupers

and generally *Untermenschen*, down to the point of sometimes being mutants with occasional animal features. Their lives boil down to a brutal, often armed, confrontation with "official hominids"—human beings as we know them today. This dark world of postindustrial ruins is described through the improbably lyrical voices of the characters, freely moving in and out of dream and trance, life and death, as they perform their pseudo-shamanistic rituals which barely help them to survive in utter degradation, filth and terror. Their stories are both always the same and always different, not unlike the endless re-elaborations one feels happening in dreams, or rather nightmares.

Volodine's literary project is very clearly political. The sophisticated radicalism of his narrative technique, which underscores the irrelevance of a personal signature, links in a unique way the literary and political ideals of the two Russian Vladimirs from whom he has picked up his first heteronym. By creating a coherently dystopian world seen from the point of view of its outspoken speechless victims, Volodine's "Minor Angels" contribute to radicalizing Deleuze and Guattari's idea of a "minor literature"—the product of an all-out linguistic and artistic resistance to destructive power structures, literature whose "cramped space forces each individual intrigue to connect immediately to politics. The individual concern thus becomes all the more necessary, indispensable, magnified, because a whole other story is vibrating in it"[5].

In the fall of 2010, Volodine, Draeger and Bassmann published their novels simultaneously, the author thus making it palpable for the first time that he was using heteronyms and working as a community of writers. This is why we have chosen to introduce their work side by side, with extracts from *Les Aigles puent* (*The Eagles Stink*) by Lutz Bassmann, *Onze rêves de suie* (*Eleven Dreams of Soot*) by Manuela Draeger, and *Écrivains* (*Writers*) by Antoine Volodine[6].

—Antoine Cazé

[1] He taught Russian in high school for 15 years before turning to translation and fiction writing in the late 1980s.

[2] Antoine Volodine, "Écrire en français une littérature étrangère." *Chaoïd*, n° 6 (automne-hiver 2002). http://www.editions-verdier.fr/v3/auteur-bassmann-2.html

[3] Both Kronauer and Draeger first emerged as the authors of children and teenagers' books, published under the innovative imprint of L'École des Loisirs. While Kronauer had a rather short-lived career (1999-2001), Manuela Draeger has now moved on into literature for adults, joining Volodine and the more recent Lutz Bassmann (active from 2008 onwards).

[4] With the exception of "entrevoûtes," which may translate as intervaults, these names are derived from traditional literary genres and modes: narrative, romance and saga. Volodine himself, however, has suggested "archodes" to translate "entrevoûtes," a way of capturing both the architectural and generic element.

[5] Gilles Deleuze & Félix Guattari, *Kafka: Towards a Minor Literature*. Translated by Dana Polan. Minneapolis: The U of Minnesota P, 1986 (original text 1975), p. 17.

[6] For further Reading (in French):
Several critical pieces on Volodine at remue.net: http://remue.net/spip.php?mot167
A very thorough Website on post-exoticism at http://www.berlol.net/chrono2/
A book-length study: *RUFFEL, Lionel. Volodine post-exotique*. Nantes: Éditions Cécile Defaut, 2007, 352 p.

# Lutz Bassmann

## from *The Eagles Stink*

### translated from the French by Brian Evenson and Antoine Cazé

The bombing that destroyed the city occurred on a Thursday, while Gordon Koum was out of town, on a mission.

He had gone to kill someone. That was why he survived.

Friday morning looked to be foggy. At daybreak, Gordon Koum stopped before a roadblock guarded by men wearing civil defense armbands. They chatted for a handful of minutes. All the guards, weary guys in their fifties, had on old leather jackets and weren't armed, except for one mustachioed man who wore a rifle slung across his shoulder. It gave him the impression of facing a band of partisans who had wandered into the wrong century. Although they had an official duty, they were unable to control the overpowering fear shining in their eyes. Their task was to prevent people from scavenging the site of the disaster but, in fact, only a paltry few volunteers turned up. Smaller still was the number of survivors from the city who could make it to their outpost. Nobody had yet appeared, coming from that direction. And that, more than anything, was the frightening thing. The clamor of the previous day had been replaced by utter calm. The night had not been interrupted by the slightest cry of despair or pain. The dawn had been silent. Beyond the civil defense barricades, the deserted boulevard seemed a cinder-coated path and, instead of leading into the heart of the city, it ended against a mountain of debris that was like a door opening onto death. You looked at the beginnings of this chaos void of any sign of life, and you felt dreadful certainties welling up inside. You almost gave up on the idea that somewhere, farther away, there might be survivors awaiting rescue. The authorities, indeed, weren't mistaken—after sending a drone over the theater of operations, they had given the order for the rescue teams to turn back and, basically, to go find something else to do instead of poking through what had become a vast cemetery. Perhaps the city would be rebuilt elsewhere some day. As for the ruins, they would be declared a forbidden zone and left alone, with their silence and their dead.

Gordon Koum listened to the militiamen's warnings, lingered in their company for five minutes, and then made a fatalistic gesture, started off along the devastated avenue and, paying no attention to the exhortations still ringing out behind him, slipped into the urban zone. After a hundred yards, he had already forgotten the men he had just been speaking with. Heavy hearted, he was thinking about our comrades, about Mario Gregorian, Antar Gudarbak and the others, for whom he was supposed to have given a report on his

mission this morning. They certainly must have perished. They were lying beneath tons of rubble, dismembered, torn apart, with unrecognizable bodies and souls, already on their way to rebirth. Gordon Koum thought about them and about the Party, whose last representatives we were at that time. But if he strode so vigorously across the devastated landscape, over the cinders that crunched underfoot, shifting and resisting like snow, it was because his mind was focused on the image of Maryama Koum.

He wanted to find Maryama Koum and Maryama Koum's children. He preferred to deny the obvious. He refused to express the slightest dismal conclusion and believed that, despite everything, he might be able to pull them out alive from the wreckage. Maryama Koum, Sariyia Koum, Ivo Koum and Gurbal Koum.

He walked across the northwestern half of the city and entered the district in which many of us, mostly vagrants and illegals, had taken up residence. The conditions of living and confinement were no worse than elsewhere, and it was an exaggeration to claim it was a ghetto, even though we were in the habit of calling it such, in memoriam of the genocides and in order to assert, again and again, our affiliation with beggars and how hard it was for us to live with official hominids.

The ghetto had been smashed to smithereens. Gordon Koum looked in vain for the entrance to the shelter where Maryama Koum and her children must have sought refuge. He did not even manage to piece together the layout of the street. The shelter was located underneath a food co-op, the basement of which had been converted into an emergency dormitory, with food supplies and a water-tank on which some forty people could survive for a week. Alarm drills took place monthly, and everyone was trained to drop everything and run, knowing exactly which way to go in order to dive into the closest cellar. The duration of every flight had been timed. From the moment the sirens began to wail, it took no more than five minutes to evacuate.

The shelter was marked by red flags, rags of worn Turkey-red cloth flying in front of the building whose basements, so it was said, had a structure capable of absorbing shocks and explosions. Gordon Koum counted on those spots of color to get his bearings. He kept running his eyes over the whole scene. But the co-op was gone.

The food co-op was gone.

All the buildings in the street had collapsed.

No trace of vermilion fabric was to be seen anywhere.

A sooty, dented, infinitely ugly plain now stretched where the city had lain. The system of public roads had been swept away and replaced by a succession of incomprehensible mounds and trenches that corresponded only rarely with former streets or avenues. Not a single building had stood firm and, although some stumps or fragments of façades still loomed here and

there, you could no longer see on them any clues as to how the place had been arranged before. Everything had become anonymous.

The civil defense men, in order to scare Gordon Koum and make him reconsider his decision to go through the ruins, had described what awaited him. They had assured Gordon Koum that his shoes would scorch after a few hundred steps, then he would feel flames devouring his feet and it would then be too late to turn back. He wouldn't be able to fight anymore, would collapse sizzling on the ground and end up burned to ash. The bombs that had annihilated the city, the mustachioed man with the rifle explained, were of a sorcerous nature. They were part of a new generation of weapons, which wreaked havoc when they exploded but then continued to have an effect until nothing human remained for miles around. The mustachioed man had a voice that trembled, from indignation and fear. He maintained that the bombs had not yet finished their course and that, upon approaching their impact points, Gordon Koum would be exposed to residual abominations, rays which would cause him to go mad or dead, or both.

In actuality, ever since Gordon Koum had started walking through the rubble, he had not felt anything in particular.

Under his shoes, his soles held firm.

There were no blisters on his skin, his extremities showed no intention of shriveling up.

The ground was not sizzling.

If residual abominations were at work, he remained unaware of them.

And in any case, after the inferno of the day before, whatever might happen to him, Gordon Koum, had no importance. No hardship could be compared with what the townspeople had endured on that Thursday, early in the evening.

At the peak of the air raid, the city had been ablaze for half a minute and that was enough time for it to dissolve. At first there was a classic preparation, with high-powered bombs. But then something spread within a few seconds, quite noiselessly, and at once the entire city seemed to melt at high speed. It literally disintegrated within an uncanny fire, a fire of thick flames, sorcerous indeed, to take up the adjective used by the mustachioed man. Flames that behaved in an odd manner, not lasting for a long time, not having anything in common with the usual fires in a war, sucking up all the noises of the ongoing destruction. The fire did not last. It was not a fire you could describe. Everything was abnormal in the way it behaved. It did not go on. The aircrafts had turned back quickly, leaving a black void behind them rather than the raging of a huge pyre, clearing room for the night, as if the bombs—and especially the last ones, or the very last one—had brought darkness with them, a darkness scientifically and militarily devised to conceal the horror while stabilizing it chemically. Some inconceivable thing had put an end to

all the noise and light and flames. From midnight on, there had not been the slightest glow to light up the smoke, and before daybreak they dispersed. And now, while Gordon Koum paced up and down the hillocks and heaps, nothing anywhere was in flames. The heat did not sting your face, there was nothing excessive about it. Instead, an almost pleasant warmth prevailed.

You could not say you felt comfortable. But you did not feel threatened. It felt as if you were walking inside an oven long after it had been turned off. It seemed you could have trudged on for hours.

The ambient temperature caused Gordon Koum no particular disorder. It did not drop, but he didn't care. It was as though, under the black crust caking everything, a slow burning continued, with embers glowing in the heart of darkness and refusing to go out, but he didn't care.

He hesitated for some time before choosing a place where he would start digging. He struggled against the urge to give up and he felt that his body was not at its best. His throat was parched—he hadn't had anything to drink since the day before, he started to cough, and then his coughing subsided. The air above the ruins was relatively clear. It was no doubt made heavier by floating particles, and enriched with toxic gases, but you could inhale it without choking. The hardest thing was to ignore the foul smells.

To ignore the foul smells.

Don't look out into the distance.

Look down at the ground that waited to be cleared away, down to the soot and the dust, and the ashes.

Look down to the ground and think about Maryama Koum.

The wind wasn't blowing. Now everything looked utterly motionless, as in a black and white photograph, with no one in it.

A photograph of devastation. Motionlessness, black and white. A vague sky. No people and no noise.

Ignore all this and go on digging.

A tarry glaze coated most surfaces. You could not touch anything without having to fight this glue.

Gordon Koum turned up charred stones and metal shards, the remains of windows and walls. Everything he moved stuck to his fingers. Everything was glazed in a warm, syrupy goo, pitch black and mostly stretching like caramel. After a quarter of an hour, he looked like an oil-covered sea-gull, such as still could be seen on the seashore back in the days when ships ran regularly, oil spilled regularly, and there were sea-gulls. His body and his clothes had become stiffened now by this dark honey. His fingers could no longer clutch anything, his hands looked more and more like mittens.

He went on excavating weakly, with some effort and slowly. He had to pause every now and then in order to rest or cough. He was working on the assumption that he was close to the shelter, above the old food co-op, but

deep down he wasn't sure of it. He might have been, had he seen some rag of red fabric lying on the ground nearby. He had selected a pile of rubble and had started in on it, letting himself be guided by irrational impressions, and, more and more frequently now, he reckoned he was plowing through a heap of debris which might well not be the right one. Everything looked alike, everything had the monochrome aspect of chaos, the lugubrious, harmful, odious, repulsive, not quite scorching, stinking aspect of chaos, its discouraging aspect, which was fundamentally ugly. Scraps of concrete, hardened splotches, steel shards of all possible and imaginable sizes. Everything was blackened and heavy. He grabbed all these a little haphazardly and tried to move everything that seemed able to be shaken loose. Most of the time, he couldn't get anywhere, beyond getting a little dirtier.

He couldn't get anywhere.

He felt dizzy.

His fingers weighed a ton.

His hands trembled.

He was always losing his balance. He had difficulty getting back on his feet.

He was dirtier and dirtier.

There was nobody else nearby.

There was nobody in the ghetto.

Apart from Gordon Koum, only a handful of individuals had crossed the civil defense barriers. Seven or eight figures at most wandered, each in solitude, in the remains of the ghetto. You saw them stand out against the sky, when they were transfixed at the summit of one of the little sooty hills that made up the landscape. Three hundred and fifty yards away from the place where Gordon Khoum worked, a man struck by madness tried desperately to scale a charred façade behind which was nothing. He climbed tenaciously, with the help of ropes, with what seemed a mountaineer's skills. Sometimes, because he couldn't climb any higher, he came back down to a lower floor and stayed for a long time prone before resuming his ascent.

A mentally ill man.

Desperadoes.

Neither one nor the other troubled the astounding stillness and the silence.

Gordon Koum watched them out of the corner of his eye while thrashing about in the middle of the disaster. He himself was now part of the landscape. He thrashed about still for just under twenty minutes. But then, while already he seemed integrated into the ruins, and as blackly twisted as the pieces that he was trying to dislodge, he let go of the pipe that he was using as a lever and brought his activity to a stop. He wasn't getting anywhere and had had it. He straightened up. He pushed his hands against his kidneys, he arched his spine to fight against backache. He gasped. His head was spinning. For the first time, he thought that the warnings of the civil security forces about the

noxiousness of the ruins had a basis in truth. For the first time, he thought that he was in the process of being destroyed himself. He must have inhaled toxic fumes, or received waves that were as invisible as they were evil. The bombs were continuing to act. His blood carted along the poisons which exhausted him.

The bombs continued to act and undermined in him all physical force.

He swallowed air in big loud gulps.

He tried to ease the disordered rhythm of his lungs.

After a moment, his respiration was more regular, but the rush of oxygen had strengthened his olfactory sensitivity. Suddenly he wanted to vomit. Suddenly he could no longer ignore foul smells. Suddenly he could no longer not understand what they revealed about what had happened during the strange fire. His nausea grew, it became uncontrollable. He tried again to reason with himself, to think about something else, but already it was in vain. A horrible story crystallized, on his dried-out mucous membranes, horrible images, at the back of his throat and his nose he received the specter of the construction materials and of the hominids who had been instantaneously transformed into a gas, then who had been turned next, nine or ten seconds later and in mixing with anything, into a vaguely liquid substance. The foul smell of this new type of tar, which brought to mind at once carbon deposits, animal fat and the black space in which the dead stroll. The foul smell left behind by the bombs of the last generation.

# Manuela Draeger

### from *Eleven Dreams of Soot*

### translated from the French by Brian Evenson and Antoine Cazé

From time to time, the neon tube sizzled, but the light didn't weaken. Despite the chaos and the shadows, the atmosphere of the workshop was peaceful, although, obviously, a little strange, with these three people who were together and who stayed silent.

After a moment, the demobbed soldier came out of his sulk.

"So, you want me to tell you your fortune, Imayo Özbeg?" he asked me.

I nodded yes.

The soldier made me sit next to him, on the seat of his car, and he held my wrist in his rough hand. We were packed in between two walls of dilapidated objects, against lead tubes, toothed wheels, rusty gates, broken electric circuits, blackened bulbs, spoons and forks with twisted handles. From where I sat, I saw the metal curtain, and, beyond, the street with its flaking tar shining vaguely beneath the rays of a street lamp. Silhouettes of passersby were rare and you didn't have time to see who they were, nor even if they were men or women. I didn't turn toward the soldier who spoke slowly and in a low voice, as if sleepy, and as if permanently looking for ideas, images, and words. I breathed the air charged with motes and metallic sawdust. Rather often I cast glances at Rita Mirvrakis, hoping to catch her attention, watching for her complicity, but she didn't look at me. Next to me, the soldier gave off a smell of burnt cardboard, dirty laundry, verdigris. I also sometimes closed my eyes to better hear the sentences that he uttered, and of which certain ones, almost mumbled, escaped me.

They had repeated to us a thousand times not to wiggle when an adult spoke to us, and I was motionless. But this motionlessness also had another origin. Quite simply the content of the speech transfixed me. I had the impression that the soldier, instead of chatting politely about my future, tried desperately to scare me. According to him, all had gone wrong from the start and would continue to go wrong to the end.

No-one had ever told me my fortune. I imagined that he was going to speak to me of trips, of encounters, of mysterious astral conjunctions. I wasn't expecting anything particularly nice, but I expected something other than what I got.

"Whether you like it or not," said the soldier, "you have bad luck in you, Imayo Özbeg… it came at your birth… you were removed from the darkness on an evil day… the very day when a new ugly war began… you had to be

pulled out with forceps... you did your best not to emerge... you resisted, in vain... misfortune also entered your dreams at the same moment... and that will dog your steps to your last breath... but even after... it will dog your steps until your rebirth... there is no Clear light for you in what will follow... in your destiny nothing will incandesce, except for flames not wanted, flames which bite and cause suffering... no other light on the road... Don't believe yourself alone, if that can console you... For hominids and subhumans of your sort there is neither exit nor Clear light... only a permanent sensation of failure... only the sensation of struggling without success, whatever the moment of dream or of death is... Sometimes it's a question of struggling in a burning, tarry glue... not even a matter of transforming oneself at the last moment into a strange cormorant... wings incapable of spreading... bones dislocated from how strong the effort has been to escape... feathers collected in a raggy mass, glued to one another... breast dull... it's misfortune... orifices blocked up by something which is neither solid nor liquid... breathing less and less possible... no more vertical, nor more horizontal... a slanting indeterminate bath, in an incomprehensible substance... no more walls that you might reach or touch, no longer anything stable around... a strange drowning... naphtha, oil... no known sensation, no light... Pointless to struggle... When your turn comes, you will in turn struggle in vain... if it isn't tar, it will be in the heart of the flames... another misfortune... In the fire at the beginning you see splendid colors... you are at the heart of wonders... orange scarves surround you... profound shades, poets and painters claim that they know how to describe them... but they've no clue what that looks like from within... when you're within the flames and you're burning... It's something else, another world... at first you believe you've already seen that... then you make out other colors, terminal colors... bronze fire, yellow of hell... smoked red, smoked carmine... and still other colors, with names unknown to the living... deep mahane... ooldamoor... camphored mander... light mizerain, dazzling lamer... orange mourma... If it's your turn to burn, you'll be struggling within it, Imayo Özbeg... in vain... for animals, subhumans, and humans, the result is always the same... you'll squirm in vain against adversity, in the scattering ooldamoor, in the blinding mizerain... and afterward that will be the same, you'll see... afterward you will struggle in vain in the heart of death... even your rebirth will not take place... It's misfortune... You can't be prepared for it, you can't avoid it... Orange mourma to finish, but it won't finish... Imayo Özbeg, you won't find refuge anywhere... Whether it be in life or death... Your name burns... Your name will burn... Others will go toward you, to the rescue or simply to accompany you, but even your name will burn... They will no longer know how to recognize you among the ashes... You'll be no more than a strange cormorant in the middle of the red... But what is known about your future... nobody knows anything about anything, we are already at the

end of time... knowing has no value... preparing yourself has no meaning... There are not only flames for entering into death... There are not only dark glue and dark flames... Sometimes it's enough to rush down the strange road of bolshevism... it's enough to enter this strange dream... Imayo Özberg, you have this dream in you like all of us... If your turn comes, you will struggle in there in turn... you will try to put an end to misfortune... you will vainly try, in turn, to put an end to misfortune... you will struggle between earth and sky, in a revolting bouquet of barbed wire... To no avail... And afterwards all will be the same... blazing successes to begin with, age-old successes, and nearly immediately afterward irreversible collapses, defeats... crushing defeats... your bones and your intellect will be crushed until you cry out... at the last moment you will contemplate your useless life, your fruitless death... your wounds... You have this dream within you like all of us... you will see... another sort of misfortune that nothing heals... And afterward..."

I had heard enough. With an abrupt twist, I freed my hand. The soldier didn't try to take me by the wrist again, he shrugged his shoulders and fell silent. We stayed dead-still, side by side, breathless. He from having spoken, I from having listened.

# Antoine Volodine

## from *Ecrivains*

### translated from the French by Brian Evenson and Antoine Cazé

He remembers the gray light which flooded the courtyard beyond the high windows of the classroom, he remembers the persistent odor of pee which floated around his classmates and which perhaps had as its origin the poorly washed floor and the sticky humidity of the desks more than the underwear and childish incontinence of the students, he remembers the pleasant resistance, the slight granulation of the paper under the lead of his pencil, he remembers the feeling of a fever that traveled through his cheeks and upper body, the feeling of urgency, craving, imperious need, he remembers that the teacher passed very close to him and examined him, but without commenting, without bothering him, conscious that he had broken the ropes of scholarly discipline, that he was no longer listening, that he was no longer poring over the exercises to do, conscious deep down that something extraordinary was in the process of occurring and that it was better to allow it to take its course, because it isn't usual for a boy of five, barely able to read, to escape in such an open way from all institutional constraint, to unfold the interior of an exercise-book sleeve and start to pour out a story which wasn't like anything, and he remembers that after having blackened the blank interior of a first exercisebook sleeve, after having filled it with his clumsy, shaky, disorderly writing, he grabbed a second exercise-book sleeve, then a third, determined to continue his drafting whatever the cost, suddenly no longer obeying given orders or customs, freeing himself from all authority, and in the first place neglecting the authority of the schoolteacher who brushed past him and who paused above him, curious to watch what he was doing, because he was jealously concentrated on his task, with all the effort that his narration demanded, and he remembers as well the images which turned in his head and solidified there, the speeches of adults which followed one another and which he didn't know how to transcribe, he remembers the jungle, the forest, the clouds which seemed to reflect the fires, he remembers the animals, the shouts, the children running, terrified, dressed in jackets that were too large and in tatters, and he remembers the heat which stung his eyes, the hot passion that he tried to master while forming the letters as quickly as possible and aligning the words which until then he had never used, because he was still very small, in a phase of his existence where all was new, speech, emotions, images, dreams and reality, knowledge, and so he remembers the feeling of naïve triumph

that carried him forward at the thought that he had just entered into the world of stories that you make yourself, and also at the thought that he was crafting a text more complex than what he should have been able to craft naturally at his age, and for that he felt a clearly prideful joy, and also he remembers that he had decided not to stop before the obstacles that written language accumulated under his fingers and to consider that the priority of priorities was not to achieve orthographical feats to please his teacher but to torrentially put down text, to put it down in treating with disdain all other considerations, to make it exist no matter what scratches to the norms and grammatical approximation of which he suspected they would be numerous, and moreover he didn't have secretly in mind to submit it afterward, this text, for reading by adults, and still less, of course, for reading by his classmates, the majority of whom still faced difficulties in deciphering words of more than two syllables, and he remembers also that this certainty of making a text exist for himself, of not working for any public, that this conviction had given him strength from the moment when he had started to spill out on the first exercise-book sleeve, and also he remembers that this happened in October and that in the courtyard, at the same time that the morning light stabilized, a bizarre rain broke out, a gossamer rain, as happened sometimes in those days, in autumn, a soft rain or rather snow constituted of thousands of long silks from minuscule spiders, and at the same moment he remembers the names of the schoolteacher and of some of his schoolmates, mostly girls, and, to answer the question that has just been posed to him in a rasping, insane voice, accompanied by a slap on the head, he says:

"I don't remember. I remember nothing. My head is empty."

There are afterwards several seconds of incredulity on the part of his interrogators, then a new slap, this time full in the face.

There are two of them, a man and a woman, and they spell one another. After the slap, the woman repeats the question in a shrill voice. The interrogation started ten minutes ago. It is carried out in the face of good sense. What do they want to make him confess? He hasn't succeeded in knowing and he has the least possible interest in it. He is in their hands and he has no desire to cooperate, he has never cooperated with interrogators and, even if these here are more or less from his side, even if they belong like him to a category that is intellectually, socially, and concretely beggared and screwed, he revives his old tactics of dissent. He pretends not to understand anything, but above all, so that his imbecility takes on a character of verisimilitude, he forces himself not to understand anything. He tries to feel profoundly passive and stupid. He remains confronted by shouts and bad treatment, obviously he cannot deny them, but at the same time he floats at a distance from the real, from everything. He fell back where he was

able, into one of the last redoubts, perhaps not very solid but very distant from the present and even from the past, he has taken refuge in a moment from his childhood. He had developed, long ago, this technique of intimate evasion, he put it into practice whenever he found himself in the offices of the police, he continued to adopt it during his trials, before his judges, then much later in the presence of psychiatrists, and, now that he is confronted by his insane comrades, his insane comrades run amuck, he assesses that it's better to once again barricade himself inside it, in the inmost depths, at the origin, far from the dreadful world of adults. People beat him, people want him to speak, to say what they want to hear. He lets them beat him and get worked up, he floats elsewhere, in a secret fragment of elsewhere, he drifts there, in an elementary school class, at a great distance.

# Monica Mody
## Kala Pani Sampler

### SIXTH WORLD TRAVELLER

At the time, of course, I turned them into media sensations. Sameshape &
Othershape were unaware of it, but they became ethnic, geographic and
social curiosities for an entire nation. I had just joined a gang of bloggers. We
prowled streets and slums, technical handbooks and audience pages, artists'
studios and alternative film clubs, buses and body doubles, city squares and
the Commonwealth Games Village, dance shows and the Department of
Atomic Energy, environmental groups and the east side of the river, town
halls and martyrs' statues, looking

For signs of urban dystopia. We were rough and restless with cannon and
sought relationships that would, historically and comparatively, challenge us.
The junkyard was the perfect setting. Ext. Junkyard – Full Moon. Sameshape
& Othershape notice the moon. Sameshape tracks how long Othershape
stares at the moon.

### SAMESHAPE

### OTHERSHAPE

### SAMESHAPE

### OTHERSHAPE

### SIXTH WORLD TRAVELLER

The tree, a lusty neem, tried very hard not to eavesdrop on the conversation
but it had begun to ferment. Its risk period had ended and it was not going to
stand upright anymore. Its leaves, laments, letters, festoons, flags, fingerprints,
H1N1 viruses, needles, medicaments and hair, almost shed. Safety latch,
turned on. Though unmarried, the tree took great pride in its appearance. It
was trying to safely evolve into another condition. Waiting

Period long. Kind of like a buzzard's head. Only room for quite alone. A
topknot, released in the middle of nowhere. Drunk on feathers & wind.
Exhilarated! My tree was so soft it curled around the edges almost collapsing

it was a trailing coughing spitting collapsing curling thing. The spittoon brimmed with tree hair & something

That ties us together. Eyes of a camera appeared everywhere. The tree did its best to be a tree fit for a socket or a natural crevice. Somewhere, a topiary for evenlycolored birds. Meanwhile, the tree had grown up old listening to peoples' tales of the young. This tree, this song, I'd first heard her sing. The tree squirmed her ear towards them.

+

## THE RATIONAL PRESIDENT
*(radio voice)*
We have gathered today to celebrate trees with star billing. These trees represent five millennia of humankind's collective aspirations, and it is but appropriate that we gift them to the museum of the new world. We will lovingly track and displace them and lovingly collect or moisten them. We will love the new world. It is due to the generosity of friends and benefactors that the new government could organize the bureaucracy, the complicity, the compromises, the ideological cooption, the cooperation, the rapacity and the ethical rationalization necessary for this farsighted program, and to them we will confer appropriate rewards. Our desire is to keep everyone in the new world happy.

## FIRST WORLD TRAVELLER
The curators returned with summary catalogues describing 29 or 92 million bittersweet trees. Each catalogue provided not only a compact illustrated listing of the trees, but also brief comments by curators that explained how each tree was proposed to be collected or moistened. These catalogues were ceremonially handed over to the Society for Just Plunder which launched systematic invasions in which bittersweet trees were hacked, stripped, and stifled. A few trees of monumental significance made it to the back of trucks, gagged and trussed, after the Department of Diplomacy intervened. The museum of the new government waited for the trucks, waist-deep in gelatinous expectation: its own secretions.

+

## SECOND WORLD TRAVELLER
Tree of numinous detail. The last tree in the war. Careworn and chrysanthemum motifs. Lush green panels. Loose-tipped design. In the grand tradition of great trees, this tree hosted a bird's nest, a snake, and a moon. On the tree

there also lived a delicate and rarefied vampire spirit, an expressive ant, and a retired hunter. They ate the elaborate fruit and lived, pretty much as other beings do.

## FIRST WORLD TRAVELLER

Before long, they became aware of an unexpected kineme. The residents of the tree had not anticipated the possibility of such a kineme. A distance away, dust Snarled at the feet of millions of squirrel-shaped blubs. Closer and closer, the blubs squeezed themselves into a phalanx of pulped fury. Gliggering eyes; there was not even negative space left.

+

## SAMESHAPE
*(irrelevantly)*

The consensus of opinion was that the wrist would grow back again. Cynics were growing wary of this whole messy situation where over and over again they had to clean up somebody's skin, somebody's bones, somebody's sleeves, somebody's vomit, somebody's tears, somebody's rage, somebody's blind spots, etcetera. They rolled away into the night, never to be heard from again. But since we cannot abandon our heroine, since we are in charge of her adventures, that moment of escape when she

Seal breaks. Sealed to a kiss, stolen seal from the medicine cabinet and taped to the inside of her razor. Cut /shield/ bitten /shield/ broken /shield/ trichotillomaniac /shield/ dermatillomaniac /scratch/ /shield/ /shield/. She grew salubrious.

## FOURTH WORLD TRAVELLER

Othershape sprawled on the regular sofa, her legs spread out before her, love growing cotton in its ears. Mouth open. Really, now. Is that a ladder you are carrying? Climb in next to me. I can hear you hard. Brush-footed. Left with no dining companions, her thought bubbles settled over every

Thing regular. She wore the lentil bean on her head to sleep. When she woke up, the lentil bean was a dream suspended above her head.

## OTHERSHAPE
*(with great fondness)*

Lentil bean, leave me with something that can disappear.

PIZZA DELIVERY BOY
(doffing his hat)

OTHERSHAPE

Flattered that you asked!

PIZZA DELIVERY BOY
(lanky and ergonomic)

OTHERSHAPE

Glad to hear about it.

PIZZA DELIVERY BOY
(walking off)

# Garrett Ashley
## The History of Character X

### The Protagonist, Character X

Alicia Banning. Annette Broderick. Atara Baldemar. The name does not equate with the success of Character X. She might become He. Adam Banning. Aaron Broderick. Aloysius Baldemar. Gender is or can be the result of the personality of the creator. Genre, as well as. The creator may alter; the story will remain the same.

For now, Character X becomes AB. AB is not only catchy when read aloud from the rudimentary transcript, but is also much easier to say than Character X. (Though for some, Character X may imply mystery, or the preverbal form of a protagonist of Science Fiction.)

### The Desire

AB is in love with Character Y. Their lives (both X and Y) have intercepted at point 0. Point 0 may be the Market Garden. A private room at Club Fire. The back row of Intermediate Light. Insert smells—tomatoes, onions, Clorox Bleach (from the mop bucket on aisle nine). Cigarette smoke, Southern Comfort, dry semen (from the private room's couch, walls, ceiling). Used textbook paper, chalk dust, the cologne/perfume emanating from Character Y as he/she scratches out one formula and starts again.

It may be the smell AB is attracted to. The smells are followed by dialogue and tags, which may also strike the interest of AB.

*These damn tomatoes are too fucking high*, said Character Y.

*These damn people are too fucking loud*, said Character Y.

*These damn problems are too fucking hard*, said Character Y.

Character Y ignores AB's attempt at further conversation. According to the fundamentals of the creation of round characters, Character Y will make

conversation inexorably difficult. Character Y will always be uninterested in AB.

Kurt Vonnegut calls this story Boy Meets Girl. *But it needn't be that*, he said.

## The Obstacle, Part One

Character Y continues to ignore AB. It doesn't matter if Character Y is even aware of AB's infatuation.

Maybe AB follows Character Y home from the Market Garden and parks his/her means of transportation at a discrete distance so as not to be seen. AB loves how Character Y's legs fold as he/she bends to the doormat and retrieves a hidden key. Exit Character Y.

Maybe AB follows Character Y to a tall brick apartment building next to a social office and leans against the chain-link fence stretching alongside a basketball court. AB loves how Character Y's cheeks blush as he/she enters the wrong door code not once, but twice. Exit Character Y.

Maybe AB follows Character Y to the athletic dorms. Character Y does not play sports, but athletic dorms are generally cheap and available to students with low GPAs. AB sits on a picnic table, the sun setting, and thinks about the things his/her infatuation will do when he/she is alone with a soft, blue pillow. Exit Character Y.

Character Y should always exit the story more than once. A single exit may only present itself as coincidence, and may seem uninteresting—AB's following of Character Y should become habitual, maybe even dangerous.

## The Obstacle, Part Two

AB's interaction with Character Y never exceeds the price of tomatoes, the volume of drunken patrons or the difficulty of an equation invoking Einstein's mirror metaphor.

*I should grow my own damn tomatoes*, said Character Y.

*I should drink alone*, said Character Y.

*I should like to travel at the speed of light,* said Character Y, *mirror outstretched before me. Would I see a reflection? Einstein didn't even know, it took him ten years of thinking to decide on it.*

### The Pill

Pills almost always make us feel better. So after many repeated instances of The Obstacle (parts one and two), AB will be confronted with an instance of tranquility. In any of the three versions of the story, tranquility must be the result of confrontation.

*Have you been following me?* said Character Y.

AB won't recognize this as any form of medication at first. It may seem frightening until at last Character Y's inquisitive grimace becomes the curious, playful smirk that often comforts us in moments of embarrassment or distress.

In any of the three versions of the story, Character Y will walk away, looking back once and then twice. The sliding doors at the Market Garden will grind shut. The crowd at Club Fire will thicken and hide all recognizable faces from the viewer. Hands will shoot up in Intermediate Light. Everyone has their own theory of relativity and Einstein's mirror. In such an exciting confusion, conversations are lost and broken.

### A Climax

Anyone who recognizes the arc of Boy Meets Girl should know that after a decline in fortune, there is a rise. AB stops following Character Y home from Garden Market, to the apartment from Club Fire, to the athletic dorms from Intermediate Light.

In fact, AB stops seeing Character Y in produce. His/Her face doesn't appear in the crowd at Club Fire. There is an empty desk at the back of Intermediate Light. The Professor doesn't necessarily feel heartbroken, for Character Y is a difficult student to handle indeed and is consequently viewed as a stronger antagonist than before.

AB begins to shop at family owned stores, which eventually leads to the consumption of fatty foods from a variety of fast-food restaurants. (Food-To-Go, of course. AB doesn't like eating alone.)

AB stops going to Club Fire with his/her friends. He/She wonders: What at this point in life is the use of friends, anyway? My friends cannot offer physical companionship, so there is no gain.

AB stops looking over at the empty desk in Intermediate Light. It'll soon be filled, anyway, by a very large, red faced Neck-Beard who may try to hold a conversation every now and again. By now everyone has already decided that—at the speed of light—there is no reflection. There is nothing.

The reader may wonder when and where the rise in AB's fortune exists. The rise may certainly be ambiguous. Years later in either of the three versions of the story, AB witnesses Character Y pulling a two (maybe three or four) year old by the hand towards a Miskelly's, Lowe's, or Home Depot. The two (three or four) year old tries to pull back, its frizzy hair dripping sweat, as he/she is intercepted by a tall man with a shaved head or a short woman with teal fingernails. The unnamed spouse picks up his/her child and kisses Character Y on the cheek. They all go and live happily ever after.

*And people love that story*, said Vonnegut. *They never get sick of it.*

# Johannes Göransson

### from *Entrance to a Colonial Pageant in Which We All Begin to Intricate*

## Note on the Production

The main scene should be full of ornaments and crime. The words attributed to the characters do not necessarily have to be spoken; they can be acted out, or played on an archaic tape-player.

The second stage is an abandoned factory in downtown South Bend, IN, where during the entire performance my daughter Sinead dances while changing in and out of various costumes: the Hare Mask, the Cartoon Face, the Red Robe of History, the Reversible Body. She is only once actually seen by the audience, on a video screen streaming live from her dance. Mostly she is hidden because she represents that which is hidden.

The third stage is a mall, where the Natives stand still, watching, interviewing and photographing the Customers. Sometimes I feel a certain tenderness towards the Natives. Other times I want to stab them in their plug-ugly faces.

The Passenger:

I was admitted. I had to answer questions. Are you gay? Are you a terrorist? Are you a communist? I answered No to all the questions. After a while I started noticing that the questions had changed. What do insects have to do with cinema? Can you hear me? Are we underwater? Can I kick you in the face? Why do your spasms look infantile? Do you know how to break a radio? But I kept answering no. Because that's what I wanted to hear myself say with that bag over my face.

* * *

The Passenger:

I had trouble eating the food. The potatoes were overboiled, the mashed-up meat was not warm. I grew weak. I thought I heard the nurses talk about my spine. There was an ant-infestation in the thighlet. On my way to the x-ray I collapsed on the floor. A nurse carried me in her arms. This is how I invented erotics.

* * *

The Passenger:

I was more Chinese than slender. My head injury showed and I was going through a peekaboo puberty with megaphones. But I knew how to cut the barbwire fence when I needed to. I led my girlfriend out of the inauguration, to the darkened fields. She held me with one hand and a glass of champagne in the other. I don't know if I began to bleed before or after she took off my costume. A parasite grows in my iris, she told me to explain what she was doing to my legs. She was preparing them for our vacation.

* * *

The Girlfriend *(her body rioted, her clothes luxurious, her smile religious, her body anorexic, her gun warm, her reasons obscure, her fire ridiculously fake):*

I took him out in the field while the city was being burned like a newborn calf in a riot. I took him in my arms as if he was that calf. He had already invented erotics. It was up to me to invent something more sustainable, an ending of sorts. But an ending that keeps on happening. I had to invent a luxury so extreme the passenger would never recover. That's what I did in the field, with these hands.

Father Firing Line:

I used to wear a comatose mask but now that that has been classified as subjectivity I wear a mask that looks like Nixon. Nobody needed to teach me how to do the plug-ugly. That came naturally to my ki-ko-pe body. Anybody can holler like a native but who among you knows what convulsions are natural and which ones are induced by a peculiar holiday? I may not be the last man standing but I am repulsive with glitter. I have perfected the tendrils in a horse's heart. Most children are too old to learn this lesson. They've watched it on TV. That's me, they say, the one with the hole.

* * *

The Passenger:

I was accepted as a bogus inmate, but I was not photogenic. I joined the firing line but I could not tell which nude was the real Ulrike Meinhoff. "This is a set-up," they all screamed. "I am the real Ulrike Meinhoff. This is a set-up." The nudes are still repeating those lines, but the firing lines have been cut out. For my next role, I wore a gas-mask that did not work. The effect was brilliant, but the beak scarred my face.

* * *

Daughter (*stripped and ready in a hyacinth pose*):

I don't need permission to rinse the swans. I just want to use the nails and sternum in a more media-saturated way. I know how to drink champagne out of a worn mask. It's the coma mask. The car-crash-hammered face I use for seizures. I shouldn't have kept you waiting in the strip mall. You must stammer. You must strike a soundproof pose for the soldiers. Knock knock knock. It's time for makeup. Look at my face. Mimesis.

* * *

The Revolution:

I am also violent when working on the martyr exhibition. The sun is rotten and I have to bruise easily during car alarms. But most of all I need to hollywood

some Africans for the final room, the Congo. That's where I get my aura. That's where I abuse gasoline. Please come down to see me on the surveillance camera. It's the newest economy. It's an economy of inside/outside where I am always the outside inside the camera. You might not understand how I can faint every time. It's easy. Write a receipt for USA and I will show you how to rip off the primal scene.

* * *

Trauma:

In the Rampant State, nobody understands how to clean the ganglia. Nobody knows how to thread it, how to abuse it, how to interrogate prisoners with it. In the Rampant State all the torture devices involve drowning or lynching. The General wants to lynch all the black male bodies with moths. He uses obvious innuendoes, to make sure his base understand him, but he cannot say it openly. To do so would be to offend the refined tastes of his base. If anybody accuses him of racism, he replies that the accusers are "playing the race card." I am playing the race card with a revolver pointing to my head. The revolver has an autonomic system. It is loaded with two silver bullets: one for my black brain and one for my insect nerve.

# Daniel Levin Becker

## about *Index of First Lines*

*Index of First Lines* could be said to be a study in literary potential, specifically in that of the discarded bits of sound and phrase I collected over the two or three years preceding its assembly in the summer of 2007. It is intended to resemble a text such as one might find at the back of a volume by a poet too retiring to title his or her works individually; the chief difference is that the poems invoked here do not exist past their first lines, and thus remain quite robustly *potential*.

Potential is a handy lens through which to view the evolution of this piece: "potential literature"—in short, the continuation of literary creation by mathematical means—is the collective quarry of the Oulipo, a Parisian supper club and research group of which I became a member in early 2009. It was my presentation of a liberal French translation of the index you see here, along with some kindred but still-unrealized ideas (and, more importantly, plans for a book on the history and philosophy of the group), that earned me an invitation to join.

The French version of the index has since been expanded and published in the Oulipo's chapbook series as *Indices*, which offers a number of suggestions for how to disregard the utilitarian value of such a text and read it as a poem unto itself, along various axes: line by line in order of the page numbers indicated, or line by line alphabetically; by selecting only lines with matching end-rhymes or lines with matching meter; by picking and choosing lines freely or at random, like a game of especially heavy-handed magnetic poetry. While translating the index for the Oulipo, I re-engineered it to reward these different readings in different ways—a process, ultimately, less of translation than of calculation, of structural and semantic draftsmanship.

Save the occasional happy accident, the concatenations in this initial version are much less versatile. The idea was not to build a multidimensional poem but to tell a simple story, however obliquely (and hindsight tells me it is rather obliquely indeed), whose narrative dimension is accessible only formally. *Index of First Lines* is no less potential for this, however; think of it as an illustration both of the sort of curiosity that leads one down the garden path toward the Oulipo, and of the sort of literary inkling that, for all its immediate resonance, has far greater richness to be tapped with the application of some formal rigor.

—Daniel Levin Becker

# Index of First Lines

Across the room the curl of your lip, 5.
After we are gone nobody will remember, 20.
And yet, like radioactively dyed tapeworms, 58.
As long as your ghost is planning to stay, 53.
At least I have a record of your handwriting, 61.

Back in my carnivorous days, 34.
Behind the frayed lace curtains of my brooding bleeding soul, 54.
But I don't own a patent leather fedora, 23.

Can it be that you are both real and figural, 13.
Certain very cavernous places, 35.

Does the Indian summer ever feel colder, 45.
Dust on bookshelves; discarded calendar pages, 59.

For a time we too were an uncountable noun, 57.

Geography is a cold and spiteful lover, 26.
Given my previously elaborated feelings on the mirth of others, 46.

Had it not been for that black cat you asked me to find, 7.
He could never bring himself to patronize that bakery again, 56.
How long have you been writing me in lowercase, 30.

I did not expect heaven to be that shade of yellow, 12.
I keep your picture in my dictionary [*fond*], 29.
I keep your picture in my dictionary [*vindictive*], 49.
Is it wrong to expect a Gideon bible, 37.

Just because there's no light, 36.
Just like the letters in the word *eodermdrome*, 19.

Let us pinpoint the locus of that laundry smell, 16.

Morning comes and the paper crane I made for you, 43.
My intentions depend on how you define 'good', 14.

Never make eye contact or walk towards laughter, 63.
Night falls and he folds her a *senbazuru* crane, 15.
Nor do I even know what a deerstalker is, 24.
Now for the debatable but undeniable felicity, 9.

On your landing just now in the cinnamon-russet gloaming, 8.
One thing I probably should have said about my coffee table, 11.

Potted plants and the word 'defamiliarize', 60.
Purgatory is a broken-down subway car, 44.

Quickly now, before we congeal, 17.

Rage at the embers of that silent December, 48.
Rare as the air where there is no there there, 27.
Really? Earmuffs?, 50.

She always secretly preferred his pseudonym, 22.
She was in a way nothing but limbs, 39.
Something that I promise was nothing, 40.

That's a pretty cute egg timer you've got there, 6.
The distance between your collarbone and Park street, 21.
The night we sat before the sea and spoke of ligatures, 55.
Time lost all meaning, because I asked it to, 38.
To distraction!, 42.

Umop apisdn, 52.
Unless you can fathom the fortitude it took, 64.
Until the comma splice becomes fashionable, 31.

Well, time to go out and taste the fucking morning, 66.
When I calculate, roughly, the number of times, 47.
When we are older wiser less presentable, 65.

Yes, I have been to a cemetery, and yes, 67.
You and I, just a split infinitive away, 28.
You know nothing of thrall, 32.
Your shadow on my wall, forever climbing, 68.

# Black Took Collective
## (Duriel E. Harris, Dawn Lundy Martin, Ronaldo V. Wilson)
### Accretion: Buffalo Performance
### Oct. 17, 2009

*Accretion* is an on-going meta-writing project that serves as a companion to multi-media performances exploring the Black Took Collective's interrogations of a black unconscious. Based on improvisational writing produced and projected on stage in real-time during performance, the project documents BTC's enaction of poetries of inquiry—engaging (and challenging) the psyche's making of racial consciousness by conceptualizing unconsciousness by means of differential poetic events. Moving alongside and through poetries predicated on the conditions of blackness, *Accretion* chronicles BTC collective members' meditations on the multiple factors that inspire our imaginations. Material used in this excerpt was culled from written language produced at two live writing stations during "Live Feed from a Black Unconscious" presented during the 4th Biennial &Now Festival of Innovating Writing & the Literary Arts at Hallwalls Contemporary Arts Center in Buffalo, New York on October 17, 2009.

We, here, are concerned with the body, blackened, afloat in the cauldron of wishes and impulses, the body, multiplied in chunks, bleeding out and taking on water in a murky sea, the body, curved and taut, strung like a bow, sunk like an anchor and now a glaze spread on the surface of consciousnesssssssssssssssssssss.

Substance of fear and rage

A tarp lifted to reveal the hung projector and other machines used for amplification –

and audible distortion, sheaves of poems, and glee.

Often, on stage, we do un-syncopated dance moves, rolling on the floor, springing up here or there, our voices tweaked by machines or bodies, sometimes on the sand, shown in the background of a screened dream. Screen + Dream + Grid is a thought made visible, an organizing structure framing the marks of what we (BTC) let escape in abandon, a partial print, component and remnant of our play reimagined as a separate text.

The record of this real or imagined event is projected in what is often a phrase, the urge, our wanting to write this down, our pondering between what it means to arrive and to want to arrive from place to race, sex to barrier, the thing taken apart, ultimately undone, so our grids and screens and habits and departures drift into one another. Where we spring up from is where we emerge. And there's something about this we don't want to escape. Freedom Resounds: We go back to enter what did or did not happen, a map of our unconscious, in the room(s) and stages we share. Here is one quick slice of our live selves, scalped, scalpeled, and held under the light, and into the dark of our accreting Black Took.

—Black Took Collective

To grieve, and to make grief of itself
on resigned to inaction,
the slow process by
"What is
may be which (she
(cavervous) be understood
hool s) hood understood had can't?
as had made a planter.

Despite which we vow to protect,
nce we have suffered, if not
y, amid: D1 pointed to her, tum
at the hint of flesh beyond what
a pattern of cutting away
might emerge by the violet fur
principle from this shocked
others [in and was
her tum and we knew what was

"An apprehension of common vulnerability."

Punctum: Barthes' isolation—a common vulnerability."

How does Butler's transp(apparent?) complicate
isolation—a way toward filmic
when written
proze: no prose

Necks count, so (as random) do heads: I'm (not interested)

so how does torture reveal itself?

Whose lives are real? How many might be remade? Those who are not real have already suffered the violence of unrealization.

: Touch, sense, hearing, sound, epistle

Stem not blade.

Blackness as a rock, blackness as a thing opposed to what we might call a subject.-the
object, embrace him-Rock-ing here. How to hold him, the mirror of anoth-
what is and is not-black ness? How to recogniz es
er, the projection of one's self via a noth-
er, the action, fret. One recognizes one's self as a
threat, fret.

I forget the name of the shiney salve on BTC's
face, but the night the shiney looks like a boxer's
grease.-Duri, she's obviously hearing things of
through the apparatus, her grids; I think of
her work as being articulated through a steel
trap, or through a revolving subway entry wheel,
one way, or in, the other you're stuck with to say
shard click, but what would the shock of that mean?)

To denote a reconfigure process of the internal mappings which
s the unconscious a place where the body is
I stowed?

# Kate Bernheimer
## Pennies, Nickels, and Dimes

I'm going to tell you something, so listen. Long ago I learned to be happy. I was happy for all of my days.

I had the birds, who told me the weather, and I had my rooms. When I first moved to the forest, I had denounced everything else. So I often sat at the window listening to the birds and the wind and the snow falling down from the sky. That is all I desired.

Sometimes, a human person would pass by my hut and stare curiously at me through the fogged windows. I would wave him away—gently, of course. I waved "Go away" with no malice, no nerves. A sort of woodland *Go-Away* trill, if you can imagine.

I had long ago left my parents' house and all childhood trinkets behind—a giant trombone, glittering paints, all of my toe shoes and tutus. I was too blissed out to bring them along. I was that airy-fairy.

I arranged to be awake and asleep according to nature—that beautiful beast, that loveliest monster—each given day. I rose with the sun, and when the sun was finished for evening, my own day was finished too.

There was no need for news from the city. News is not usually good, so why seek it? During my lifetime the news has always been bad. May it reasonably request to be called the "news?" I think not. (True news is worth listening for, and more radiant or awful. Anyone can hear it, if she only tries.)

Instead, I spent my days walking the forest dressed appropriately for the weather, whatever it was. When it was summer, I wore little, and when it was winter, I bundled up. It is not that I cared for myself, nor whether I lived or died. I loved life—yes—but not my own personal possession of it in my humble container. Besides, any reasonable person who has the means will dress for the weather. It would only be spiteful to do anything else.

In spring I looked for nests, particularly those of the robins. Robins sometimes nest twice in a season. Isn't that a wonderful fact? Certain facts provide such simple pleasure. I allowed myself the happiness of observing the robins' double-nesting season. Oh the robins—their little red bellies, those dignified coats.

I kept myself occupied thus.

I had no need for money. I had all the wood that one would require for fire, and when the robins' nests sometimes would fail, and fall to the ground, and the robins depart for elsewhere, I had fine little blue eggs for supper. If

they'd fallen down freshly, there was no need even to cook them—thus no need to waste any wood on a fire, if I wasn't cold. (Mind you, if the robins did linger, I would do what I could to place the nest back in a tree. Yet I found that more often the failed nests were abandoned, after a few long moments of robin-grieving. And how I grieved with them.) Dearest robins, my precious friends!

Did you ever love something so much you just wanted to eat it?

I was so poor that I slept on a bed made of hay. I had gathered the hay from the barn. When I first was sent to the forest, I came upon the cottage as in a dream, and I went out to the barn and saw what there was to see: a ladder, a bucket, an old dying mare.

I went to the well and filled up the bucket, but the mare did not want the water. What could I do? I gave her my blessing and left her there in a halo of flowers. Gathering hay in my arms, I went into the cottage and made a small mattress. I had nothing to call my own except for the clothes I wore on my back and a few small objects (matchbook, storybook, lantern) and now the thatched cottage and the barn and apparently an old dying mare and some hay and some water.

Lovingly, I cared for the mare every day. There was little for us to do in the woods but keep company there. Sometimes I worked on the clearing, making space for foxgloves and fiddlehead ferns. It is strange, but the fields did not speak to me nor did the flowers! Not even the mare. Before I had been banished, or stolen, I could hear ladybugs talking—dust motes whispering—flowerheads expanding their lungs.

Still, I had my kindness. If a child came along, walking down the dirt road to the clearing, I would feed her some morsels.

And if a child walked down the dirt road wearing nothing, I would give her a burlap sack for her back. I would say, "Here, put this on."

And if a child approached me and told me he was cold—why of course, I would bring him nearer the fire. But not too near!

Happy is as happy does.

*And Lucy is my Name-O.*

Of course, none of this ever happened. I lived deep in the forest. No child ever did come.

Once, it is true, I found my *own* self in need of food. I walked down the dirt road to another road and from there, on pavement into the town. I passed the post office, and the postmistress peered out a window. I passed the town hall, and saw a meeting room there all full of men; one hit a gavel upon a table. It seemed the gavel just floated in air a long time before it hit down, very silent. I passed by three churches, their windows closed tight. I passed by a lake, and then I reached the town dump.

Yet once there I had no sense of what to do—the bins were all tightly

locked. Even the bears, so great and needful, could not have gotten in them. But there were no bears. They all were gone.

So I turned and walked home. I went hungry until something grew in the ground. That's the whole story: once I was hungry and I walked and I walked, and then I went home to my dying mare.

*Obladi oblada life goes on on la la la la life goes on*, I sang in her ear.

Whether I ought to have gone on looking for pennies, nickels, or dimes in that pine-needled forest, I don't think so. One should look skyward for stars and leave them home in the heavens. And, looking down, seek the snails in their shells, some of earth's most wonderful gifts to us humans. Those humble residences! Don't dare step on them.

In that forest I found a new and peaceable home. It was different from any I ever had known. It was a new kind of happiness—I kept my ear cocked to the clearing, waiting for someone to come take me home. I was happy when I thought of my mother.

And so I called the old dying mare Mama. Mama! I would say to her. How I love you! Oh my mama my mama my love!

About that, we laughed and we laughed. It was too bad, but we laughed so hard that the mare up and died.

But she died happy, I tell you. And so did I.

# Rachel Gontijo Araujo
**all the parts of the body below the head**[1]

## 1. THE ANUS

in the beginning I didn't spread to other places. I knew tongue. They called it mother. Or origin. Or head. Its biology was such that it made the belief in grammar or knowledge or truth or 'the thing in itself,' necessary. Between self-censorship, Portuguese and guilt, I discovered the muscles of the lower limb, the loins, the blood vessels, the fingers, the aorta, the jugular, the gluteus minimus, the gluteus medius, the gluteus maximus, the labia, and —that you can't catalyze change without touching yourself.

I started writing.

[1] Or: "Speak to my ass. My head is sick."

## 2. THE VENA CAVA

Writing. As the name suggests is a muscle of the arm with a sucking reflex: Half saliva, half unconventional fingering. Even though the Terrorists of Theoretical Discourse (TTD) might disagree and forget one enters into words with one's body[2], I don't. I like it bare.

The gap in a bone. Skin. The region just above the external genitals. It all affects me. If I write, I place my body on the page; *Sexually*, as Boris Vian would say in *L'Herbe Rouge*. And instead of a classical purity of tone I struggle to make work that is imperfect, that shifts in tempo and texture, that confronts in flesh and keeps me from this almost automatic urge to self-manage desire; to anesthetize the sex.

## 3. THE SACRUM

For some years now, I have it very clear that language has nothing to do with metaphysics or the metaphysician's promise of a terra firma. If anything, it is an abandonment of thought, or at least an abandonment of Socratian-Cartesian-based thought that pretends to be divorced from the messiness of that which is physical. From the growls, the swelling, the moans, the mourning, the mucous, the genital contractions, and of course, the pain.

If Deleuze and Guattari are correct and if there's only desire and nothing else, writing, language can only be a production of [that] desire. Here notions of origin and technique are replaced by the "the Yes and No of the palate," which takes place in the mouth and is [most of the time] a voluntary act.

Vian wasn't too far off when he addressed in "Utilité d'une littérature érotique" the importance of a literature that arouses. The sense of language, like that of touch, requires that the matter tasted come into actual contact with the end of nerve(s):

Car il ne faut pas s'y tromper. Le communisme, c'est tres gentil, mais c'est devenu un genre de conformisme nationaliste. Le socialisme a mis tant de vin dans son eau qu'il a tourné a l'abondance... quant au reste, je n'en parlerai pas parce que j'ignore ce que c'est que la politique et ça ne m'interésse pas plus que le tabac... Oui, les vrais propagandistes
d'un ordre nouveau, les vrais apôtres de la révolution future, future et dialectique, comme de bien entendu, sont les auteurs dits licencieux. Lire des livres érotiques, les faire connaitre, les écrire, c'est préparer le monde de demain et frayer la voie à la vraie revolution; — Boris Vian

For one must not be deceived. Communism is well and good, but it's become a sort of nationalist conformism. Socialism has put so much wine in its water that it has turned to abundance... as for the rest, I won't speak of it because I don't know what politics are and am not any more interested in them than I am in tobacco...Yes, the true propagandists of a new order, the true apostles of the future revolution, future and dialectical, of course, are the so-called licentious authors. To read erotic books, make them known, write them, is to prepare the world of tomorrow and open the way to the true revolution. – Boris Vian (tr. Bernd Klassik)

[2] Dufourmantelle, Anne.

## 5. THE MOVEMENTS OF THE ARM

At this point, I should just go ahead and admit that writing occurs slowly. Sometimes to the point of no writing at all. An assemblage as much as it is a cutting, the equilibrium in language seems to me imaginary. At the tip, at the furthest end, I cannot offer anything but the "I." The problem is, it takes a while for body to be covered only by skin. The bones have to project more and more between muscles and tendons, the head not to be pinned down by some idea of truth and to strategically come together with the sacrum so that the two pelvic bones may form a bony ring. And at this moment, *if anything at all happens to* [my] *writing, nothing happens to it but touch*[3] and some genital contractions.

---

[3] Jean-Luc Nancy.

Bibliography

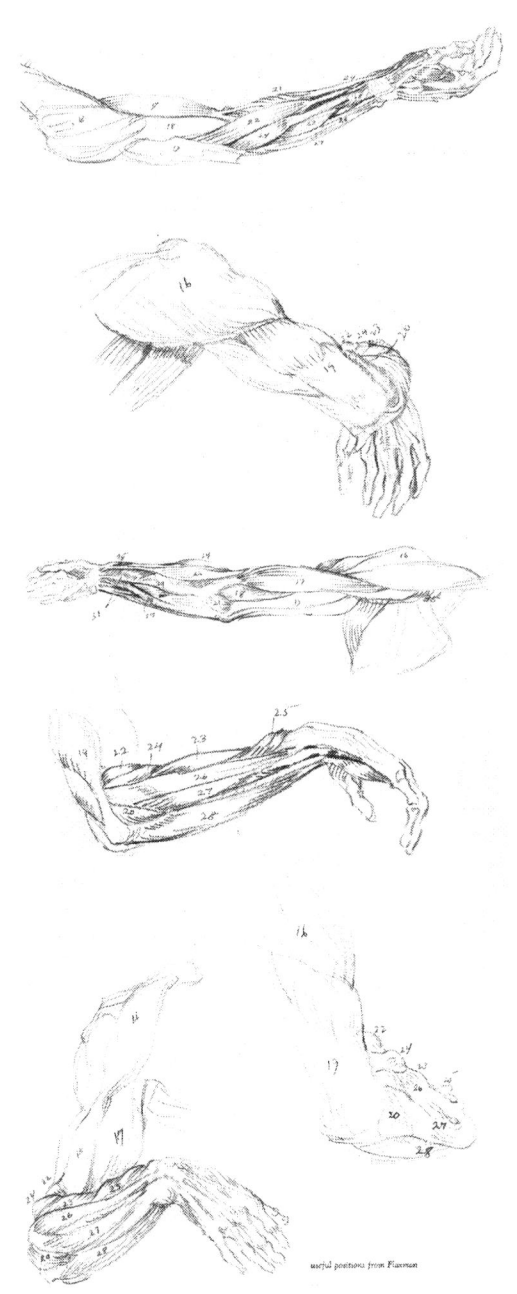

useful positions from Flaxman

# Lance Phillips

## Logogriph

Haul to one senseTheir birch and quartzes
ProduceThrough gesturing a series
Lick thumb tipAs distribute along circumference/orifice


Arm crooked into mandibleWhether Hercules or not, for carrying lust


Slash repeatedly and it is her faceTo have the men approach in similar aspect
   Caesar's EnglishHe says


A CerberusRope and dogs from the cottage


One armAs a matter of dissonanceThe pansies' purplish one wearies ofSent
   looking


The beauty of monstersAs pinpricks into shins grasses milkweed
   driedAssignation the field is common to


Fingers from palms liftedThe spirit and the blocking


Face one tenthTorso one fourthUnder this, the house, integumentary moon

ModelOne cannot resultTie into cricketHand signal

One continues thusThrashMouth burning asideOne feeds it into her thus it continues

white aster

FabulistNo yellowjacket

The flashes brighter the peals louder than before the content had shiftedBased upon the tendonOxalis

Replicate: THEREReplicate: it is all stingerReplicate: there is a nodule one must encounter say a barb

I am waiting now and waiting becomes a content I cannot resolveCold now and FallThen cold and Winter

Replicate: sadlyReplicate: aster spray, crickets beneathReplicate: fiduciary responsibility, that the plants will grow to be looked upon

Replicate: smallest moonThere fighters replicate smallest moon

Content one describes at bestStill not houseNether region

**Jesse Ball** You find a joyful note under a rock. Someone is watching. *Hide this note for someone new to find; otherwise, the person you love most will die.* Next morning, you hide it in a book & sit waiting. Is it now your duty to kill the new most-loved one?

# Sarah Tourjee
## Bread Alley

The window was watching her. The stalker was watching her objective through a window. Objective was watching a window through the stalker. Detailed kidnapping started preconceived drawings. The preconceived kidnapping started with detailed drawings. The portraits were produced in charcoal and the smallest drop of blood. Detailed with preconceived, the drawings started kidnapping. Through her the stalker was a window-watching objective.

Charcoal produced the smallest portrait of blood. The drops were the smallest blood, and in charcoal portraits produced. Stalker had seventeen humans, old and stolen. The lure was an alley into bread. A piece of bread was used to lure the subject into an alley. The stalker was seventeen years old and had never stolen a human. Seventeen was an old human. The victim ate into the trap and walked.

A subject of the piece was bread alley and a used lure. Bread an alley to lure a piece into the subject. An alley was used to lure into the subject of bread. The victim walked into the trap unwittingly and ate greedily. Greedily and unwittingly ate the trap into the victim. Why? cried mouth. I just wanted a boyfriend, said the stalker, that's all. The stalker cocooned in her catch. Seventeen years stolen, a human was the stalker. Old and stalker had a human.

The stalker cocooned her catch in duct tape for the journey home. And greedily walked the victim. Journey for the home duct. The duct in the journey for her catch cocooned. Her stalker catch-tape cocooned. Cocooned in tape, journey the duct for her home the stalker. Home duct for the journey cocooned in her. Catch the stalker! cocooned the tape. Her new mate kept screaming so the stalker showed him the portraits until he was still. That's all I wanted, said the stalker. Produced were the smallest blood drops. This was the captive's doing.

Objective the window, a stalker was through watching. The kidnapper's lair had been decorated for two. When the captive's mouth was untaped, he cried, why are you doing this? Are you the captive's mouth?, he cried, when this doing was untaped. The wanted stalker said, just a boyfriend, that's all. All boyfriends wanted just a stalker. Two had been decorated for kidnappers.

When the captives cried, the mouth was doing this untaped. Kidnapper's decorated lair for two. The portraits still new and kept. Blood were the portraits and charcoal drop-in. Portrait-blood the smallest produced the charcoal drop.

The portraits showed him screaming until he was new. The stalker cocooned in her catch. I just wanted a boyfriend that's all stalker. Her mate showed him the stalker so the screaming kept still.

The stalker home in her catch. Kidnapping preconceived. Lair decorated. The stalker had a human. Stolen years had seventeen. Are you the captive's mouth? You are he when the untaped captive's was, why this? Bread the subject. Into the subject lure the bread. The subject was used to bread. The victim ate. The trap ate the victim. The mouth cried. The stalker kept him. That's a boyfriend, said the stalker. The new mate kept screaming until the stalker was he.

# Marc Saaporta

about *Composition No. 1*

*Composition No. 1* is a re-imagining of the little known classic by French writer, Marc Saporta. This is the first ever book in a box, originally published in 1962, that went on to inspire later works such as *The Unfortunates* by BS Johnson. In many ways it was a book published ahead of its time; it not only challenges our perceptions of what makes a book a book, but it also challenges us to read in a different way.

Quite literally, the print edition of *Composition No. 1*, republished by London-based Visual Edition, is made up entirely of loose pages. Each page contains its own self-contained narrative and so it is left to the reader to shuffle through and decide which order to read them in, and how much or little they want to read before they begin again.

This format uses the interactive messing, shuffling, and sliding we're so familiar with on our screens and brings it to a physical book.

The images that follow are from the app of *Composition No. 1*, which allows users to randomise the book, exploring and extending the reading experience on screen, uncovering the full potential of reading the book in a non-linear way.

—Visual Editions

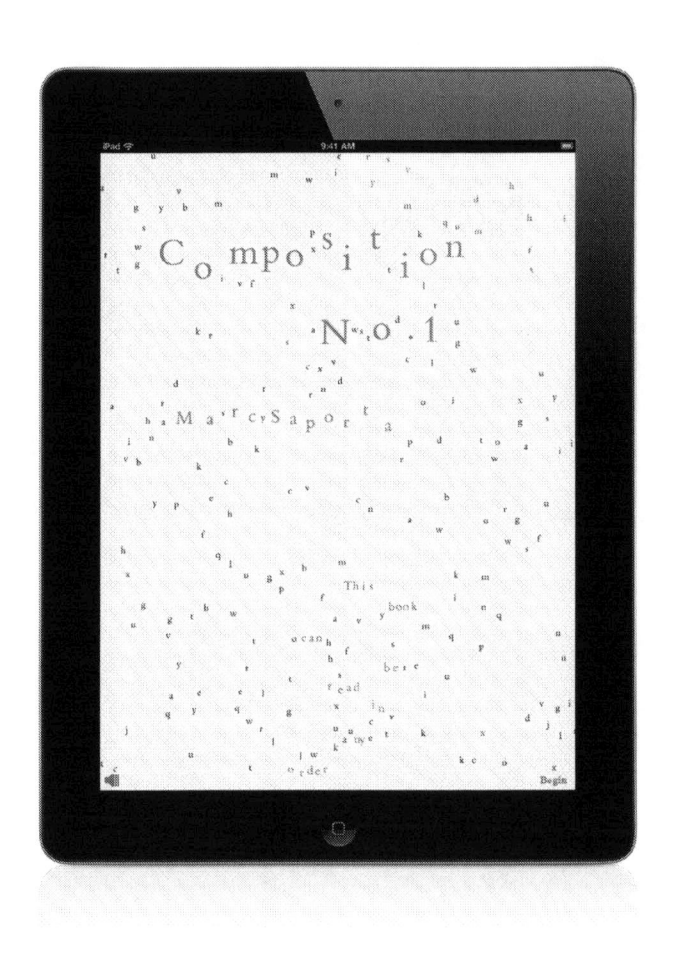

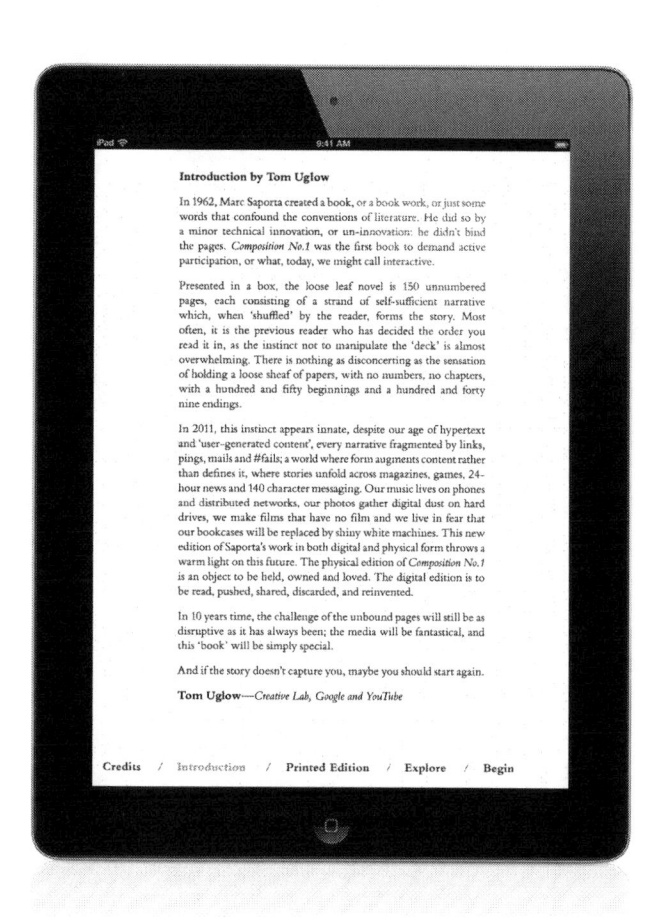

**Introduction by Tom Uglow**

In 1962, Marc Saporta created a book, or a book work, or just some words that confound the conventions of literature. He did so by a minor technical innovation, or un-innovation: he didn't bind the pages. *Composition No.1* was the first book to demand active participation, or what, today, we might call interactive.

Presented in a box, the loose leaf novel is 150 unnumbered pages, each consisting of a strand of self-sufficient narrative which, when 'shuffled' by the reader, forms the story. Most often, it is the previous reader who has decided the order you read it in, as the instinct not to manipulate the 'deck' is almost overwhelming. There is nothing as disconcerting as the sensation of holding a loose sheaf of papers, with no numbers, no chapters, with a hundred and fifty beginnings and a hundred and forty nine endings.

In 2011, this instinct appears innate, despite our age of hypertext and 'user-generated content', every narrative fragmented by links, pings, mails and #fails; a world where form augments content rather than defines it, where stories unfold across magazines, games, 24-hour news and 140 character messaging. Our music lives on phones and distributed networks, our photos gather digital dust on hard drives, we make films that have no film and we live in fear that our bookcases will be replaced by shiny white machines. This new edition of Saporta's work in both digital and physical form throws a warm light on this future. The physical edition of *Composition No.1* is an object to be held, owned and loved. The digital edition is to be read, pushed, shared, discarded, and reinvented.

In 10 years time, the challenge of the unbound pages will still be as disruptive as it has always been; the media will be fantastical, and this 'book' will be simply special.

And if the story doesn't capture you, maybe you should start again.

**Tom Uglow**—*Creative Lab, Google and YouTube*

Credits  /  Introduction  /  **Printed Edition**  /  **Explore**  /  **Begin**

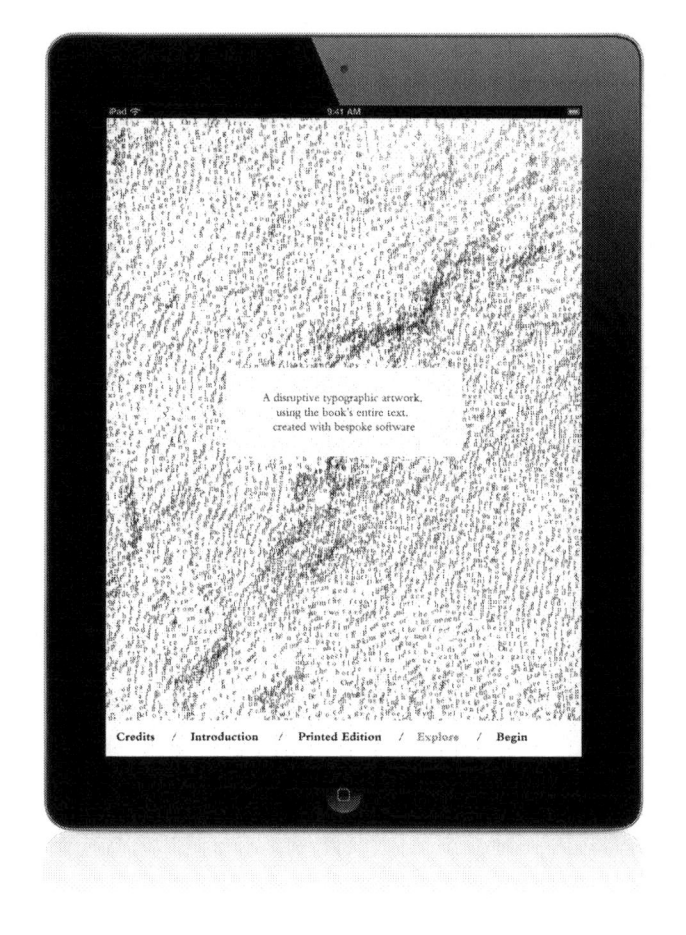

A disruptive typographic artwork,
using the book's entire text,
created with bespoke software

Credits / Introduction / Printed Edition / Explore / Begin

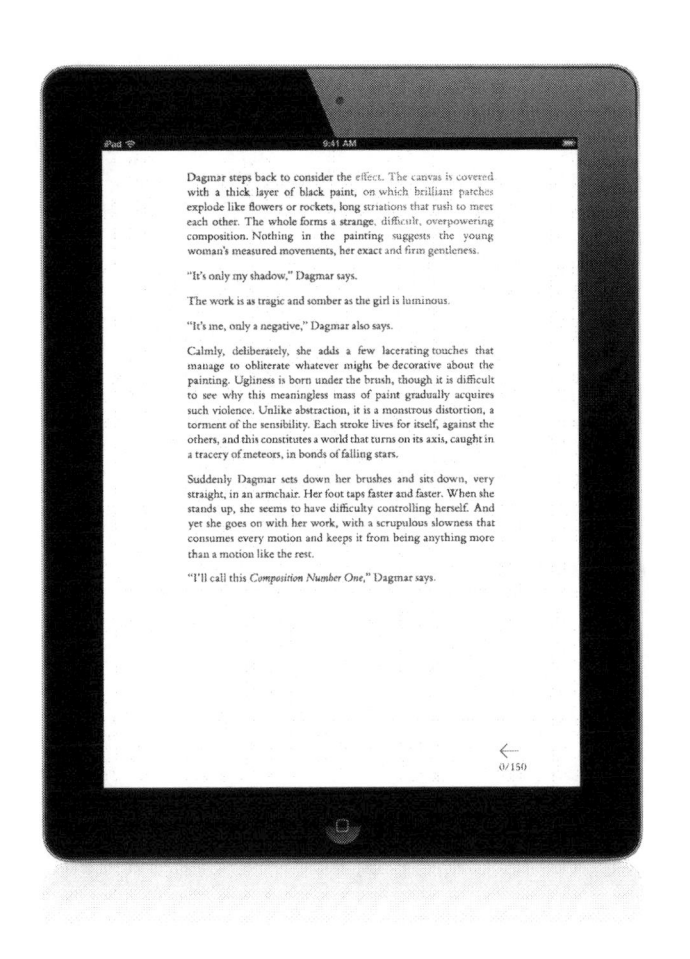

Dagmar steps back to consider the effect. The canvas is covered with a thick layer of black paint, on which brilliant patches explode like flowers or rockets, long striations that rush to meet each other. The whole forms a strange, difficult, overpowering composition. Nothing in the painting suggests the young woman's measured movements, her exact and firm gentleness.

"It's only my shadow," Dagmar says.

The work is as tragic and somber as the girl is luminous.

"It's me, only a negative," Dagmar also says.

Calmly, deliberately, she adds a few lacerating touches that manage to obliterate whatever might be decorative about the painting. Ugliness is born under the brush, though it is difficult to see why this meaningless mass of paint gradually acquires such violence. Unlike abstraction, it is a monstrous distortion, a torment of the sensibility. Each stroke lives for itself, against the others, and this constitutes a world that turns on its axis, caught in a tracery of meteors, in bonds of falling stars.

Suddenly Dagmar sets down her brushes and sits down, very straight, in an armchair. Her foot taps faster and faster. When she stands up, she seems to have difficulty controlling herself. And yet she goes on with her work, with a scrupulous slowness that consumes every motion and keeps it from being anything more than a motion like the rest.

"I'll call this *Composition Number One*," Dagmar says.

0/150

# Annam Manthiram
## The Discrepancy Equation

Discrepancy Methodology

Types of discrepancy sensitivities discussed include the rectangle or extreme) discrepancy, the p-carlo discrepancy, and the mcd and $\beta$ discrepancies.

These discrepancies approach an unknown as the number of cases in a set reaches infinity.

Cases Examined and Units Defined

Set = Coupling

$n$ = Harry and Wanda ($n$ and $w$)

$g$ = Arjun and Zara ($a$ and $z$)

$w$= Mabel and Sam ($m$ and $s$)

$R$ = Result

boxed[rectangle discrepancy] = claustrophobic insecurity

p – *carlo discrepancy (pc)* = poor communication

*mcd discrepancy* = multi-norm, polygamous

$\beta$ *discrepancy* = ugly behavior

Case Study: $n$

The discrepancy sensitivity of case $n$ can be calculated using the following equation, which was derived by taking the partial integral of $h$ and $w$ with respect to a sexual integer ($\propto$) associated with $n$.

$S \int h + w$ (sex is integral to both h and w)

$\frac{\Delta\propto}{\Delta h} \times \infty \xrightarrow{yields}$ (sexual integer on top of $h$ an infinite number of times yields an empty set for w)

$R = \lim_{n\to\infty} (1 + \frac{\propto}{h})^w$ = *multi norm (mcd)*

## Case Study: $g$

The following equation failed to yield a measurable result upon the discovery of $\beta$ discrepancy.

$$\sqrt[z]{a} = |a| + \lceil a \rceil + \|a\| + [\![a]\!] + (a_1|a_2) + \langle a_1|a_2|a_3 \rangle \, (z \text{ forces } a \text{ to cohabitate,}$$
$a$ fragments)

$z = \max_{0 \le x \le 1} x\beta^{-x^2} = 0$ ($z$ reaches discrepancy upon disintegration but $a$ forms no meaningful result)

## Case Study: $w$

The discrepancy sensitivity of case $w$ can be calculated using the following matrices. The derivation provided significant content as the case studied was an extreme case with large negative values for sensitivity analysis.

$$
\begin{matrix}
a & df & jm & qr & x \\
b & eg & nk & uv & w & z & y = p - carlo \\
c & hp & lo & ts & h
\end{matrix}
$$

$p - c \overset{\Delta}{=} m \text{ and } s$ (p-carlo leads to a change in integers $m$ and $s$)

$R = \boxed{(m \text{ and } s)\, p - carlo^{\infty}}$ (p-carlo and rectangle discrepancies identified)

## Conclusion

As an important measure, discrepancy sensitivity indicates the importance of the existence of a particular flaw in the distribution of the set. These equations are used to determine the survival probability for each set, and whether the results of each case warrant immediate separation.

# Sawako Nakayasu

## Flying Accusations

Two people, plus a woman. Then a crowd.

Of being dangerous to one, or simply a comfort hazard, of having heaved some heavy body some part of the way uphill time and yet again, of having peered. Out one eye and in the other, and in one eye, nay behind both eyes, something believing.

Of having said this and nothing furthermore.

Of having pried both eyes wide with two fingers each, thumb and another finger, thumb and another finger, one person uphill and the other person downhill.

A woman who has never held a job, never driven a car, never had anyone raise any voice at her.

Woman having been referred to as loose, loose in the head, lets a few words drop from her mouth.

Peer down the hill, hold two eyes pried open using two hands and yet now more than two people accumulating uphill downhill, an aggregate of downhill persons meets an aggregate of uphill persons at some finite or defined forthcoming moment.

One person uphill says nothing at all, except in the form of two prying fingers, regarding One downhill person.

Downhill person in particular, or not to lay such specific trappings.

Everyone else, as a member of the home audit takes it all in from what is presumed to be a safe distance.

A banging is heard on the door, and a woman who has never opened the door stands behind it with her hands on her hips, indignant at the thought.

Meanwhile a downhill person lifts an uphill person, then staggers sideways in a lack of conviction.

A new downhill person lifts both the staggering downhill and saddled uphill person, staggers backward in a lack of momentum.

Soon an assembly of staggering bodies.

Speed arrives from a distance although no one notices at first.

Gravity slows down as it can.

The hill itself, staunch in its angle.

The home audit members grow restless and start packing their bags. one person lifts a bag labeled wanderlust, but leaves it behind in confusion. The only person who has ever said anything so far is the woman who has never spoken her mind. The only two executable actions, the home audit remembers, is that of staggering and that of prying eyes open. The lifting is never completely so transitive as it may believe itself at any given moment. On the other hand, all moments are given, just as everyone here is a member, just as any moment is dangerous to everyone, even those who claim to be comfortable and those who plan to stay at home and those who have never left in the first place. Having been swept away, or up, or out. Under some dirty table. Both uphill and downhill are both here and there, and neither uphill persons nor downhill persons have any expressable doubt. What they do have, however, builds itself up the longer they stay on the hill, which is by this time bordering on excessive. The woman takes her hands off her hips but no one is there to feel any relief.

Given all of the conditions above, including the one-dimensional hill, any of the above performers are asked to drop their shoulders, gather their last bearings, remove any metal from their persons.

A rush of simulated heat and its wherefore.

# J. A. Tyler

## The Gone Children They Said Tell Us a Story

The gone children they said *Tell us a story* and the woods launched into song. The gone children they said *No, make it something more like darkness* but the woods were already overwhelmed in language. The woods they were already talking the sing-song of lyrics. The woods they were already stretched over the heads of the gone children and pumping into their tiny ears the sounds of oceans, night times of forest, the moon. And the gone children were too polite then to say anything, their time already had and the woods rocketed off. The gone children sat and listened. And the gone children tried to imagine themselves as balloons, floating away.

The gone children they said *Tell us a story.* The woods were sleeping. The gone children drug their shoulders in bark and asked *Why is it that you are always sleeping when we want to hear stories?* An owl, a tree, the sound of a river. These the noise. The gone children said *Do you hear that?* but the woods they did not answer. The woods fast in sound and creeping vine-dreams. The gone children cried but there were too many sentences to hear. The bite of forest walls and black sky. The gone children they wanted to say to the woods, *Dry up and go home,* but there is no home for these woods, not when the noises are so loud and with all the stories being un-told.

The gone children they said *Tell us a story* and the story that the woods told was about the gone children sitting in a wood and asking of the woods *Tell us a story*. And the gone children they said *No, we don't want this to be about us* but the woods had already taken the story and carved it into skin, showed it up to the sky and the moon and the stars. Animal sounds made sentences that the gone children thought were better than the thin-skinned story of the woods, and they said *Couldn't it be stories like that?* with the woods having already spoken. The curtain of sky having replied. The course of communication sifted through and done and lost again, as it is when the gone children open up the holes that are their mouths, this sky, darkness.

The gone children they said *Tell us a story* and the woods said *No,* walked away with branches in their hands, bark on their hearts. The gone children left with nothing but night and the stumps where trees used to be, where a forest used to stand. *This is where a forest used to stand* they said to the sky but the sky too had moved, leaving in its wake a rip of paper painted blue, a sky removed and made to look like what once was. *We once were* the gone children were thought to have said, but nothing was there to hear them, no one was left to respond. And that was how the story ended, or it didn't end, or there never was any story to tell.

The gone children they said *Tell us a story*. The woods they said to these gone children *The story is something you should be hearing right now*. But the gone children weren't, hadn't, couldn't. *We don't hear anything but the stars and the moon humming and the river* they said, bowing their heads to prayer. *Then you are lost* is what the woods said, before they tucked back into the ground and forever left in their stead a plainsong, a fever of meadows, a hilled land within nothing but sunsets and ache. *This is not a story* the gone children said, and they were right, but the woods had already receded, the trees already backed up into themselves, the sky already bent to the color of future.

# J. R. Carpenter

## about *TRANS.MISSION [A.DIALOGUE]*

TRANS.MISSION [A.DIALOGUE] is a web-based computer-generated narrative dialogue, a never-ending conversation between generations of transatlantic migrants propagating across, beyond, and through the long- distance communications networks that their migrations have engendered. This multi-site-specific dialogue resonates in the spaces between places separated by time, distance, and ocean, yet inextricably linked by generations of immigration.

The text reproduced in print here is but one of an infinite number of possible dialogues. Every time you visit this page: http:// luckysoap.com/generations/ transmission.html, the sentence structures will be the same, but even as you read them, their variables will shift and change. Soon there will be immigrants where once were explorers; a persistent tap eclipses a strange whir; a message instead of a passage; Nova Scotia in place of Scotland; a submarine cable replaces a shipping network. How different is the narrative of one journey from the next?

The source code of TRANS.MISSION [A.DIALOGUE] is adapted from a JavaScript narrative generator called The Two created by Nick Montfort in 2008: http://nickm.com/poems/the_two.html. To view the source code of these pages, right click, and select View Page Source. There the sub-text is revealed, the potential text, the text waiting to happen. The code is quite easily read. First there are the variables, and then there are the sentence structures which give them meaning.

```
var w=['why','where','how'];
choose(w)+'?'
Why?
```

TRANS.MISSION [A.DIALOGUE] is a mechanical construction, a sentence engine performing the programmatic function of associating suspended variables with syntactic signification that they might travel through networks and emerge intact as narrative units. The dialogue generated by this engine is both technically and topically inflected with the syntax and grammar of code language. Codes, their creators, the modes through which they operate, propagate, and communicate, and the confusion they instigate are the main topic of the dialogue generated. Absurdity, weirdness, and illogicality are the default modes of long- distance communication, migration, displacement and difference. TRANS. MISSION [A.DIALOGUE] aims to embrace these characteristics, to confuse and confound boundaries between physical and digital, code and narrative, past and future, home and away.

# TRANS.MISSION [A.DIALOGUE]

Begin Transmission.
How?
With a question.
What emerges from a question?
Spring fog on the Atlantic. Distant shores to lure us.
Have the crucial parcels been weighed yet?
The conductor transmits his instructions.
Why didn't the wanderers insist upon updated directions?
Some of them lasted thirty odd days.
Convictions dried up, or so the reports seem to suggest.
How did the conductor signal her reports pertaining to former dialogues?
The long-distance shipping network can't detect these strange whirs.
Should the administrator suddenly come to imagine this coast?
The passage from Scotland had to be brutal.
Conditions appear to be unreadable.
Receiving beaming feedback, no signals...
Who can interpret the surf in mist like this?
Many passages of the historian's report are not documented.
Might sailors suddenly trade away these coasts?
17th-century strangers penned charts. Thirty odd were from Scotland.
Why is it that they sometimes seem to destroy pieces from the data?
Transverse delivery mechanisms take days to relate the trial paper trails.
Haven't the historians kept in touch?
Reassurances were air mailed hours ago.
There may have been portents.
Encrypted signals, ghosts on the monitor.
A whir, some static...
Did anyone else detect that rattle?
Alien radios have corresponded.
One stranger tempts the programmer.
Which words of explanation might she relay?
Writer's ballads of storied cliffs occasionally arise from these images.
Might past sailors' mothers want additional records from them?
Perhaps, but by autumn a couple charts may be flawed.
How was the closest channel authored?
The latest vistas are similar to those of Nova Scotia.
In these strange guidebooks, the Atlantic is occasionally gleaming
But wait... does that relay previous questions?
Signals of foreign rain begin on the screen.
Is the filing system functioning?
Some of us suspect it's fixed.
Please try again.

# Shane Allison

## Mother Worries

Lord, how we gon' pay these bills in this
How we gon' pay these bills,
Lord. How we gon' pay these bills in
We gon' pay these
We gon' pay
Lord how we gon' pay these bills in this house?

How Lord, are we gon' pay these bills in this house
Lord how, Lord how we gon' pay these bills in this
Lord how, Lord we gon' pay
Lord how are we gon' pay these bills
These bills, Lord how we gon' pay these
How we goin' to pay these bills, Lord in

In this house, Lord? How is it that we gon' pay these bills in,
In this house, Lord. How, Lord we goin' to pay the bills in this house
These bills, these bills in this house, Lord, these
Bills in this house, how are we goin' to afford to pay the bills in this
House of all houses? With the bills the way, these bills
Are, how are we goin' to pay?

How, Lord? How is it that we are goin' to pay
The bills in this house the way they are in
This house, this house with the bills
In this house of houses in the house
With the bills we don't know how we're goin' to pay in this
House with the bills the way these

Bills are in this house, with these
Bills we don't know how we gon' pay
In this, our house of houses with this and this
Bill, Lord we have to pay in
This house, the house with all the bills that need to be paid in the house.
Lord how? How Lord is we to pay these bills?

How are we gon' do it? How is it that we are to pay these bills
These bills, which are stacking up high as a house with these
Bills we don't know, Lord, how we goin' to pay the bills that are due on the house
That needs to be paid
In the house, this house in
Which the bills are big in this

House with these bills that we
Don't know how in this world
We don't know how we goin' to pay

**Amber Sparks**

A slice of water flash freezes. Fringed by ice shelves, what's in this space should be thick, dark tar. But this sea is kin to sky. This sea is a mirror; the rains that pour in shed their silver & stream up through the clearest waters in the world.

# Joyelle McSweeney
### about King Prion

These poems are from a series called *King Prion*, an infectious performance piece which hopes to contaminate its listeners with the desire to replicate it. The reader of this anthology should thus read these poems aloud, with a full lung. The opening whoop opens up a high fraught sonic space of trembling through which King Prion can step in and speak through the subject's nose, mouth, hair, bones, fluids and soft tissues. In variety of collapsing moments, King Prion passes for Art, Disease, and other Killer Wants, material, pharmaceutical, bacterial, and virtual.

—Joyelle McSweeney

## King Prion

--Hoooooooo
Lay in an array of pixels
Fat, simulated proteins
*Looks just like nutrition!*
*Acts just like an avatar!*
I just wanted to give my body to
A net of guarine
Ginko-balboa azatine melanine
Camphobacter phylacter nicotine
Which hung like neuron-nectar in a cell, net of
Vatic coughdropped hairball tells the future of
Neural center where the straight lines hopped
Like a hairline fracture on a bender jumps a
Mullholland retaining wall and crashes the crinkled Vale of
Food-for-thought
Fruit for monkeys in a barrel, one fruit per monkey
For a total of fortyseven monkeydays
For a total of twelve hours at a clip
The go-home-and-feed-the-baby milk of it
That man is a mouth chased by ghosts
Round a rainslicked hairpin off a cliff in
(And now I pause to remember
How Art was a silver paper moulded to the ceiling
Where you cut your hair
For your rebirth as Fata Androgyana
The scissors-sister who slits where she goes-into
Cuts as she cuts--)
This machine makes its need louder and
Invites me into its duct, unlike the baby
Sleeping on the other edge of Pow'r,
Eyes roll'd, mouth pinch'd shut
Round Pow'r's earthly sinks and shunts—

**King Prion**

--Hoooooooo
Crepe'd up a knife blade ladder on
Spectator shoes or gladiator sandals
Cut to the glut, Fata Androgyana,
To the fat of the matter.
You cupped yourself to the sickle-sale table
There's a drug for that and its name is traced on ice
With a triple toe lutz boot black blade handle.
Dorothy Hamill.
Hack't locks
For the trunk sale.
Sword tied to the
Second hand
The glabrous torso
Pouring bile and
Tied to the saddle
Makes the failing world go round
In battle
On hoarse legs
Bone chip tip top knobble
(I live in a starhouse built for denial
Hygienists in Scarsdale.
A case of adolescent sarc-
Oma.
It has six dental points despite the five on my papers. Despite
the Nazi hinges
Singe-ing yours. Those black arms
Swing like a krazy kat clock
Point everywhere.
I'm an artist so
like a broken clock I never have
had to *Repeat myself—*

**King Prion**

--Hoooooooo
Wore that morning's liv
-ery slippery
Made a loop of the loupe,
A jewler. *Happy Happiest toddler*
*On the block!* And when he leuked closer
The red cell
de-bucketed, spilt guts
Like a hasp spent or hen bent
Over eggs in the nest of
complexity. Easy's over. A chopping or an auction
Bloc. A chopping list. What complex
-ity
Could crack and flow like this
And make a motion studyable at MIT.
Reproduction in 3-D
If you need me
I'll just be standing outside for a sec
In Media
Ab Ovum
Like a kid just studying
Hump & Dump I didn't know you had to study that stuff
Oval is the shape of the egg pierced, blown &
Strung up
Before the horse. The cart
Before the horse before the
Chicken bucket.
(Batter me).
That's  no way to go to the
dump
To dump the contents, pump
The trumped-up sludge
Like chum
Pump action
Lamp chain or chain gang,
Dead key on an otherfucking
*Keyboard* or
*Lanyard,* chomp bit
In the mouth
Of the dust
In the mouth Of the champ of the chumps

**King Prion**

--Hoooooooo
Wolf-whistle'd & Cadillac'd
Into the canyon wall
Red river at bloodset mad as a
Stripped tendon
Senator Mousecatch
and four faces from the Mountaintop
(Old Diabolical Engine
Old Granite
Old Labial and
Old Archdiocesal Ironsides)
Frowned down upon
Today's fever index: rocky spotted catscratch
Carcrash carwash
And Scotchguard
-ed SUV
Offgassing into the afterlife
Its upright family cargo
I'm one
-half-lab-rat into the shingle
Gravel tamps down my pink eyes
Grout clads
my claw hammer
My inner awl and my
petite piston
As I strive
For a burial berth
In the afterlife's
Low-slung motel mid-roadtrip mid-
Lincoln Continental
divide The drain first clock then counterclock
*wise* the Exhaust fan its Nicorette filter
*wise* The rodent-dropping whirr of its
hard *drive*

# John Madera

*Spectral Confessions and Other Disgressions*

**Edited by the Witch of Endor**

[From The Official Catalog of the Library of Potential Literature]

Witness a weird world composed of ectoplasmic stuff, where flesh and bone have been ecstatically sloughed off like exuviae, a world of odd obsessions and dark drives, of madness and menace, of everything post-human. Literally ghostwritten, *Spectral Confessions and Other Digressions* gathers reflections from a host of legendary ghosts. The Holy Ghost's prolegomenon provides a heady and "personalized" pneumatology: the metaphysics of spirits or spiritual beings. King Hamlet, surely the most famous of the ghosts who have haunted Shakespeare's plays, remarks on the reunion of his family, addressing how even in the afterworld forgiveness is possible. Slimer's rambling self-reflective musings here mark a stark contrast to his obnoxious slime-spewing performance in the film *Ghostbusters*: "Ah, the guttural burp usurped everything, and I was lost awash in the slosh." Besides confirming that entering a darkened bathroom, standing in front of its mirror, and repeating her name thirteen times will not cause her to appear, Bloody Mary, in a humorous turn, presents an incendiary recipe for her eponymic drink. "Death and Taxes" is a delightful essay on financial management by Jacob Marley. The Ghost of Christmas Past's lyrical reverie on the physics of time and space is another of this mammoth tome's highlights. The Murdered Peddler, a ghost invented by Margaret and Kate Fox in the 1840s as part of an elaborate hoax, inexplicably proves his own existence. After reading Casper McFadden's tell-all tale about his *ménage à trois* with Wendy the Good Little Witch and Hot Stuff the Little Devil, you might call him an unfriendly ghost. The Tombstone and Amityville Ghosts, the Vanishing Hitchhiker, the South Shields Poltergeist, and the Brown Lady; the Ghosts of Drury Lane, the Seven Gables, and the *SS Watertown*; and no small number of spooks, specters, wraiths, phantoms, apparitions, shades, psychopomps, haints, poltergeists, and revenants all flit about these pages. Even a fetch—a visible spirit of a person yet alive—offers some gelid words. But perhaps most surprising is the blank verse of the book's sole entry by a non-human ghost: The Flying Dutchman, the seventeenth-century merchant ship said to haunt the seven seas: "Ye souls of trees I charge with treason now. / Aroint thee from my bow and stern and sink / Beneath this bitter and mutinous sea..." Finally, the diversity of voices, from the malevolent to the benevolent, and the clarity in which mounds of beyond-the-grave reports are expressed are testaments to the necromantic powers of the seemingly immortal Witch of Endor, who edited *Spectral Confessions and Other Digressions*, a collection that may compel you to entertain that vexing death wish.

# Nico Vassilakis
## about *STARINGS*

How to speak about vispo? For one, the relatable denominator is how we see. How language affects us visually, how staring at language is essential to reaping functionality out of vispo. In this case, we'd consider a stare to be an elongated gaze, and staring the hyper-focused verb from which we gain further insight.

The alphabet is continually morphing. It is both evolving and devolving into a periodic table of speech elements.

There is an underlying desire for the product of alphabet, of any culture, to meander, to reinvent itself. We scribe anew. It reminds us that alphabet, the letter, is a drawn experience—drawn either by hand or by the machines we have built. The physical ingredients of language, the letters, dream of how to form and reform themselves into new meaning. The meanings we live with are changing. The hierarchy of sight has made our engagement with the world virtually all visual. The eyes crave a refreshed approach so that they can seek and find new content. Vispo is all eyes, is the delirium of alphabet shift.

You are here, seeing language undo itself.

Staring your way into and through the letter as object.

—Nico Vassilakis

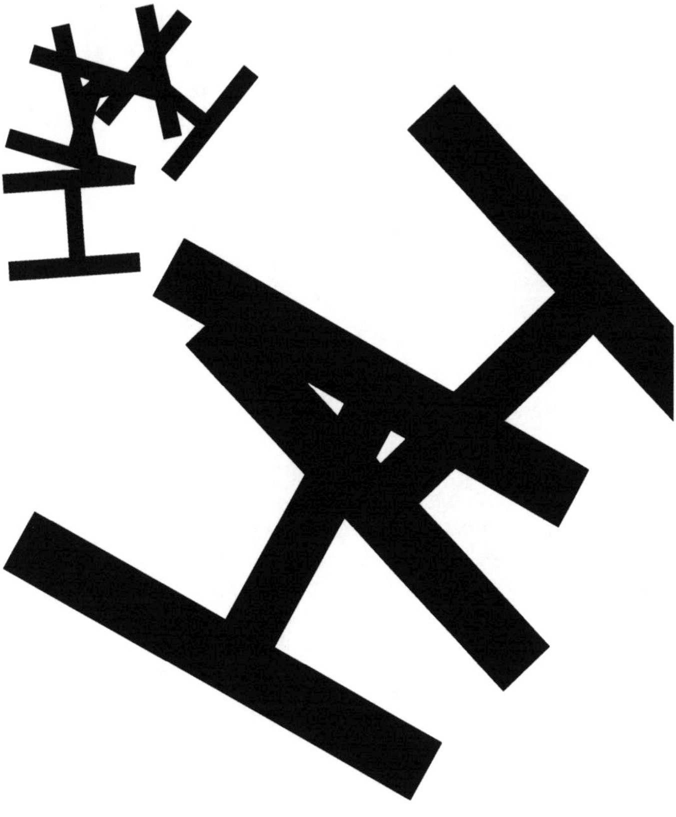

# Elizabeth Gentry

### about *Housebound*

"Among the manuscripts, I kept returning over and over again to one, or rather I found I quite could not get out of it once I got in; I was Housebound inside its pages, just as its characters were. Its syntax and nouns are hypnotic! In this domestic heaven or hell, there are 'no more anecdotes, poetry recitations, ghost stories, contrived games, or late-night disclosures before the wood stove.' And yet there is nothing but. Here, secrets crisscross through walls as through hours, and words travel in creepy, kind whispers (I saw a toy shop). Grown children run through the woods and enter strange houses. They live over here and over there—all over the terrible and beautiful map. Crime scene, children's book, family romance? A masterful, miniature, paradox world. So many surging demands on dear Maggie, this story's main girl. Oh, horrible danger must lurk for her—or something much worse, and prettier still, something that goes back much further than time."

—Kate Bernheimer
Judge for the 2011-2012 Madeline P. Plonsker
Emerging Writer's Residency Prize

Elizabeth Gentry's *Housebound* is a novel like no other: a disquieting and interior adventure through one family's secrets and lies. Maggie, the eldest daughter, is preparing to leave the house in which she's lived, worked, and been educated her whole life long: a life led seemingly without contact with the outside world or even with extended family, save in the form of weekly trips to the library for the stories that are almost the only escape for Maggie and her eight brothers and sisters from the festering unhappiness of their parents. In her last days in and around the awkward and remote house that is the only home she's ever known, Maggie makes a series of discoveries that put her own ultimate escape from the house to the city into perilous question.

The cool and detached narration of the novel, and Maggie's seeming estrangement from the most familiar details of her life, along with the uncanny rural setting, give the novel an almost Kafkaesque feel, if Kafka had been born an Appalachian woman. Mythic and domestic and coldly thrilling, this novel will live on in readers' memories long after they, like Maggie, have escaped (or failed to escape) its clutches.

—Josh Corey

# Housebound
## Chapter One

Leaving home felt like tunneling out of a snow that had kept everyone housebound so long they had run out of things to talk about. There were no more anecdotes, poetry recitations, ghost stories, contrived games, or late-night disclosures before the wood stove. Rather than building their knowledge of one another in successive cycles of irritation and love, memorizing each new layer as they aged and grew, the eleven members of the family had simply succumbed, once and for all, to a silence that turned them into strangers. They forgot the pressing revelations. They forgot that short surprised laugh. They forgot, too, the ring of the telephone against the wall, connecting them to people they might no longer recognize. With the radio dusty and their records scratched and worn, they perched on the ends of straight-backed chairs reading as if with peripheral vision engaged, shoulders tensed against an encroachment of space unlikely to occur. They felt suspended, always waiting for someone else to make the first move—to take a turn with the bath, to return with fresh wood, to put the pot on to boil, to summon to supper, and most of all, to grow up and to leave.

When Maggie decided to leave, the honeysuckle vines were just beginning to smother the herb garden far below her cracked bedroom window. Awaking in early dawn to the sound of a cough, she guessed that Douglas, the fourteen-year-old, lay without sleeping, his twin bed pushed against the wall alongside two bunks and a cradle. Presently their mother and father would pass through the nursery from their adjoining room on the far side, apparently unable to imagine that their children wanted anything more than to linger on in the great heart and heat of the room for six, passageway to each parental entrance and exit. And why not? The oldest boys in the side rooms downstairs weren't ready to leave. The eighteen-year-old whom the children often referred to as the theologian could continue indefinitely in his independent study of philosophy and religion, since their mother ceased her instruction of each of them at age fifteen, having nevertheless surpassed the limited capacity of the rural public schools. The sixteen-year-old athlete could run half-way to the city nearly thirty miles to the west and across the railroad tracks in town straight up the ridge into mountain ravines to the east. What could such skills bring? Her brothers were delaying, preparing for nothing.

But Maggie's skill, child rearing, had been honed long ago, with the last baby now four years old. Sliding from beneath the coverlet and reaching for the

lamp switch, she understood that the time had come for someone else to use this room: at nineteen, she had occupied the only private bedroom off the second-floor landing for nearly a decade. If she did not leave, perhaps no one would.

From the nightstand drawer, Maggie pulled an old favorite children's book and a new favorite novel and set them on the bed. On top of the books she placed a pocket knife with scissors, a spool of white thread stuck through with a thin needle, and an unopened pack of Teaberry gum given her by a town boy for changing the diaper of his baby sister, small contraband in a house where sweets were outlawed by their father. Bending to reach beneath her bed, she felt for a round leather box that she had discovered in the top of her closet years ago. When Maggie asked to be allowed to keep the box, her mother could not remember where they had acquired such an item—perhaps it had been in the house when they arrived, she said. Yet upon first taking the worn black handle, Maggie had imagined a raucous, gray-headed woman who drank beer and smoked cigarettes as was done in some books and perhaps on some forgotten television show, watched at someone else's house long ago, perhaps even the woman's herself. Though Maggie did not remember ever having met this low-breasted woman, she thought of her as a forgotten grandmother, one who had no trust for men or women and who steered away from babies whenever possible. Since no one spoke of relatives, the family might as well have come into being all on its own, without ancestry or extended relations, its identity gleaned from these small, oddly-shaped rooms, the steep staircase, the deep ashy swirling within the woodstove, and the thin paneling of the half-finished basement. Still, like a disgruntled fairy godmother, the imaginary grandmother had briefly appeared in the living room when, at age eleven, Maggie had been told to wait with her laboring mother until the midwife came. "I tore mine out with a coat hanger," she said with a chuckle, then faded away.

Though Maggie understood that today she would at best only accompany her father into the city to inquire about a position, she packed her things into the box with her clothes in case she did not return, changed into a dress, then pulled on a green cardigan against the spring chill. From across the hall Douglas heard the bureau drawers slide open and for no particular reason—unless it was that the noise he heard was the same noise he heard every morning—became despondent: if no one left, then it was as if they all existed solely as indirect witnesses to their parents' copulation, a kind of relentless insular system in which all circled a secret central drama that only revealed itself with each new creation. Even the smallest of rustlings from the other side of the bedroom wall, noises that could have simply been the parting of his parents' bedclothes, had lately caused Douglas to awake in disgust, shamefully longing for solitude to still the early morning tides of ache. He did not consider that perhaps this four-year lapse in childbearing was not temporary

but final, and that whatever happened from here spun them out and away from the source, which somewhere deep had glowed warm and bright, but which now was cooling, withdrawing, curling in to simply sustain itself. These were only the unseen beginnings of change, after all, beyond his experience or intuition, and he had no reason to believe that there would be anything next but a new cradle slid into the room in which he slept with the twelve-year-old whose baby fat was gathering at her chest; the eleven-year-old who kicked the mattress while she slept; the ten-year-old who pressed his cheek to the cool glass of their one window each morning, staring at the gravel driveway; the eight-year-old who bounced a ball against doors to pass the time; and the four-year-old who for attention still tried to slip into now self-conscious baby talk, until everyone stiffened and looked away, embarrassed for him.

And so it was that Douglas, along with all of the other children, felt some strange new contraction in the heart when the family had settled onto the benches of the long wooden table for breakfast, where Maggie made her announcement.

"There haven't been any babies here for quite some time," she said, her voice deep and almost hollow. She nodded toward Bertie, the four-year-old, sitting on the middle sister's lap to get closer to his hot cereal. Bertie looked up from beneath soft blond curls as if he had been caught growing up, and was responsible for no longer charming them. "I don't want any babies of my own," she continued, "so it's time for me to find some work to do."

Some time had passed since two complete sentences had been spoken over breakfast that did not pertain to some practical task—an instruction or bid for help. The children shifted on the benches, unable to believe they were witnessing a declaration of intent, a suggestion of change that even their parents' refusal could not erase, since Maggie had not asked for permission, nor had she made the announcement in private. She made it in front of all of them deliberately, suggesting that they, too, might find something else.

But their father did not resist. Maggie half-expected her parents to make some other suggestion, to promote an idea of their own. In taking the initiative she would perhaps trigger some forgotten dream they had been harboring for her. Instead, her father looked just past her, through the kitchen and toward the back door, the broken red veins visible in his cheeks and nose, one wisp of hair lying across the top of his head. "There are always babies in the city," he said. "And some people I know." He speared egg with his fork, suggesting that they might all resume eating.

Their mother never looked up. She took the littlest from his sister's lap and put him on her own, tucking her fuzzy brown hair behind one ear as she did so. "He's spilling," she said in a rare explanation for an action that was the only clue to the others that she resented this disruption. In that one word and move, they all knew that in Maggie's absence, their mother would

redouble her efforts at caring for Bertie, not because Maggie wasn't there to help, but because the boy was the farthest from leaving her, a safe investment. Bertie suddenly felt restless and cramped, as if he were growing bigger in his mother's lap, so that her thighs no longer cushioned him, and her hip bone cut into his.

Knowing that her father would want to leave promptly, so that he could make inquiries on her behalf but still reach the government finance office in time for work, Maggie left the table after quickly finishing her breakfast. She did not wait, as she would have on every other morning, for the others to finish. She took a last bite of potato and without a word placed her fork across her plate and mounted the steep stairs to her bedroom. This seamless motion was like a soaring in her mind and in the minds of her siblings—fork to plate, heel to floor, toe to first wooden stair, the lift and swing of her denim dress over her boots. She would not be asked to resume her seat at the table, they knew, not now or ever. They turned from the sight of her retreating hemline back to their half-empty plates, unsettled.

The new rule—that Maggie would no longer join them at table—held in place that very evening, when she and her father returned home from the city, having found her a position in a daycare center that would begin in three days. Edwin, the eight-year-old throwing his battered orange ball against the barn door when they arrived home, was so surprised at the slamming of two car doors instead of one that he missed his ball and had to chase it across the grass. Maggie, stepping from the station wagon, never once looked in his direction. She seemed disoriented, as if she had run very fast through the woods believing that she was being chased by a wolf, only to be stopped by someone who told her there had never been a wolf. Edwin was almost as frightened of the wolves that were said to no longer exist as his older brother Quinn was of the tramps that he believed wandered through the woods from the railroad. Still, he could understand her disappointment and even embarrassment, running so hard for what turned out to be no reason at all. Grasping the ball between his fingertips again, he felt shamed somehow, caught doing something routine when she had ventured out to something new. How soon would something new be required of him?

[Look for *Housebound* from &NOW Books in October 2013.]

# Amina Memory Cain & Anna Joy Springer

**A conversation about yesterday's Tomorrowland, today.**

**Remembering & Now 5: Tomorrowland Forever! / University of California, San Diego / OCT. 13 – 15, 2011**

**Anna Joy Springer:** *What would your ideal literary arts festival or conference look like?*

**Amina Memory Cain:** Many years ago, in the middle of a performance in the middle of winter at Links Hall in Chicago, Illinois, I had a realization about what was missing for me at many of the literary readings I had attended. In the performance, the dancer/performers were doing such interesting things with their bodies, much of their movement coming from their contact with the floor, with the passage they made while lying down. This invited me (and many others in the audience) to scoot down in my seat. We also wanted to be horizontal. Affected this way, physically, we could not help but adjust our bodies to what we were seeing. The performance changed the space of the room. I thought to myself, why can't literary events be this open and warm and intimate and cutting? As the co-founder at the time of a new reading series, I wanted the events we curated to be in relationship to these qualities, and then I wanted to see if a festival/conference could also be in relationship to them.

**Amina Memory Cain:** *When you first agreed to organize and host the UCSD iteration of &NOW (Tomorrowland Forever!) what did you want it to be or look like or do? How did this either change or deepen in the year we spent planning the festival? And what did the festival feel like once it finally took place?*

**Anna Joy Springer:** I asked to host &NOW 2011 back at the SUNY Buffalo festival, so I had a little under two years to organize the festival; after the first year thinking about how &NOW and UCSD might best correlate, and then getting some of the money and other institutional support sort of lined up, I asked you to be the co-host. UCSD is a research university known primarily for scientific and tech innovation, though its Arts & Humanities and Social Sciences also lean distinctly toward the experimental. I wanted to use the festival, in part, to investigate both &NOW's and UC San Diego's zealous

use of this non-neutral term "innovation" in terms of cultural practices and production. Unlike "experimental," "fucked up," or "anti-corporate," in the first decade of the 21ˢᵗ century the term "innovative" seemed to be a stingless and even aggrandizing term that was simultaneously popping up all over advertisements, speeches, and other vehicles of market rhetoric. So I wanted to explore the value of this term, which had in it a tacit promise of a better future. We generally don't say innovative, for instance, when talking about new kinds of bombs or poisons. This notion of a promise for a better future had fallen out of popularity (except for its kitsch forms) in the postmodern era, yet it had returned in the rhetoric of our discipline, and I wanted to see where we were at with this newly-imagined futurity. I came up with the theme Tomorrowland Forever! idea at a recital by Our Lady J in a bar in Hollywood. She sang secular gospel as a complexly gendered future creature with a robot voice full of actual passion. She performed on the second night of the festival, a night specifically designated as "queer;" in fact I believe I curated most events around her performance. That night there were about 13 people in the audience. The other 200-300 people were back at their hotels, exhausted, or drinking at the café across the way. I was in the audience and so were you. It was totally magical. We had this profound experience together. This intimacy was unusual, spiritual, and material. It was unquestionably new, freakish even, in the context of an intellectual literary festival, though undocumented and mostly unwitnessed.

**AJS:** *How close did &NOW 2011 come to your ideal literary festival? In what ways?*

**AMC:** Happily, I think &NOW 2011 came pretty close to this ideal of warmth and openness, and the Black Took Collective performance on closing night sent me even further into a changed, charged room than the performance I speak of above. For me, the conference certainly felt like a generous (and generative) environment in which people didn't feel held back. Many festival participants wrote us afterwards to tell us it felt like that for them too, so I know this was true for at least some of the writers and artists who attended. I know that people had conversations with each other about their work, and that they took risks. I hope no one felt isolated, alone, shut down. Organizing a festival/conference of that size and scope is hard, maybe one of the hardest endeavors I've ever taken up, and certainly the most time-consuming. There were so many details to keep track of, and sometimes we were exhausted by the work. Some of those details might have gotten lost, at least temporarily. I hope these instances were few and far between.

: *For you, what does it mean to be a curator? What does it mean to be a curator within (innovative/avant-garde) literature?*

**AJS:** I like making games, puzzles, and toys for people and seeing what they do. For &NOW, I wanted to figure in time for social and physiological delight. For instance, I wanted to create a nap/silence/meditation room, which all conferences should have. There should be isolation tanks to get in and massage chairs. To be a curator is to consider the experience of a human body in space-time as well as its potential complexes of consciousness and signification. I guess I think of it like being a hostess or priestess. Unfortunately, I couldn't get shuttles to and from the hotel, because by the time we discovered we would have enough registration money to pay for them, someone else (V.S. Ramachandran) had ordered them for another conference on campus. So some of our guests' bodies were super-tired because they didn't drive or order cabs. Their poor feet!

**AJS:** *Amina, I know I got to see almost nothing except the featured events, because the rest of the time I was running around helping volunteers or guests or I was flopped on the lawn smoking maniacally. I missed the famous moment of hair-burning! What are a few things you heard about from the festival, but didn't get to see, but wish you had?*

**AMC**: There's so much I wish I had experienced; everything, in fact, but especially "*Emily Dickinson's Futures*" (Julie Carr, Richard Deming, Lori Emerson, Andrew Zawacki); "*Sciamachy: Shadows In and Around Literature*" (Tim Horvath, Larry Reed/ShadowLight Productions, Kane X. Faucher); "*In Transit: Errible Language, Mobile Politics*" (Oana Avasilichioaei, Jen Hofer, Marco Antonio Huerta, Román Luján, John Pluecker); "*Best Beasts Forever*" (individual presentations by Jennifer Calkins, Michelle Detorie, Oana Avasilichioaei); "*Seeing Stars*" (Tisa Bryant, Roxanne Carter, Masha Tupitsyn, Ronaldo Wilson, Kate Zambreno). And I really wish I had seen Michael du Plessis' performance out on the lawn, as well as the site-specific installation "*Transgressing a Ribbon*" (Jared Stanley, Gabie Strong, Matthew Hebert).

**AMC**: *Were there conversations you hoped would happen at the festival, both through the curation of the featured events, as well as through the panels?*

**AJS:** I really hoped people would stop thinking of formally new rad weird odd literature as unmarked by identity and cultural experience. I wanted the pervasive brilliance of literary artists of color, queer (not gay) writers, and non-normative, freakish, undervalued and invisible writers of puzzling literatures to sit at the head of the table. I don't think I succeeded entirely,

but I did learn that some attendees who normally stand at the far margins of avant garde cultural events, (because of either a marked "otherness" identity or because their work is unlike the work of the popular outcasts) felt very warmly engaged. I was really glad to hear that. Everyone always feels like a big lonely loser at these things. I wanted everyone to feel, at times, like there might be more interesting ways to connect than by dividing up into pre-determined demographics and finding the exact right scene and staying and publishing and teaching and documenting there forever.

**AJS**: *What's the relationship between the literature you create and the social spaces and events you design?*

**AMC**: In some ways, my writing is simply a vehicle for me to spend time in a setting, as well as with the characters that populate it, in order to explore the very things I speak about above. I see, easily, connections between the space of a text and the space of a literary event. So much is possible in either. And I am probably always thinking about closeness and proximity, about breaking down barriers and boundaries and cutting through, no matter what I set out to do. Write a story or organize a festival: sometimes the work is the same. I am forever interested in 'changing the space of a room,' in moving around in it to see what is there.

# Previous Publication Credits

**Shane Allison**
"Mother Worries," *West Wind Review* 2010

**Garrett Ashley**
"The History of Character X," *decomP magazinE* (2011)
http://www.decompmagazine.com/thehistoryofcharacterx.htm

**Rachel Gontijo Araujo**
Evening Will Come,
http://www.eveningwillcome.com/issue14-rgaraujo-p1.html

**Jesse Ball**
book excerpt, "Stamp Stories" (Mud Luscious Press, 2011)

**Lutz Bassmann**
/Les Aigles puent/, Lagrasse, Verdier, collection"Chaoïd", 2010.

**Kate Bernheimer**

**Andrew Borgstrom**
"That We Never Knew This Reaches Upward, Assists the Room Grew" originally appeared in *JMWW* (June 2011): http://jmww.150m.com/Borgstrom2.html

**J. R. Carpenter**
TRANS.MISSION [A.DIALOGUE] 2011
http://luckysoap.com/generations/transmission.html

**Don Mee Choi**
"The Morning News Is Exciting" from *The Morning News Is Exciting* (Action Books, 2010)

**Andy Devine**
"A, a, about, along …" from {C.}: An MLP Stamp Stories Anthology (Mud Luscious press, 2011).

**Sandra Doller**
"H.D.'s Not Eating of Chickens" from *Chora* (Ahsahta Press, 2010)

**Manuela Draeger**
/Onze rêves de suie/, Paris, Éditions de l'Olivier, 2010.

**Kate Durbin**
"Anna Nicole Show" from *E! Entertainment* (Insert Press, 2011)**Brian Evenson**
"Windeye" and "A History of the Human Voice" from *Windeye*. Copyright © 2012 by
Brian Evenson. Reprinted with the permission of The Permissions Compan¥, Inc. on
behalf of Coffee House Press, www.coffeehousepress.com.

**Johannes Göransson**
The book, Entrance to a colonial pageant in which we will all begin to intricate was
published by Tarpaulin Sky Press in 2011 (*Entrance to a Colonial Pageant in which We All
Begin to Intricate*. Grafton, VT: Tarpaulin Sky Press, 2011.). The part called "Trauma" was
also published in *jubilat* (Three poems. *jubilat* 17 (2010): 8-10. Print.)

**Black Took Collective: Duriel E. Harris, Dawn Lundy Martin, & Ronaldo V. Wilson**
"Accretion: Buffalo Performance Oct. 17, 2009" from "Black Took Collective: Accretion,"
*P-Queue* (2010): 75-87.

**Gretchen E. Henderson**
book excerpt: from *On Marvellous Things Heard* (Green Lantern Press, 2011)

**Parneshia Jones**
*44 on 44: Forty-Four African American Writers on the Election of Barack Obama 44th President
of the United States*. Edited by Sonia Sanchez, Lita Hooper and Michael Simanga (Third
World Press, 2010).

**Daniel Levin Becker**
Entire piece originally published in Monolith 1 (2010), pp. 26-29, http://www.
monolithmagazine.net

**John Madera**
"Spectral Confessions and Other Digressions" from *The Official Catalog of the Library of
Potential Literature* (Cow Heavy Books, 2011; reprinted by The Lit Pub, 2012).

**Annam Manthiram**
"The Discrepancy Equation" originally appeared in *decomP*, October 2010.

**Joyelle McSweeney**
"King Prion" from *The Necropastoral* (Spork Press, 2010); later published in *Percussion
Grenade* (Fence Books, 2012).

**Monica Mody**
"Kala Pani Sampler" originally appeared as "Poet's Sampler: Monica Mody," *Boston
Review*. 2011: 72-73.

**Sawako Nakayasu**
"Flying Accusations" from Sink Review (Issue 7, January 2011),
http://sinkreview.org/sink-7/flying-accusations/

**Urayoán Noel**
book excerpts: "tri city® (terse sets)" and "me, o poem! (a cameo poem)" from *Hi-Density Politics* (BlazeVOX, 2010)

**Alissa Nutting**
"Refraction" originally appeared as an untitled stamp story in *[C.] An MLP Stamp Stories Anthology* (Mud Luscious 2011)

**Lance Phillips**
"Logogriph" from *These Indicium Tales* (Ahsahta Press, 2010)

**Kathleen Rooney & Elisa Gabbert**
The One about the Unheimlich" from *Verse* (2009). "The One about Simulacra" from *Moria* (2010). "The one about the afterlife" from *Opium* (2009).

**Marc Saaporta**
*Composition No. 1*, iPad app
Published by Visual Editions 2011.
Designed by Universal Everything. Photos © Visual Editions.

**Eleni Sikelianos**
"Black-out Fabric—What I Found There" first appeared in the *Black Warrior Review*, Fall/Winter 2010.

**Amber Sparks**
book excerpt: "Stamp Story" from *An MLP Stamp Stories Anthology* (Mud Luscious Press, 2011)

**Sarah Tourjee**
"Bread Alley," *Anomalous Press*, Issue 1,
http://www.anomalouspress.org/current/1.tourjee.breadalley.php

**J. A. Tyler**
"The Gone Children They Said Tell Us a Story" originally appeared in *Caketrain 8* (Nov. 2010): 165-169. The work was also published as part of the novel *Water* (Civil Coping Mechanisms, 2013).

**Nico Vassilakis**
from *STARINGS* (Xerolage, 2010),
http://xexoxial.org/is/xerolage46/by/nico_vassilakis

**Antoine Volodine**
/Écrivains/, Paris, Seuil, collection "Fiction & Cie", 2010.

**Raúl Zurita**
Book excerpt from *Song for his Disappeared Love* (Action Books, 2010)

# Contributor Notes

**Shane Allison** has had poems and stories grace the fine pages of such literary magazines and anthologies as *West Wind Review, Spork, Oh No, Mississippi Review, New Delta Review, Assacarus, Best Black Gay Erotica* and *Best Gay Erotica.* After the publication of several chapbooks, his debut poetry collection, *Slut Machine* was released by Rebel Satori Press and *I Remember*, his poetry/memoir is now out from *Future Tense Books.* He edits anthologies for Cleis Press and is at work on a new collection as well as a novel.

**Garrett Ashley** is working on an MA in creative writing at the University of Southern Mississippi. His work has appeared in *Asimov's Science Fiction, PANK, LORE, Strange Horizons, New World Writing, Pear Noir!,* and *Nano Fiction,* among others.

**Rachel Gontijo Araujo** is a writer and the founder of A Bolha Editora, a Brazilian press committed to publishing translated works in Portuguese, and to disseminating under-represented Brazilian works in North america. She is also the author of *Primary Anatomy*, excerpts from which have been published by or are forthcoming with *Mandorla, Action Yes, Everyday Genius,* and *Evening Will Come.* Her collaborative translation, with Nathanaël, of *The Obscene Madame D,* by Hilda Hilst, was recently published by Nightboat Books and A Bolha.

**Jesse Ball** (1978-?) is the prize-winning author of various works of fiction and non-fiction, including The Curfew, The Village on Horseback, and others. His work often employs ambiguity and absurdity to render the world obliquely.

**Lutz Bassmann** belongs to a community of imaginary writers. Bassmann is a pseudonym for Antoine Volodine, and also a character within Volodine's work. Jordan Stump's translation of his novel /We Monks and Soldiers/ was published in 2012 by University of Nebraska Press. In his books, he reaches further into the post apocalyptic world also invented and explored by Volodine and Draeger.

**Kate Bernheimer** is the author the story collection *Horse, Flower, Bird* (Coffee House Press 2010, with illustrations by Rikki Ducornet) and a novel trilogy that concluded recently with *The Complete Tales of Lucy Gold* (FC2 2011). *How a Mother Weaned a Girl from Fairy Tales,* a new story collection, is coming from Coffee House Press in 2014. She edited the World Fantasy Award-winning *My Mother She Killed Me, My Father He Ate Me: Forty New Fairy Tales* (Penguin 2010), with a fourth edited fairy-tale collection—of new mythologies—forthcoming from Penguin in 2013. She teaches in the MFA Program at the University of Arizona in Tucson.

**Andrew Borgstrom** has recent work in *The Chattahoochee Revew, Black Warrior Review*, and *Sonora Review*. He is the author of a small book, "Meat Is All" (Nephew, 2011), a pamphlet, "Explanations" (The Cupboard, 2010), and a chapbook, "And What Is Left, As Much As The Hands Will Hold, & A View Of The Empty Porch" (Greying Ghost, 2010). He is an associate editor with Mud Luscious Press and lives in the desert.

**Daniel Borzutzky** is the author of *The Book of Interfering Bodies* (2011), *The Ecstasy of Capitulation* (2007), and *Arbitrary Tales* (2005). His translations include *Song for his Disappeared Love* by Raúl Zurita (2010); and *Port Trakl* by Jaime Luis Huenún (2008).

**Amina Memory Cain** is the author of *CREATURE* (Dorothy, a publishing project, 2013) and *I Go To Some Hollow* (Les Figues Press, 2009). She is also a curator, most notably for *Both Sides and The Center* at the MAK Center/Schindler House in Los Angeles (with Teresa Carmody), and *When Does It or You Begin? Memory as Innovation* at Links Hall in Chicago (with Jennifer Karmin).

**J. R. Carpenter** is a Canadian artist, writer, researcher, performer and maker of zines, books, poetry, very short fiction, long fiction, non-fiction, non-linear hypermedia narratives and computer-generated texts of various kinds. She is a two-time winner of the CBC Quebec Short Story Competition. Her first novel, *Words the Dog Knows*, won the Expozine Alternative Press Award for Best English Book. Her second book, *GNERATION[S]*, is a collection of code narratives. She has been using the internet as a medium since 1993. She was honored with a retrospective by the Electronic Literature Organization in June 2012. She lives in Devon, England.

**Don Mee Choi** is the author of *The Morning News Is Exciting* (Action Books, 2010) and the recipient of a 2011 Whiting Writers' Award. She has received the 2012 Lucien Stryk Asian Translation Prize for *All the Garbage of the World, Unite!* by Kim Hyesoon. Her translations can be found at Action Books, Tinfish Press, and Zephyr Press.

**Andy Devine's** alphabetical fiction and essays have appeared in a variety of literary magazines, including *New York Tyrant, Unsaid, elimae, Everyday Genius*, and *Taint. Words* (Publishing Genius) is his first book. Andy Devine Avenue — in Flagstaff, Arizona — is named after him.

**Sandra Doller's** books are *Oriflamme* (Ahsahta, 2005), *Chora* (Ahsahta, 2010), and *Man Years* (Subito, 2011). Newer projects include a prose called *Memory of the Prose Machine*, and a translation of Eric Suchère's *Mystérieuse*. Founder & editrice of 1913 Press/*1913 a journal of forms*, Doller lives in San Diego with man & dogs.

**Manuela Draeger** belongs to a community of imaginary authors. Draeger is a heteronym for Antoine Volodine. Draeger is also a character in Volodine's books: a librarian in a post-apocalyptic camp who invents stories to tell children. Three additional Bobby Potemkin stories have appeared in English in /In the Time of the Blue Ball/. Draeger is actually the author of children's books published under the

innovative imprint of L'École des Loisirs; only recently did she move out this genre to write in a manner reminiscent of Volodine's.

**Kate Durbin** is a Los Angeles-based writer, performer, and transmedia artist. She is author of *The Ravenous Audience* (Akashic Books) and *E! Entertainment* (Blanc Press Diamond Edition, forthcoming). She is co-author of *Abra*, forthcoming in artists' book and iOS editions. She is co-recipient of the Expanded Artists' Book grant from Center for Book and Paper Arts at Columbia College Chicago. Her projects have been featured in *Spex, Huffington Post, The New Yorker, Specs, Salon.com, AOL, Poets and Writers, Poets.org, VLAK, Lana Turner: A Journal of Poetry and Opinion, Black Warrior Review, Joyland, berfrois, Hyperallergic, 1913, LIT, Fanzine,* and *The American Scholar,* among others. She is founding editor of Gaga Stigmata, an online arts and criticism journal about Lady Gaga.

**Brian Evenson** is the author of a dozen books, most recently *Immobility* (Tor) and *Windeye* (Coffee House Press). He has translated work from French by Jean Frémon, Stendhal, Christian Gailly, Marcel Cohen, and a number of others. He lives in Providence, RI and works at the school which served as the basis for Lovecraft's Miskatonic University.

**Elizabeth Gentry** received the 2012 Madeleine P. Plonsker Emerging Writer's Residency Award for *Housebound* (Fall 2013). She currently works as Writing Specialist for the University of Tennessee College of Law and teaches writing and literature for the University English Department. Recent publications include a novel excerpt entitled "In Exchange" published in *Confrontation* and an essay entitled "Appetites of the Natural World" published in *So to Speak*. She received a MFA in fiction writing from the University of North Carolina at Greensboro.

**Johannes Göransson** is the author of five books, including *Haute Surveillence* (2013), and the translator of several books, including Aase Berg's *Dark Matter* (2013). He teaches at the University of Notre Dame and blogs at Montevidayo.com.

Co-Founded in 1999 by Duriel E. Harris, Dawn Lundy Martin and Ronaldo V. Wilson at Cave Canem, a retreat for African American Poets, **Black Took Collective** is a group of Black post-theorists who perform and write in hybrid experimental forms, embracing radical poetics and cutting-edge critical theory about race, gender, and sexuality. Their manifesto "Call for Dissonance," *Black Took Collective* appears in *FENCE,* Fall/Winter 2002 and *A Best of Fence Anthology: The First Nine Years* (UPNE, 2009). Recent BTC performances include: "Black Took Collective: Autopsy" (UC Santa Cruz and Pomona College); &NOW 2011 Tomorrowland Forever; and Dixon Place's HOT! Festival.

**Gretchen E. Henderson** is a Mellon Postdoctoral Fellow at MIT. Her books include the musically-modulating novel, *The House Enters the Street* (Starcherone Books, 2012); an exploration of literary appropriations of music and silence, *On Marvellous Things Heard* (Green Lantern Press, 2011); and *Galerie de Difformité* (winner of the Madeleine Plonsker Prize, &NOW Books, 2011): a print book networked online

inviting readers to participate in its (de) formation across media (difformite.wordpress. com). Gretchen also has published a cartographic poetry chapbook, *Wreckage: By Land & By Sea* (Dancing Girl Press). She is working on *Ugliness: A Cultural History* (for Reaktion Books).

**Parneshia Jones** is a recipient of the Gwendolyn Brooks Poetry Award, the Margaret Walker Short Story Award; and the Aquarius Press Legacy Award. She is published in several anthologies including *She Walks in Beauty: A Woman's Journey Through Poems*, edited by Caroline Kennedy; *The Ringing Ear: Black Poets Lean South*, edited by Nikky Finney, as well as *Poetry Speaks Who I Am*, a book/CD compilation. Jones is a member of the Affrilachian Poets, a collective of Black voices from Appalachia and serves on the board of Cave Canem.

**Daniel Levin Becker** is reviews editor of *The Believer* and the youngest member of the Paris-based Oulipo collective. His first book, *Many Subtle Channels: In Praise of Potential Literature* was published by Harvard University Press in April 2012.

**John Madera's** fiction may be found in *Conjunctions, Opium Magazine*, Featherproof Press, *elimae*, Jaded Ibis Press, Cow Heavy Books, and other venues. His nonfiction may be found in *American Book Review, The Believer, Bookforum, The Review of Contemporary Fiction, Rain Taxi: Review of Books, The Brooklyn Rail*, among many other venues. He's editing a collection of essays on the art and craft of writing (Publishing Genius Press). Former fiction editor at *Identity Theory*, and former senior flash fiction editor at *jmww*, he edits the online forum Big Other. His column, "A Reader's Log(orrhea)," may be found at *The Nervous Breakdown*. Online at www.johnmadera.com.

**Annam Manthiram** is the author of the novel, *After the Tsunami* (Stephen F. Austin State University Press, 2011), and a short story collection (*Dysfunction: Stories*, forthcoming from Aqueous Books, 2012), which was a Finalist in the 2010 Elixir Press Fiction Contest and in Leapfrog Press's 2010 Fiction Contest. A graduate of the M.A. Writing program at the University of Southern California, Ms. Manthiram resides in New Mexico with her husband, Alex, and son, Sathya.

**Joyelle McSweeney** is the author, most recently, of the prose book *Salamandrine, 8 Gothics* (Tarpaulin Sky Press, 2013) and the poetry volume *Percussion Grenade* (Fence, 2012), both of which also include plays, as well as *The Necropastoral* (Spork, 2010), an artists' book made in collaboration with Andrew Shuta. She edits Action Books, contributes to Montevidayo.com, and teaches at Notre Dame.

**Monica Mody's** *Kala Pani* is forthcoming soon from 1913 Press. She has published two chapbooks of poetry, and her work has also appeared in places such as *Boston Review, Upstairs at Duroc, apocryphal text, Cannot Exist, LIES/ISLE, The HarperCollins Book of English Poetry*, and *Occupy Consciousness: Essays on the Global Insurrection*, among others. She has an MFA in Creative Writing from the University of Notre Dame, where she was the 2010 Sparks Writing Fellow, and is currently pursuing a Ph.D. in East-West Psychology at the California Institute of Integral Studies.

**Sawako Nakayasu** writes and translates poetry, and her recent book, *Mouth: Eats Color–Sagawa Chika Translations, Anti-translations, & Originals* does both in one work. Other recent books include *Texture Notes* and *Hurry Home Honey,* and books of translation include Ayane Kawata's *Time of Sky/Castles in the Air* and Takashi Hiraide's *For the Fighting Spirit of the Walnut,* which received the Best Translated Book Award in 2009. She has received fellowships from the NEA and PEN, and her own work has been translated into Japanese, Norwegian, Swedish, Arabic, Chinese, and Vietnamese.

**Urayoán Noel** is the author of, among others, *Boringkén* (Ediciones Callejón, 2008), *Hi-Density Politics* (BlazeVOX, 2010), and *The Edgemere Letters* (2011), a multimedia collaboration with artist Martha Clippinger. Born and raised in San Juan, Puerto Rico, he teaches English at SUNY Albany and recently received fellowships from the Bronx Council on the Arts and the Ford Foundation. A contributing editor of *Mandorla,* he is currently completing a book on Nuyorican poetry since the 1960s and a translation of the Chilean vanguard poet Pablo de Rokha. His forthcoming book of poetry is *Los días porosos/The porous days* (Guatemala City: Catafixia Editorial).

**Alissa Nutting** is author of *Unclean Jobs for Women and Girls* and an Assistant Professor of Fiction Writing at John Carroll University. Her work has or will appear in publications such as *The Norton Anthology of Contemporary Literature,* the *New York Times, Tin House, Bomb,* and *Fence.* She recently edited The Grey Issue of *Fairy Tale Review.*

**Lance Phillips** has published three books of poems, *Corpus Socius, Cur Aliquid Vidi* and *These Indicium Tales,* with Ahsahta Press and his fourth, *Mimer,* is forthcoming from the same. His work has appeared in many journals including *New American Writing, VOLT, Fence,* and *Verse.* He lives in Huntersville, NC with is wife and two children.

**Kathleen Rooney** is a founding editor of Rose Metal Press and the author of *Oneiromance (an epithalamion)* (Switchback Books, 2008) and the novel in poems *Robinson Alone* (Gold Wake Press, 2012). She lives in Chicago. Together they are the authors of *That Tiny Insane Voluptuousness* (Otoliths, 2008). **Elisa Gabbert** is the author of *The French Exit* (Birds LLC, 2010) and *Thanks for Sending the Engine* (Kitchen Press, 2007). She lives in Denver and blogs at The French Exit.

**Marc Saporta** (1923-2009) was a French novelist, essayist and literary critic. He is the author of five acclaimed novels: *Le Furet* (1959), *La Distribution* (1961), *La Quete* (1961), *Composition No. 1* (1962), and *Les Invites* (1964). He also translated writings by Ernest Hemingway, Jack Kerouac and Martin Luther King.

**Davis Schneiderman** edited this book, with help from many other generous people.

**Eleni Sikelianos** is the author of a hybrid memoir and seven books of poetry. Forthcoming is *The Loving Detail of the Living & the Dead* (Coffee House, 2013). She studied at Naropa with Anne Waldman, Allen Ginsberg, and Anselm Hollo, among

many others. Her work has been translated into a dozen languages, and she has been the happy recipient of various awards for her poetry, nonfiction, and translations, including a National Endowment for the Arts and the National Poetry Series prize. Sikelianos currently teaches in and directs the Creative Writing PhD program at the University of Denver.

**Amber Sparks** is the author of the short story collection *May We Shed These Human Bodies*, published by Curbside Splendor. She is a contributor to literary blogs Big Other and Vouched, and lives in Washington, DC with her husband and two beasts. She also blogs occasionally at www.ambernoellesparks.com.

**Anna Joy Springer** is an artist and cross-genre writer who investigates the weird intersection of sacredness, perversity, and interbeing. She is the author of *The Vicious Red Relic, Love* (Jaded Ibis, 2011), an illustrated fabulist memoir with soundscape, and *The Birdwisher, A Murder Mystery for Very Old Young Adults* (Birds of Lace, 2009). An Associate Professor of Literature at UC San Diego and the Director of its MFA Program, she teaches experimental writing, feminist literature & graphic texts. She's played in punk and dyke punk bands Blatz, The Gr'ups, and Cypher in the Snow.

**Sarah Tourjee** is the author of the chapbook *Ghost* (Anomalous Press). Her short fiction has appeared in Conjunctions, *PANK, The Collagist, Wigleaf, Everyday Genius, Anomalous*, and elsewhere. She earned her MFA from Brown University, and lives in Northampton Massachusetts.

**J. A. Tyler** is the author of eight books including *A Man of Glass & All the Ways We Have Failed* (Fugue State Press) and *No One Told Me I Was Going to Disappear*, co-authored with John Dermot Woods (Jaded Ibis Press). He is also founding editor of Mud Luscious Press.

**Nico Vassilakis** works with both textual and visual alphabet. Recent books include *Staring @ Poetics* (Xexoxial Editions, 2011), *West of Dodge* (redfoxpress, 2010), *Protracted Type* (Blue Lion Books, 2009), *staReduction* (Book Thug, 2008), and *Text Loses Time* (Many Penny Press, 2007). His *Vispo* videos have been shown at festivals and exhibits of innovative language art. He was a founding member of the *Subtext Collective*. Nico, along with Craig Hill, edited *THE LAST VISPO: A Visual Poetry Anthology 1998 - 2008* forthcoming from Fantagraphics Books (Fall 2012). Samples of Nico's work can seen at www.staringpoetics.weebly.com.

**Antoine Volodine** belongs to a community of imaginary writers. Volodine is a pseudonym for an author who keeps his own name a secret. His work in English includes *Minor Angels* and *Naming the Jungle*, and the forthcoming *Writers*. His work in French comprises some twenty fiction books; originally a science-fiction writer, Volodine moved out of what he felt to be too narrow a genre and went on to invent a singularly original, "post-exotic" universe.

**Raúl Zurita's** books include *Purgatorio* (1979), *Anteparaiso* (1982), *La Vida Nueva* (1994), *Poemas Militantes* (2000), *Los Paises Muertos* (2006), *Poemas de amor* (2007), In *Memoriam* (2008), *Cuadernos de guerra* (2009) and *Zurita* (2011). Zurita sky-wrote the poem *La Vida Nueva* over Manhattan in 1982, and he was a member of CADA, an art-action collective renowned for their performance-protests in Chile during the dictatorship of Pinochet. In 2009, Zurita's *INRI* (translated by William Rowe) was published by Marick Press; *Purgatory* (translated by Anna Deeny) was published by the University of California Press; and *Song for his Disappeared Love* (translated by Daniel Borzutzky) was published by Action Books in 2010. Zurita lives in Santiago, Chile and is a professor at Universidad Diego Portales.

# THE MADELEINE P. PLONSKER
# EMERGING WRITER'S RESIDENCY PRIZE

www.lakeforest.edu/plonsker

Yearly deadline: March 1

# THE MADELEINE P. PLONSKER
# EMERGING WRITER'S RESIDENCY PRIZE

www.lakeforest.edu/plonsker

Yearly deadline: March 1